AF626794

Tran Hong Hanh

Local Knowledge and Food Security among the Red Yao Ethnic Group in Vietnam

Spektrum

Berlin Series on Society, Economy and Politics in Developing Countries

edited by

Volume 95

LIT

Tran Hong Hanh

Local Knowledge and Food Security among the Red Yao Ethnic Group in Vietnam

A Case Study in Sa Pa District, Lao Cai Province, Vietnam

LIT

Bibliographic information published by the Deutsche Nationalbibliothek
The Deutsche Nationalbibliothek lists this publication in the Deutsche Nationalbibliografie; detailed bibliographic data are available in the Internet at http://dnb.d-nb.de.

ISBN 978-3-8258-9639-3
Zugl.: Berlin, Freie Universität, Diss., 2006

A catalogue record for this book is available from the British Library

Fresnostr. 2 D-48159 Münster
Tel. +49 (0) 2 51-620 32 22 Fax +49 (0) 2 51-922 60 99
e-Mail: lit@lit-verlag.de http://www.lit-verlag.de

Distribution:

In Germany: LIT Verlag Fresnostr. 2, D-48159 Münster
Tel. +49 (0) 2 51-620 32 22, Fax +49 (0) 2 51-922 60 99, e-Mail: vertrieb@lit-verlag.de

In Austria: Medienlogistik Pichler-ÖBZ GmbH & Co KG
IZ-NÖ, Süd, Straße 1, Objekt 34, A-2355 Wiener Neudorf
Tel. +43 (0) 22 36-63 53 52 90, Fax +43 (0) 22 36-63 53 52 43, e-Mail: mlo@medien-logistik.at

In Switzerland: B + M Buch- und Medienvertriebs AG
Hochstr. 357, CH-8200 Schaffhausen
Tel. +41 (0) 52-643 54 85, Fax +41 (0) 52-643 54 35, e-Mail: order@buch-medien.ch

Distributed in the UK by: Global Book Marketing, 99B Wallis Rd, London, E9 5LN
Phone: +44 (0) 20 8533 5800 – Fax: +44 (0) 1600 775 663
http://www.centralbooks.co.uk/html

Distributed in North America by:

Transaction Publishers
New Brunswick (U.S.A.) and London (U.K.)

Transaction Publishers
Rutgers University
35 Berrue Circle
Piscataway, NJ 08854

Phone: +1 (732) 445 - 2280
Fax: + 1 (732) 445 - 3138
for orders (U. S. only):
toll free (888) 999 - 6778
e-mail: orders@transactionpub.com

Gedruckt mit Unterstützung des Deutschen Akademischen Austauschdienstes

TABLE OF CONTENTS

Acknowledgements

First, I express my profound thanks to the Deutscher Akademischer Austauschdienst (DAAD) for financial support during my study in Germany.

I specially thank my two supervisors: Dr. Elisabeth Meyer-Renschhausen (Institute for Sociology, Free University - Berlin) and Prof. Dr. Friedhelm Streiffeler (Faculty of Agriculture and Horticulture; Humboldt University of Berlin) for providing me with the main scientific contributions. Their ideas and criticisms, always accompanied by encouragement, have been of inestimable value to me and my study.

My heartfelt thanks go to Prof. Dr. Helgard Kramer, Prof. Dr. Manfred Schulz, Dr. Ulrike Schultz (Institute for Sociology, Free University-Berlin) and Dr. Thomas Sikor (Faculty of Agriculture and Horticulture, Humboldt University of Berlin) for their interest in my study and their helpful, useful comments and suggestions.

I offer my sincere gratitude to my colleagues in the Institute of Anthropology-Hanoi (Vietnam), especially to Prof. Dr. Khong Dien (former Head of Institute), Prof. Dr. Pham Quang Hoan (Head of Institute) and Dr. Hoang Huu Binh (Chief of Personnel Department) and Dr. Vuong Xuan Tinh (Editor-In-Chief of Anthropology Review) for encouraging me to study in Germany; to Mr. Doan Viet for conducting fieldwork with me in 2003 and surveying household economy by a set of questionnaire; to MA. Nguyen Thi Hong Nhi and Ms. Tran Thu Hieu for giving me many chances to have several books on loan from the library of the Institute. I additionally thank Dr. Vuong Xuan Tinh for his helpful comments and suggestions.

Honestly, I express my appreciation to the following friends: Mr. Huynh Van Chuong and Mr. To Xuan Phuc, who are Ph.D students in the Faculty of Agriculture and Horticulture (Humboldt University of Berlin), for their helpful discussions; Mr. Bernd-Michael Kabioll, Mrs. Judith McDowell and Mrs. Anna Gyorgy for their corrections of my first draft. My additional thanks go to Huynh Van Chuong for his technical guidance.

I am extremely grateful to the local communities, particularly the Red Yao people in my research areas, for their enthusiastic involvement in different interviews and discussions to share their knowledge and experiences with me. They have great contributions to my study.

Finally, I honestly extend my deepest thanks to all members of my family for their psychological supports and encouragements.

Thank you very much for all of your distributions.

LIST OF FIGURES

LIST OF TABLES

LIST OF MAPS

ABBREVIATIONS AND EQUIVALENTS

1. Abbreviations

CEMMA	Committee for Ethnic Minorities and Mountain Areas
GDP	Gross Domestic Product
FAO	Food and Agriculture Organization of the United Nations
IFPRI	International Food Policy Research Institute
LUC(s)	Land Use Certificate(s)
MOLISA	Ministry of Labour, Invalids and Social Affairs
NGO	Nongovernmental Organization
TRIPS	Trade-related Aspects of Intellectual Property Rights
UNDP	United Nations Development Programme
USD	United States Dollar
VND	Vietnamese Dong
WB	World Bank
WHO	World Health Organization
WTO	World Trade Organization
ha	hectare

2. Equivalents

dong	Vietnamese currency unit, 1 USD = 15,800 dong (2005)
1 ha	= 48 kg of local rice seeds
	= 36 kg of new rice seeds
	= 25 kg of maize seeds

Chapter 1
INTRODUCTION

1.1 Justification

Although the issue of food security has been a concern since the 1970s, it remains a central global challenge. According to statistics from the FAO, 815 million people are undernourished and experiencing food insecurity, while 24,000 die of starvation everyday, three-quarters of these children under the age of five.[1] Therefore, food security remains a worldwide focus of conferences and research. Food security is understood in various ways depending on the persons and organizations involved. It is normally linked with the issue of low household income, malnutrition, food scarcity and poverty. However, in principle, the sustainable different livelihoods are indispensable to achieving food security. Moreover, the diversifications of livelihoods are different from country to country, from region to region, and even from community to community.

It is a fact that economic growth and globalization do not automatically guarantee to food security over the world, particularly in developing and low-income countries. Therefore, in these countries, economic growth is essential but insufficient to reduce hunger. Nevertheless, agricultural growth has a much greater impact on hunger reduction than industrial growth. This is also the case in Vietnam, where three-fourths of the country is hilly and mountainous and about 80 percent of the total population is involved in farming.

Vietnam's economy began to develop steadily in recent years in comparison with that of other countries in East and Southeast Asia. Remarkably, Vietnam reached a GDP growth rate of 8.43% in 2005, and ranks second in GDP growth rates in Asia, after China. However many regions of the country still experience severe poverty. In addition, although Vietnam is the world's second largest rice exporter, many areas have a shortage of food, mainly rice.

Most poor and food insecure people in Vietnam live in the rural and mountainous areas. They suffer from inequitable access to schools, health care, roads, technology, institutional support and markets. In the rural areas, the people depend mainly on agriculture for their livelihoods. In comparison, apart from agriculture, the uplanders depend on the forest for their additional livelihood. Therefore, agricultural production and resource use have a close relation with poverty in the mountainous areas. Moreover, food security and improved access to productive resources for the poor in these areas are fundamental prerequisites for sustained poverty reduction.

Various policies and development projects to eradicate hunger and reduce poverty, then to achieve food security have been implemented in the rural and mountain regions of Vietnam. Although there were remarkably successful results with some of the development projects, many of them failed or did not achieve the desired results. The macroscopic plan for a nation usually fails in the

---

[1] FAO (2005). *Agricultural trade reform offers benefits, but the poor could be left behind*, Rome: Italy. Also available at http://www.fao.org/newsroom/en/news/2005/1000173/index.html (7/12/2005): 80.

process of its execution and management in the local level.[2] There are many reasons, both subjective and objective, for these effects.

Sometimes solutions recommended in certain projects do not fit in with the knowledge of the local people, who could possibly suggest better alternatives for development projects. The people who design and implement development projects are not aware of the true value of the local knowledge. Development based on imposing plans without the farmers' participation creates great pressures on land, water, forest and other natural resources. This situation increases poverty and environmental degradation.

Through the above lesson learned, it is essential to recognize the importance of the farmers' knowledge and their experience in socio-economic development. Their local knowledge must be considered as a valuable regional and national property as well as the key to development at the local level. This is especially important for Vietnam to rid itself of the threshold of low-income country by 2010.

To achieve the desired effects, it is crucial to promote comprehensive development in every region of Vietnam, particularly in the rural and mountainous areas. This development contributes to bridging the gap between the uplands and the lowlands. To do this, it is important to use and develop the potentialities of labour, land and professions in the rural and mountainous regions based on their traditional economy.

It is indispensable to study, select, inherit and develop the valuable knowledge of the local people, which may suggest alternatives appropriate to their ecological and socio-economic circumstances. However, in some cases, under the burden of hunger and long-term poverty, the small farmers may use the natural environment in unsustainable ways that increase the vulnerability of the conditions for their livelihoods. Thus, it is important to have a combination between advantages of their local knowledge and the strength of modern technology to achieve sustainable development, as a counter to projects planned and designed solely by scientists and policy-makers.

1.2Research sites

The research region of this study is Sa Pa district, Lao Cai province. This northern province, bordering on China, is one of the seven poorest provinces in Vietnam.[3] Its capital, Lao Cai city, lies some 300 km northwest along the Hong (Red) River from Hanoi. The district includes nine different ethnic groups. Among them, the Red Yao ethnic minority was chosen as the subject for this research as this group has extensive experience in producing food and earning cash income through different livelihoods. Their standard of living is thus relatively higher than that of other ethnic minorities in the same district. The

---

[2] Neil L. Jamieson, Le Trong Cuc, and Terry Rambo (1998). "The Development Crisis in Vietnam's Mountains". Honolulu: East-West Center. *Special Reports*, No. 6: 14.

[3] Six other poorest provinces of Vietnam include Ha Giang, Cao Bang, Lai Chau, Son La, Bac Kan, and Kon Tum provinces. See more: Parliament Council of Ethnic Groups. Session X (2000). *The policy and law of ethnic groups of the Vietnam Communist Party and the government.* Hanoi: National Culture Publishing House.

Red Yao are second in population size among the local ethnic minorities, behind the Hmong. They live in three regions: in the highlands, the central area and the lowlands. The research includes all three regions, examining one representative community in each. Tả Phìn commune is in the central lands of Sa Pa district, Bản Khoang commune in the highland of Sa Pa, and Nậm Cang commune is representative of the lowlands of Sa Pa (see: Map 1.1 and Map 1.2).

Map 1.1. Map of Lao Cai Province

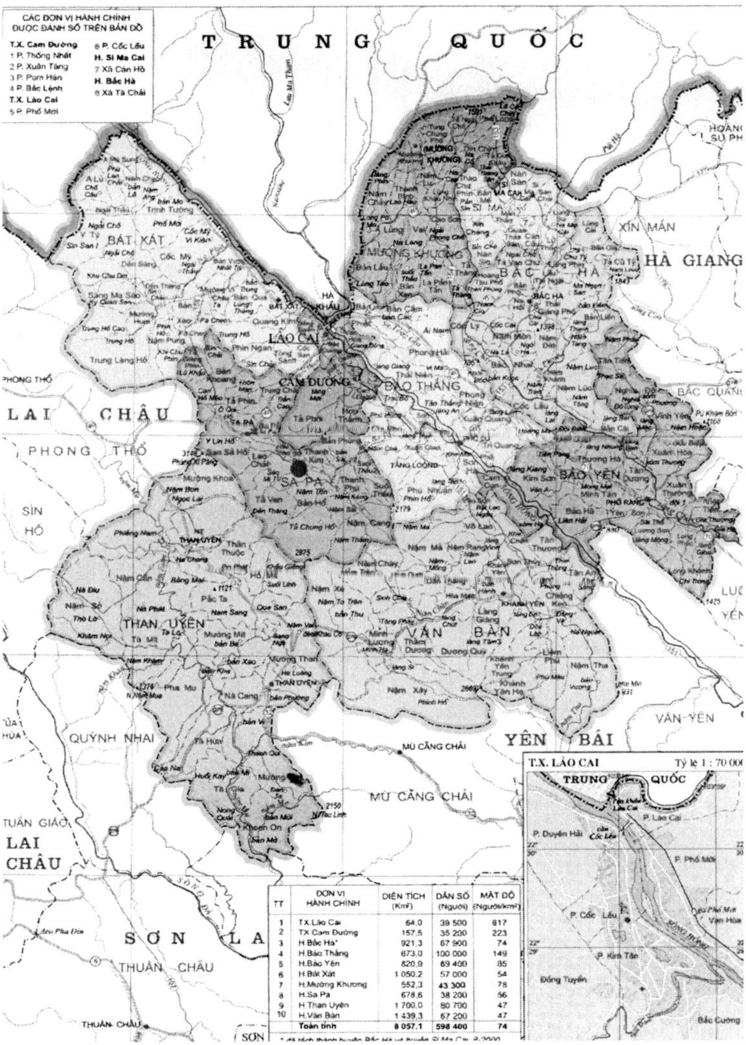

Source: Administration map of Vietnam

Map 1.2. Location map of the research areas

Source: Administration map of Vietnam

Tả Phìn commune is 12 km north of Sa Pa town. Because of its location near town, it is easy to reach with public transportation and is strongly influenced by tourism. It is known for its natural beauty, cultural diversity and traditional crafts, based on skills handed down from one generation to the next. Poverty in this commune is most remarkable because farmers have a shortage of productive sources (mainly cultivable land) and high population density. The income from tourism is unstable and insufficient to solve poverty.

Bản Khoang commune is 18 km West of Sa Pa town, near the forest. In this commune there are many people related by marriage to the Red Yao of Tả Phìn commune. It is possible and a potential for the local people to develop agro-forestry in combination initiatively with the development of tourism due to an abundance of forests, a very nice mountain landscape and diverse cultures of ethnic groups. Their living standard has improved in the recent years through the development of agro-forestry; however, poverty is still a question for many of them.

Another research site is Nậm Cang commune, 45 km southeast of Sa Pa town, in the most remote part of Sa Pa district. Despite the distance from town, bad roads and public transportation, especially in the rainy season, the living standard of the Red Yao in Nậm Cang commune is much higher than those of other communes and is the highest compared with those of other ethnic minorities in Sa Pa district. This is because farmers in this commune have a lot of forest land and good agricultural land that create a good condition for them to grow *thảo quả* (Amomum tsao-ko Crev. et Lem.)[4] as a cash crop and medicinal herb.

1.3Research objectives

This thesis addresses the following research questions:

- What do Red Yao farmers produce and who produces what? (with attention to labour division and gender roles in economic activities)
- How has land tenure in the Red Yao communities changed in different periods and how have these changes influenced the production of local farmers?
- What kinds of food resources are available to the local people, and how do they have access to them?
- Finally, what opportunities and challenges do small farmers meet to maintain their local knowledge and to achieve food security?

All these objectives aim at learning about the role of the Red Yao people's knowledge in accessing food and in managing their livelihoods to achieve food security for their households. In addition, this study identifies opportunities and challenges for the local people and communities to get food security in transition nowadays.

Based on that, I give policymakers and development project planners and practitioners the documentary basis which can help with determining future actions and decisions. By this way, it is hopeful that the local people will have more opportunities to benefit from development projects and ensure their food security in coming years.

[4] See: Do Tat Loi (1991). *The Vietnamese medical herbs and ingredient medicaments.* Sixth Edition. Hanoi: Scientific and Technical Publishing House.

1.4Thesis outline

Apart from the introduction, this thesis is divided into seven main chapters.

The second chapter on local knowledge of food security is the theoretical framework of my study. This chapter refers to various conceptions of local knowledge and food security as well as the different approaches to food security practiced by organizations, professions and individuals, internationally and in Vietnam. Based on that, we can recognize a complexity and a diversification of these conceptions and approaches. However, each country or each region has its own specific characteristics. Therefore, criteria of food security and poverty are different from country to country, from region to region, and even from community to community.

The third chapter mentions the methodology which is applied to collect data in the field and analyze these data.

"Red Yao people and socio-economic situations of the research areas," the fourth chapter, first introduces readers to the Red Yao people in the ethnic structure of Vietnam and of the research areas. The physical conditions and political, socio-economic and cultural situations that influence the Red Yao's knowledge and their food security are also included in this chapter.

In the Red Yao communities in the Sa Pa district, agriculture plays an indispensable role in the local people's existence. Therefore, it is necessary to refer to the Red Yao's cultivation and their local knowledge of this sector. This is also the content of the fifth chapter. Up to now, although the local farmers have applied some modern techniques to their production, they still practise their traditional methods of cultivation, based mainly on their own experience and knowledge which are transmitted from generation to generation. This manifests itself in different steps of their production process. In addition, government land policies have influenced the farmers' land use and contribute to promote them to increase their capital, labour and intellectual investments in production.

In addition to cultivation, animal husbandry also plays an essential role in producing food and foodstuff for the Yao ethnic group. In addition, their livestock breeding and their cultivation are closely interrelated. These connections are addressed in the sixth chapter of this study.

The Red Yao people in Sa Pa district are mountain people. Therefore, it is obvious and indispensable for them to depend as well on the forest and forest products. In addition to agriculture, the forage economy also contributes to their livelihood. Food and resource gathering plays an important supplementary role to the food security of the local communities, particularly in the period between harvests. However, the farmers' rapid population growth and the nearly exhausted exploitation of the forest in some communes have put pressure on natural resources and there have thus been some negative impacts on one of the important occupations for local farmers. It is thus essential to refer to the forage economy of the Yao people, as is done in the seventh chapter.

As the innovation of the country progresses, Vietnam has remarkable advances in different sectors, mostly in terms of socio-economic development. Many changes in Vietnamese government policies concerning ethnic minorities have influenced the socio-economic situation of the mountain areas, including the Red Yao's communities. These policies aim at targeting the poorest segments of the population in rural and urban areas. In spite of efforts at all levels of government and the population, many difficulties remain in the Yao small-scale society. The final chapter presents all challenges and possibilities that the Red Yao people meet to achieve food security and develop their household economy. This also contributes to reflecting the current socio-economic situation of some other ethnic minority people in the same region. Based on that, this part of my study interprets the relationship between knowledge, food security and development, and offers suggestions for the next larger-scale projects, in terms of both interdisciplinary and transnational research.

Chapter 2
LOCAL KNOWLEDGE AND FOOD SECURITY: CONCEPTUAL FRAMEWORK

2.1 Local knowledge

2.1.1 Definition of local knowledge

Local knowledge is defined as scientifically and intellectually grounded systems of classification, additionally it is understood as "the logic of the concrete", wisdom of common sense - a special thought framework and different from this region to another.[5] This kind of knowledge is also considered systems of knowledge and practice, developed over generations, in a particular field unique to a specific culture and society, and an information base of a society.[6]

Giving attention to agriculture and agricultural practises of the farmers, many researchers have surveyed local knowledge regarding these issues. Therefore, their definition of local knowledge is closely related to the farmers' agriculture. Richards defines local knowledge as a reference to the strength of peasant production in a particular context.[7] Anan Poltanee, a Thai scholar, remarks that "practice and knowledge of peasants are closely connected with the local agro-economic system which is regarded as valuable, rational and most appropriate to their circumstances of life... Their indigenous knowledge has provided them a wealth of extremely rich and creative information".[8] Additionally, local knowledge is referred to as "customs and habits" in many Vietnamese ethno-monographs published mainly in the 1970s and 1980s. This is also one of the two main categories of local knowledge divided by John Ambler (1996).[9] According to John Ambler, the first category can be called "technical knowledge", and the second category involves "local regulations", "customs" or "habits". The technical knowledge of people living in the highlands involves detailed knowledge of the humidity of the local area, the natural potential of the

---

[5] Claude Lévi-Strauss (1979). *Myth and Meaning*. New York: Schocken Books.
- Clifford Geertz (1975). "Common Sense as a Cultural System". *Antioch Review*, 33: 47-53.
- Clifford Geertz (1993a). *Local knowledge: Further essays in interpretive anthropology*. FontanaPress-An Imprint of HarperCollins Publisher.
- Clifford Geertz (1993b). "Local Knowledge" and Its Limits: Some Obiter Dicta". *The Yale Journal of Criticism*, 5: 129-135.

[6] Dennis Michael Warren (1989). "Introduction". In: Paul Richards, L. Jan Slikkerveer, and Adedotun O. Philips (1989), *Indigenous Knowledge Systems for Agriculture and Rural Development: The CIKARD Inaugural Lectures*. Studies in Technology and Social Change, No. 13; Iowa State University Research Foundation: 1-3.
- Dennis Michael Warren (1995). *The cultural dimensions of development, indigenous development system*. Leiden.

[7] Paul Richards (1985). *Indigenous Agricultural Revolution: ecology and food production in West Africa*. London: Hutchinson, Great Britain.

[8] Anan Poltanee (1992). *Framer as Scientist: Bringing Farmer Knowledge for Researchers*. In J. Mc. Kinninged, Marginalization in Thailand.

[9] John Ambler (1996). "Experiences for study of mountain development: Some general characteristics from Asia". In: *workshop on appropriate use for sustainable mountain management in Vietnam*, edited by Le Trong Cuc, Dao Trong Hung and Tran Duc Vien. Hanoi: CRES and HUAF, Agricultural Publishing House.

land, techniques of plant production, of the selection of seeds, and the knowledge of different kinds of plants and animals. Meanwhile, "customs" and "habits" can also lay down rules, for example, which water resources can be used for watering the land, who is allowed to exploit which area of forest, how many buffaloes and cows will be allowed to graze a private plot of grassland, and which cultivation techniques are acceptable.[10]

In a narrower sense, local knowledge is also referred to as popular knowledge and folk knowledge, or folk culture.[11] According to Ngo Duc Thinh, a Vietnamese folklore researcher, folk knowledge is a non-school knowledge, a sum of experience accumulated by human beings through a long process of activities designed to adapt themselves to, and alter the natural and social environment in a way that benefits their materials and spiritual interests. Such a fund of knowledge exists and develops not through learning by books, but mainly through personal communication and memory; expressions, sayings, proverbs and through interaction in daily labour, other occupational activities of fishermen, peasants, livestock breeders, and artisans, etc.[12] Nguyen Van Truong considers that local knowledge derives from experience of the people striving to survive in a non-sustainable eco-system, and must be amended, improved and further developed.[13]

The World Intellectual Property Organization (WIPO) set the indigenous knowledge and folklore under the scope of local knowledge. As a result, local knowledge is considered as a part of a heritage. According to WIPO (2000), local knowledge is understood to have a close relation to a term of heritage. Furthermore, knowledge can be separately developed by a succession realm. Afterwards, it exposes the appearance of folklore that sometimes has a synonym with a cultural expression. This can be understood as a mode of cultural explanation, which reflects definitions of culture of a community.[14] WIPO continue to state that systems of knowledge, including all scientific knowledge, knowledge of agriculture, technology and ecology, can be identified as one of the moveable cultural property.[15] The UNESCO also assumes consideration of knowledge as an aspect of culture when they identify the culture.

The concept of "indigenous knowledge", "traditional knowledge" and "local knowledge" is often used interchangeably. In a study of definitions and role of indigenous knowledge, Hoang Xuan Ty (1998) equates the definition of

[10] John Ambler (1996). *ibid*: 36-37, 39.
[11] Stephen B. Brush (1996). *Valuing local knowledge: indigenous people and intellectual property rights*. Washington D.C.: Island Press: 4.
- Ngo Duc Thinh (1995). "Folk knowledge and development". Hanoi: *Lecture for training workshop in CRES.*
[12] Ngo Duc Thinh (1995). *ibid.*
[13] Nguyen Van Truong (1994). "An approach to concept of mountain development of natural resources in Vietnam at commune and village levels". *Hanoi workshop presentation.* October 14-16, 1994.
[14] WIPO (2000). "Draft Report on Fact-finding Missions on Intellectual Property and Traditional Knowledge (1998-1999)". *Draft for Comment*, 3rd July 2000: 26.
[15] WIPO (2000). *ibid*: 27.

these three knowledge systems.[16] However, in fact, there is a little difference between them. In a study by John Mugabe (1998), he explains that "indigenous knowledge" is knowledge "that is held and used by a people who identify themselves as indigenous of a place based on a combination of cultural distinctiveness and prior territorial occupancy relative to a more recently-arrived population with its own distinct and subsequently dominant culture. Traditional knowledge is, on the other hand, that which is held by members of a distinct culture and/or sometimes acquired by means of inquiry peculiar to that culture and concerning the culture itself or the local environment in which it exists." He concludes, "Indigenous knowledge fits neatly in the traditional knowledge category but traditional is not necessarily indigenous." Therefore, indigenous knowledge automatically is traditional knowledge but traditional knowledge is not necessarily indigenous. Traditional knowledge thus is the total of all knowledge and practices, whether explicit or implicit, used in the management of socio-economic and ecological factors of life.[17] In another thought, indigenous knowledge systems constitute a practical thought. This means the way in which ideas, conceptions, and attitudes are developed by people in order for them to carry out their everyday activities... Practical thought has its impetus in the exigencies of life producing food, etc.[18] Therefore, to recognize indigenous and traditional knowledge, it is firstly important to recognize who owns such system of knowledge, indigenous or traditional people. This is a relatively complicated question raised by demographers. In addition, other criteria, including the temporal criterion, for identification of indigenous, traditional and local characters should be questioned. I will address the problem of indigenous, traditional, and local people in a later part of this chapter that refers to a relation between knowledge and people.

In attempts to distinguish "local" and "indigenous" knowledge, a Thai anthropologist Pinkaew Laungaramsri shows that indigenous knowledge is normally referred to traditional knowledge. Therefore, she does not differentiate clearly between indigenous and traditional knowledge. It seems that they are considered as synonymous. Meanwhile, local knowledge is identified as the knowledge, including modern knowledge, the people apply and then adapt to their modern world. In her study, local knowledge encompasses both common knowledge and specific knowledge because it consists of dynamic interaction between the "native" and "modern" modes of knowledge.[19] Her definition of

---

[16] Hoang Xuan Ty (1998). "Part 1: Definitions and Roles of Indigenous Knowledge". In: Center for Ecological and Forest Studies (1998), *Indigenous knowledge of agriculture and natural resource management among the people in the uplands*. Hanoi: Agricultural Publishing House: 11.

[17] John Mugabe (1998). "Intellectual Property Protection and Traditional Knowledge: An Exploitation in International Policy Discourse". *Paper prepared for the World Intellectual Property Organization (WIPO)*, Geneva, Switzerland. [Available at http://www.acts.or.ke/paper%20-%20intellectual%20property.htm 18.07.2003]: 4.

[18] Charles F. Keyes (1999). "Approach To The Study Of Indigenous Knowledge System: Some Preliminary Thoughts", *Paper prepared for Thai - Vietnamese training workshop on anthropological methodology* held in Chiang Mai University, Thailand: 1-2.

[19] Pinkaew Laungaramsri (2001). *Karen Ecological Knowledge and the Challenge to the Modern Conservation Paradigm*. Chennai: Earthworm Books: 6-7.

local knowledge seems to coincide with the definition of traditional knowledge by Carlos M. Correa (2001). According to him, traditional knowledge includes the information about different kinds and functions that is developed during the past and continuously improved and adapted. It can be addressed in written and unwritten forms. It maybe also has the commercial value depending on its potential and current use.[20] In sum, there is always a shift from indigenous knowledge to traditional knowledge, then to local knowledge.

The overlapping utilization of the definition of "indigenous", "traditional", or "local" knowledge is relatively common and understandable. John Mugabe, in his study, also mentions various efforts of researchers to differentiate such knowledge systems. However, there is no universal definition of these systems. He writes, "There have been various efforts to define the concepts of traditional knowledge, indigenous knowledge, and indigenous peoples, but there are so far no universally adopted definitions." He continues that different persons have their own concepts depending on their intellectual persuasion and professional interest.[21] In agreement with difficulties and differentiations of concepts of such knowledge, WIPO state, "terms are not neutral, and the choice of a term is neither arbitrary nor irrelevant. The choice of term may be perceived as sending certain messages or value judgements, even if this is inadvertent."[22]

This knowledge is different from the formal knowledge and specialist knowledge that are identified as the elite and the profoundness of sciences, professions and intellectual of both Western and non Western societies.[23] Hoang Xuan Ty, a Vietnamese ecological-experienced researcher has the same thought as Brush. He considers academic knowledge to be created mainly by scientists, systematized and transmitted by books. Meanwhile, knowledge of indigenous people communities is created directly from the working process of the people. It is gradually perfected and handed down from one generation to the next by oral communication in the family, in the village, or through sayings, proverbs, epics, and local regulations, etc.[24] It came into being through "groping in the dark," not

[20] Carlos M. Correa (2001). "Traditional Knowledge and Intellectual Property. Issues and options surrounding the protection of traditional knowledge". Quaker United Nations Office Geneva. [available at http://hostings.diplomacy.edu/quaker/new/doc/tkcol3.pdf 18.07.2003]: 4.

[21] John Mugabe (1998). "Intellectual Property Protection and Traditional Knowledge: An Exploitation in International Policy Discourse". *Paper prepared for the World Intellectual Property Organization (WIPO)*, Geneva, Switzerland. [Available at http://www.acts.or.ke/paper%20-%20intellectual%20property.htm 18.07.2003].

[22] WIPO (2000). "Draft Report on Fact-finding Missions on Intellectual Property and Traditional Knowledge (1998-1999)". *Draft for Comment*, 3rd July 2000.

[23] Stephen B. Brush (1996). *Valuing local knowledge: indigenous people and intellectual property rights*, Washington D.C.: Island Press: 4.

[24] Hoang Xuan Ty (1998). "Part 1: Definitions and Roles of Indigenous Knowledge". In: Center for Ecological and Forest Studies (1998), *Indigenous knowledge of agriculture and natural resource management among the people in the uplands*. Hanoi: Agricultural Publishing House: 12.

through systematic experiments;[25] or through its encoding into an oral discourse (not in literary language and the use of sensual (especially visual) demonstration.[26]

In the literature, Rural People's Knowledge (RPK) (or local knowledge) is considered in three contrasting ways. The first is that RPK is "primitive", "unscientific", "wrong", etc. Formal research and extension must "educate", "direct" and "transform" rural people's production and livelihood strategies to "develop" or "modernize" them. The second, RPK is a "valuable and under-utilized resource" and needs to be intensively and extensively studied, and "incorporated" into formal research and extension practice to make agriculture and rural development strategies more "sustainable." The last way is that neither RPK nor Western science can be regarded as unitary "bodies" or "stocks" of knowledge. Instead, they represent contrasting multiple epistemologies produced within particular agro-ecological, socio-cultural and political-economic settings. The interaction of RPK makes current research and extension practice address fundamental issues of power and need in development.[27]

Obviously, knowledge of local, traditional, or indigenous people has some limitations. IDS workshop assembles the limitations of indigenous knowledge (ITK) in the following description:[28]

- ITK and innovative capacity is unevenly distributed within and across communities.
- The ability of individuals to generate, implement, and transfer ITK varies greatly.
- Social groups and economic stratification affect the type and extent of ITK in rural societies (for example, richer individuals are likely to innovate more in aggregate, but poorer people may be forced to innovate by their poverty).
- The transfer and use of information is sometimes constrained and error prone where it has to be passed on orally and held in the heads of practitioners.
- The scope for improvements from "pure" ITK is limited to what can be done with the local pool of techniques, materials and genetics resources, plus whatever is produced casually.
- Many genetic possibilities are not exploited within the informal system, such as the crossing of self-pollinating crops where specific plant-breeding techniques are required.
- Finally, ITK may break down when people are faced with an environmental crisis or external interventions.[29]

---

[25] Le Trong Cuc (1996). "The role of local knowledge to sustainable highlands development". In: *Agriculture on sloping lands: challenges and potential*, edited by Tran Duc Vien and Pham Chi Thanh. Hanoi: Agricultural Publishing House: 27.

[26] Georg Elwert and Lazare Séhouéto (1999). "Local Knowledge and the Improvement of Food Production – A Case Study in Bénin". In: Uwe Kracht and Manfred Schulz (eds.), *Food Security and Nutrition: The Global Challenge*. Münster: LIT VERLAG: 238.

[27] Ian Scoones and John Thompson (1994). "Knowledge, power and agriculture-towards a theoretical understanding". In: Ian Scoones and John Thompson (eds.) (1994), *Beyond Farmer First: Rural people's knowledge, agricultural research and extension practice*. Intermediate Technology Publications: 17-18.

[28] IDS: Institute of Development Studies (University of Sussex, Brighton, East Sussex, BN1 9RE, UK.

Apart from these, other limitations of indigenous knowledge are mentioned in Hoang Xuan Ty's study including that due to the high local character of IK, it is hard to disseminate widely IK of this region to another. In addition, similar to the last limit of IK addressed by Farrington and Martin (1987) in the IDS workshop, Ty states that often indigenous knowledge does not fit to the current social situation and the changing environment nowadays any more.[30] Therefore, it is reasonable that the knowledge of the people is always dynamic, changeable and adaptable to the changing environmental and social circumstances. Afterwards, the indigenous knowledge is gradually developed into traditional knowledge, and into local knowledge under the impact of an external system of the new and modern knowledge.

The contradiction of these two knowledge systems does not prevent the fluidity and the permeability of knowledge and culture boundaries because both encompass acceptable parts of each other. Therefore, local knowledge as common sense is considered as a cultural system or as traditional cultures.[31] Similarly, Tran Binh points out that knowledge of economic activities is considered as a part of the cultural systems of ethnic groups. Due to living in different natural environments, each ethnic group has its own behaviour to subsist and develop. Even each community has its mode of thought and action despite of their share of the same environment.[32]

Thanks to the consideration of indigenous knowledge as cultural knowledge, according to Paul Richards (1985, 1986), Moock and Rhoades (1992), the cultural knowledge produces and reproduces mutual understanding and identity among the members of a farming community, where local technical knowledge, skills and capacities are inextricably linked to non-technical ones (such as cultural, ecological and sociological factors).[33] It is obvious that cultural aspects of different kinds of the farmers' knowledge involve in folk wisdom and

---

[29] IDS workshop (1989). "Farmers' knowledge, innovation, and relation to science". In: Robert Chambers, Arnold Pacey, and Lori Ann Thrupp (eds.), *Farmer First: Farmer Innovation and Agricultural Research*. Intermediate Technology Publications: 37.

[30] Hoang Xuan Ty (1998). "Part 1: Definitions and Roles of Indigenous Knowledge". In: Center for Ecological and Forest Studies (1998), *Indigenous knowledge of agriculture and natural resource management among the people in the uplands*. Hanoi: Agricultural Publishing House: 25.

[31] Clifford Geertz (1993a). *Local knowledge: Further essays in interpretive anthropology*. FontanaPress-An Imprint of HarperCollins Publisher.

- Le Trong Cuc (1996). "The role of local knowledge to sustainable highlands development". In: *Agriculture on sloping lands: challenges and potential*, edited by Tran Duc Vien and Pham Chi Thanh. Hanoi: Agricultural Publishing House: 21.

[32] Tran Binh (2001). *Customs of economic activities of some ethnic groups in the Northwest of Vietnam)*. Hanoi: National Culture Publishing House: 6.

[33] Paul Richards (1985). *Indigenous Agricultural Revolution: ecology and food production in West Africa*. London: Hutchinson, Great Britain.

- Paul Richards (1986). *Coping with hunger: Hazard and Experiment in an African Rice-farming System*. London: Allen and Unwin.
- Ian Scoones and John Thompson (1994). "Knowledge, power and agriculture-towards a theoretical understanding". In: Ian Scoones and John Thompson (eds.) (1994), *Beyond Farmer First: Rural peoples knowledge, agricultural research and extension practice*. Intermediate Technology Publications: 18.

ritual ceremonies which are often considered as superstition by the scientists and the policy-makers.

One important question raised by IDS workshop (1989) is how to deal with indigenous knowledge that is apparently tinged with myth and superstition. Although scientists may respect farmers' interventions such as a modified hoe which saves labour, they are likely to ridicule the idea that the moon influences plant growth or that injections can encourage a plant to fruit, because these make no obvious sense to them. Indeed, such ideas provide ammunition to scientists who are tempted to dismiss local knowledge as worthless.[34] The reason for this undervaluation of local knowledge is that scientists often trust only in the modern scientific achievement. Additionally, they assess the farmers' ideas and perceptions as absolute outsiders. They rarely, or not at all, make a reckoning of the spiritual life, traditional ways of temporal and weather forecast (an aspect of the ethnic culture) of the local inhabitants, whom they communicate with and study. As a result, their denial of the farmers' conceptions and interpretations is obvious. However, it is very important to recognize that the people have lived in their own communities and the environment for a long time. To survive, they apply all their skills and experiences to their living. Additionally, their belief in several spirits has helped them to overcome many difficulties in their lives. In reality, the economics of the local people is mostly based on the agriculture that was completely dependent on the natural environment in the previous period, and is still dependent mostly on it in recent years. Therefore, their experience with the weather forecast to practice the productive activities is utilized commonly in various ethnic groups that have a tradition of age-old agriculture.[35] Over and above, the ideology and the persuasion contribute to creating and influencing the characteristics of traditional knowledge of the people.[36] This coincides with the statement of Jonathan Rouse when he mentions characters of traditional knowledge and that it is not necessary for them to operate in the same cosmology as western science.[37]

In opposition to the ideas of mocking farmers' knowledge, Nguyen Van Truong states that criticizing and denigrating local knowledge betrays a lack of

---

[34] IDS workshop (1989). "Farmers' knowledge, innovation, and relation to science". In: Robert Chambers, Arnold Pacey, and Lori Ann Thrupp (eds.), *Farmer First: Farmer Innovation and Agricultural Research*. Intermediate Technology Publications: 36.

[35] Bronislaw Malinowski (1935). *Coral Gardens and Their Magic-A Study of the Methods of Tilling the Soil and of Agricultural Rites in the Trobriand Islands*. London: George Allen and Unwin Ltd. Ruskin House, England; American Book Company.

- Nong Trung (1971). "Chapter VII: Folklore and indigenous knowledge". In: Be Viet Dang, Nguyen Khac Tung, Nong Trung and Nguyen Nam Tien (1971), *The Yao in Vietnam*. Hanoi: Social Science Publishing House: 294-327.

- Ly Hanh Son (1999). "Chapter VIII: Indigenous knowledge". In: Pham Quang Hoan and Hung Dinh Quy (eds.) (1999), *Traditional culture of the Yao in Ha Giang province*. Hanoi: Social Science Publishing House.

[36] M. M. Ahmed (1994). *Indigenous Knowledge for Sustainable Development in the Sudan*. Khartoum: Khartoum University Press: 13.

[37] Jonathan Rouse (1999). "Global Dissemination of Indigenous Knowledge - Contradiction, or the Way Forward?". Available at: http://www.worldbank.org/afr/ik/global_1k99061.htm.

understanding of the scientific, socio-economic and ecological basis of a way of life, and spiritual and intellectual shallowness."[38] In principle, no knowledge is naturally bad. The question is how to use it correspondingly. Indigenous knowledge does not contradict modern knowledge, but they supplement each other in order to achieve a much better sustainability instead of mechanical applications of all outside things.[39] Similarly, traditional knowledge and decision making share many of the attributes that modern management theory is trying to promote the flexibility, the fluidity and the responsiveness. Modern management principles, as with local agriculture practice, conflate the roles of specialists and generalists.[40]

Based on the analysis of difference of "indigenous", "traditional", and "local" knowledge, I suggest a figure of the model of the mutual interaction of these three knowledge systems and their relations to modern knowledge. However, depending on each rural people community, the level of interaction of these systems can be clear, strong and remarkable or not.

In short, local knowledge, in this study, is understood as the knowledge, both indigenous and traditional, that is accumulated and transmitted from one generation to another and interacted by the new or modern knowledge. To adapt to the changing environment, including naturally, socio-economically and culturally, the people inherit available long-term knowledge in combination with the application of modern knowledge to their daily lives. Gradually, through this combination, the new knowledge is localized by the people appropriate for their living environment and becomes their experience. Therefore, local knowledge of rural people is not immutable, untouchable or unchangeable, but obviously dynamic. It is changed by the invention and innovation of the local people as well as by relations to other knowledge systems. As a convincing evidence of the dynamic character of local knowledge, rural people in many areas of the highlands partly shift their modes of thought and actions in order to achieve a better life.

2.1.2 Local knowledge and local people

In principle, suggested John Mugabe (1998), this knowledge changes its character when the needs of the people change. It is thus very difficult to isolate traditional knowledge from traditional people.[41] Tran Quoc Vuong and his colleagues also mention the similarity when they focus on the role of people in

---

[38] Nguyen Van Truong (1994). "An approach to concept of mountain development of natural resources in Vietnam at commune and village levels". Hanoi workshop presentation, October 14-16, 1994.

[39] Hoang Xuan Ty (1998). "Part 1: Definitions and Roles of Indigenous Knowledge". In: Center for Ecological and Forest Studies (1998), *Indigenous knowledge of agriculture and natural resource management among the people in the uplands*. Hanoi: Agricultural Publishing House: 33.

[40] David Marsden (1994). "Indigenous management and the management of indigenous knowledge". In: *Beyond Farmer First: Rural People's Knowledge, Agricultural research and extension practice*, edited by Ian Scoones and John Thompson with a foreword by Robert Chambers. Intermediate Technology Publications: 56.

[41] John Mugabe (1998). "Intellectual Property Protection and Traditional Knowledge: An Exploitation in International Policy Discourse". *Paper prepared for the World Intellectual Property Organization (WIPO)*, Geneva, Switzerland. [Available at http://www.acts.or.ke/paper%20-%20intellectual%20property.htm 18.07.2003]: 5.

generating their culture. According to them, the people are both the subject and the object of the culture.[42]

The relationship between knowledge and people is also reflected in several definitions of knowledge systems, including "indigenous", "traditional", or "local" knowledge. Therefore, indigenous knowledge is usually referred to in parallel and together with indigenous people. According to the Article 1, part (b) of the ILO convention, "peoples in independent countries who are regarded as indigenous on account of their descent from the populations which inhabited the country, or a geographic region to which the country belongs, at the time of conquest or colonisation or the establishment of present state boundaries and who, irrespective of their legal status, retain some or all of their own social, economic, cultural and political institutions."[43] Similarly, a reference of "traditional" or "local" knowledge is closely related to the "traditional" or "local" people. In this study, the local people are, not so complicated as identification of indigenous people, implied as the people who have been living in a certain region.

In short, knowledge systems have a close and profound relation to the people because, like the culture in general, knowledge cannot generate itself. On the contrary, it is always an intellectual produce of a certain ethnic group, a group of people or an individual. In addition, a survey of "indigenous", "traditional", or "local" knowledge concerns about the historical migration of the people in the research area.

2.1.3 Local knowledge and context

Most anthropological and ethnological studies of traditional knowledge or local knowledge have been conducted within the general frameworks of "human and cultural ecology" and "ethnoecology". The term "human ecology" has had many meanings when used in different disciplines by different scientists at different points in the history of their disciplines. However, human ecology is normally used to refer to interactions between agroecosystems and human social systems, or between forestry and social systems.[44] It is found that a subset of human ecology refers to the study of the interactions between ecologically economic systems and human social systems. It is not quite different from the term of human ecology, "ethnoecology" as a part of ethnoscience, according to D. L. Hardesty (1977), is defined as "the study of systems of knowledge developed by a given culture to classify the objectives, activities, and events of

[42] Tran Quoc Vuong (ed.) (2000). *Vietnamese cultural basis*. Second Edition. Hanoi: Educational Publishing House: 9.

[43] Convention 169 (1989). *Indigenous and Tribal Peoples Convention*, 5/9/1989.

[44] T. P. Bayliss-Smith (1982). *The Ecology of Agricultural Systems*. Cambridge: Cambridge University Express.

- A. Terry Rambo and P. E. Sajise (eds.) (1985). *An Introduction to Human Ecology Research on Agricultural Systems in Southeast Asia*. Los Banos: University of the Philippines.

- Gerald G. Marten and Daniel M. Saltman (1986). "The Human Ecology Perspective". In: Gerald G. Marten (ed.) (1986), *Traditional Agriculture in Southeast Asia*. Boulder and London: Westview Press: 20-53.

- CH. Agrawal and S. Saigal (1996). *Joint Forest Management in India: A Brief Review*. Society for Promotion of Wastelands Development, India.

its universe."[45] Therefore, ethnoecology refers to the study of how traditional groups organize and classify their knowledge of the environment and environmental processes.[46] It is thus concise that study of ethnoecology has the same meaning with the study of how a particular ethnic group views the world it inhabits and how this helps this group to interact with the environment. Definitions of "human ecology" and "ethnoecology" include the term "cultural ecology" because both of them reflect interactions of the people with the environment and ecosystems. By this way, their culture is exposed. The relationship of the people and the environment as well as socio-economic circumstances is more understood in the following texts, excluding in the second part of food security and accessibilities to food of this chapter.

People exist in close relation to nature. The relationship between people and nature, therefore, is a basic aspect of culture. It is a multidimensional, adaptable, inadaptable and changeable (naturally, socially and by the people themselves) kind of relationship. The common trend of people is to adjust to the available natural environment and cope compatibly with the challenges made by them themselves.[47] Although the natural condition does not determine the development process of the society, it influences the choice of productive tools and implements of the people as well as the distinction of their manners of production.

In addition, the people live not only with nature, but also with each other and within the society. They are not able to live separate from their society. In their small-scale society, culture is created, preserved and developed from generation to generation.[48] As a basic social unit, the family is the first cultural environment for an individual to absorb the culture of his community.[49] Having the same opinion of Tran Quoc Vuong and his colleagues, Ian Scoones and John Thompson (1994) identify the extremely significant role of the people and their society in holding, controlling and generating the culture, including local knowledge. They write that "no knowledge can exist in a cultural, economic or political vacuum... Knowledge is socially and politically constructed; it requires a socially differentiated, politically astute analysis to comprehend."[50]

[45] Cited in J. Peter Brosius, George W. Lovelace, and Gerald G. Marten (1986). "Ethnoecology: An Approach to Understanding Traditional Agricultural Knowledge". In: Gerald G. Marten (ed.) (1986), *Traditional Agriculture in Southeast Asia*. Boulder and London: Westview Press: 187.

[46] J. Peter Brosius, George W. Lovelace, and Gerald G. Marten (1986). *ibid*: 187-188.

[47] Tran Quoc Vuong (ed.) (2000). *Vietnamese cultural basis*. Second Edition. Hanoi: Educational Publishing House: 9-30.

[48] Arun Agrawal (1995). "Dismantling the Divide Between Indigenous and Scientific Knowledge". *Development and Change*. Volume 26, No. 3: 416.

- Jonathan Rouse (1999). "Global Dissemination of Indigenous Knowledge - Contradiction, or the Way Forward?". Available at: http://www.worldbank.org/afr/ik/global_1k99061.htm.

[49] Tran Quoc Vuong (ed.) (2000). *Vietnamese cultural basis*. Second Edition. Hanoi: Educational Publishing House: 36-41.

[50] Ian Scoones and John Thompson (1994). "Knowledge, power and agriculture-towards a theoretical understanding". In: Ian Scoones and John Thompson (eds.) (1994), *Beyond Farmer First: Rural peoples knowledge, agricultural research and extension practice*. Intermediate Technology Publications: 25.

The relationship between local knowledge and its socio-ecological context is also emphasised in a case study of the farmers' knowledge in Kenya presented by Juma (1987). According to Juma, local knowledge about plants and seeds of the people can be better understood if we recognize that it is based on a distinctive epistemology that is unique to these people's culture. Their knowledge and practices have co-evolved over time as adaptations to particular environmental, socio-economic, and political circumstances and pressures. This epistemology is also associated with religious beliefs about the plants and their uses. In this sense, their religion is partly a way of treasuring values resources.[51] M. M. Ahmed (1994) has a similar viewpoint as Juma has when he examines the context in which the traditional knowledge of the people exists and is found.[52]

In general, it is found that local knowledge and local people have a close relation to each other. Moreover, people have also a very close and deep relationship with their natural, socio-economic, and political environments. Those environments are indispensable for the generations and the development of the culture. Therefore, as a cultural aspect, local knowledge should be recognized as a systematic entire in order to interpret the relationship between people and nature, people and society. These two important factors are always referred to in parallel to local knowledge presented in the next chapter of this study.

2.1.4 Classification of local knowledge

Local knowledge includes various types of knowledge. Like traditional knowledge, kinds of local knowledge can be distinguished based on the accompanying factors, potentials and practices of knowledge, on individual or collective ownership and its legal circumstance. The literature on local knowledge suggests that local knowledge encompasses information about the conception of the people of the world, cosmology and spiritual life, including application of witchcraft, and hermaphroditism. This information is always connected to the context in which it appears and exists. For example, witchcraft practices relate to magic disease treatment or to ritual ceremony of herbal medicine collection and use. Cultural aspects of witchcraft and religion are presented in many publications.[53]

Ngo Duc Thinh (1994) classifies folk knowledge of ethnic groups, a broader term of local knowledge, into the four following types: 1) Knowledge of nature and the environment; 2) Knowledge of human beings; 3) Knowledge of production; 4) Knowledge of the management of community and society. This

---

[51] IDS workshop (1989). "Farmers' knowledge, innovation, and relation to science". In: Robert Chambers, Arnold Pacey, and Lori Ann Thrupp (eds.), *Farmer First: Farmer Innovation and Agricultural Research*. Intermediate Technology Publications: 33.

[52] M. M. Ahmed (1994). *Indigenous Knowledge for Sustainable Development in the Sudan*. Khartoum: Khartoum University Press: 13.

[53] Grant Evans (ed.) (1993). *Asia's Cultural Mosaic - An Anthropological Introduction*. Singapore: Prentice Hall.

- Cecil G. Helman (1990). *Culture, Health and Illness: An Introduction for Health Professionals*. Second Edition. Wight Publisher.

- Peter Brown, Kendra Hatfield Timajchy, and Jun Hu (1997). "Medical anthropology". In: *Blackwell Dictionary of Anthropology*, edited by Thomas J. Barfield. Oxford: Basil Blackwell: 316-318.

classification is influenced by the Soviet science of ethnic groups.[54] In a generalizing way, Hoang Xuan Ty (1998) considers that this kind of knowledge includes many different fields relating to agro-forestry, management of natural resources and of community.[55] Dennis Michael Warren points out that each society has its own variety of knowledge systems. Some of them regard the natural and physical environments (such as soil taxonomies); some concern about cognitive and ideational environments; some others refer to the social circumstances (such as kinship systems).[56] Similarly, regarding to agricultural practices, local knowledge concern the farmers' classification of plants and soils. Local people use many categories in different parts of the world to describe types of land, landscape, crops, wild plant species and other natural resources. The categories and names used by them usually differ from those used by scientists.[57] In another research by Dennis Michael Warren, he uses the term of indigenous technical knowledge to limit the scope of indigenous knowledge. To him, this knowledge system consists of knowledge of cultivation, livestock breeding, forest and community natural resource management, nutrition and human health, and community administration and transmission of experience to the younger generation.[58]

In general, local knowledge deals with various issues of human life, from the process of agricultural production, techniques to spiritual life and art of the local people. In other words, local knowledge is a pattern of response and behaviour, and adaptability of an ethnic group to the ecological and human environment. Local knowledge can be owned by an individual or by some members of a group or by all group members. Therefore, there are three overlapping types of knowledge: popular, folk and professional.

Many different issues of local knowledge were referred to and discussed about. However, it is still a question of what local knowledge on food security means because of the complexity and the broad term of food security. To answer this question, first, we should clarify what is the key issue of food security in the world, including in Vietnam, particularly for ethnic minorities. Based on that, we can recognize aspects of local knowledge in this field.

---

[54] Cited in Pham Quang Hoan (1999). "Local knowledge on natural resource management of ethnic minorities in Vietnam". Hanoi: *Vietnam Social Sciences*, No. 3: 43.

[55] Hoang Xuan Ty (1998). "Part 1: Definitions and Roles of Indigenous Knowledge". In: Center for Ecological and Forest Studies (1998), *Indigenous knowledge of agriculture and natural resource management among the people in the uplands*. Hanoi: Agricultural Publishing House: 11.

[56] Dennis Michael Warren (1989). "Introduction". In: Paul Richards, L. Jan Slikkerveer, and Adedotun O. Philips. (1989), *Indigenous Knowledge Systems for Agriculture and Rural Development: The CIKARD Inaugural Lectures*, Studies in Technology and Social Change, No. 13. Iowa State University Research Foundation: 1.

[57] IDS workshop (1989). "Farmers' knowledge, innovation, and relation to science". In: Robert Chambers, Arnold Pacey, and Lori Ann Thrupp (eds.), *Farmer First: Farmer Innovation and Agricultural Research*. Intermediate Technology Publications: 31.

[58] Cited in Hoang Xuan Ty (1998). "Part 1: Definitions and Roles of Indigenous Knowledge". In: Center for Ecological and Forest Studies (1998), *Indigenous knowledge of agriculture and natural resource management among the people in the uplands*. Hanoi: Agricultural Publishing House: 12-14.

2.2 Food security

2.2.1 Definition of food security

Food security has been the concern of many people since the 1970s. However, the common concept of food security remains controversial. Maxwell (1996) points out that there are about 200 definitions of food security depending on the approach of each person and each organization. In 1986, the World Bank defined food security as "access by all people at all times to enough food for an active, healthy life." The FAO and WHO (1992) define food security in its most basic form as the access of all people to the food needed for a healthy life at all times.[59] According to the Plan of Action of the World Food Summit held in Rome in November 1996, food security exists when all people, at all times, have physical and economic access to sufficient, safe and nutritious food to meet their dietary needs and food preferences for an active and healthy life. Achieving food security means ensuring that sufficient food is available, that supplies are relatively stable and that those in need of food can obtain it. Therefore, the dimension of food security is one of the three essential elements of a sustainable and equitable agriculture policy.[60]

In general, in my view, food security could be understood as access for all people to sustained livelihood sources in order to get food or an amount of money equivalent to food purchase. However, depending on each region and each country or even each small-scale society, the livelihood resources vary. We can recognize this by determining and analyzing aspects of food security in the following section.

2.2.2 Aspects of food security

Food security can be also understood in another way. It is *an issue of low household income*, poverty and not just inadequate aggregate food production, challenges programs which encourage women to just growth more food crops to improve their food security.[61] There are two types of food insecurity. They are chronic and transitory food insecurity. Chronic food insecurity is a long-term problem caused at the household level by lack of income or of assets to produce or buy food adequate for the household. Meanwhile, transitory food insecurity is a short-term food security problem caused by a shock to the food production or economic system, where income or resources necessary to adjust to the shock are not available.[62]

---

[59] Cited in Joachim von Braun (1999). "Food Security - A Concept Basis". In: Uwe Kracht and Manfred Schulz (eds.) (1999), *Food Security and Nutrition: The Global Challenge*. Münster: LIT VERLAG: 41.

[60] According to Shiva, the two other essential elements of a sustainable and equitable agriculture policy are the dimensions of ecological security and of livelihood security. See: Vandana Shiva. 2002. "Globalisation of Agriculture, Food Security and Sustainability". In: Vandana Shiva and Gitanjali Bedi (eds.), *Sustainable Agriculture and Food Security: The Impact of Globalisation*. New Delhi: Sage Publications: 11.

[61] Christina H. Gladwin, Anne M. Thomson, Jennifer S. Peterson, and Andrea S. Anderson (2001). "Addressing food security in Africa via multiple livelihood strategies of women farmers". *Food Policy*, Volume 26, Number 2: 179-180.

[62] Christina H. Gladwin, Anne M. Thomson, Jennifer S. Peterson, and Andrea S. Anderson (2001). *ibid*: 180.

Joachim von Braun (1999) links food security to nutrition. Household income therefore is referred to as an important condition for the people to access to food. He writes, "increasing the incomes of households that have malnourished members can improve their access to food. Increases in income are strongly related to non-staple food consumption, particularly of meats."[63]

The current thinking of food security regarding to *poverty* is increasingly common. It is obvious to determine or define poverty in correlation to the definition of food security. Poverty means a condition of absolute or relative deprivation of material and cultural resources. In the developed world, poverty is "more likely to be relative (the lack of resources in comparison with other members of a given society) than absolute (the condition in which the basic resources necessary to sustain life are lacking), in that basic needs are met even for the poor. In less developed countries, poverty is also likely to be absolute. Lack of adequate nutrition, housing, and health care are primary concerns, especially lack of food. Adequate food, health, and basic education have all been consistently demonstrated to be important foundations for economic development."[64] Robert Chambers and Melissa Leach (1989) also show the synonym of poverty as deprivation in normal professional usage. When they reflect the urban and industrial origins of poverty studies, poverty is defined in terms of low incomes and outlays.[65]

However, according to Joachim von Braun and Rajul Pandya-Lorch (1992), poverty is essentially, but not always, a matter of low incomes, where the cost of acquiring a certain commodity bundle determines the income or expenditure-based poverty line. An income-based indicator is an indirect means of measuring poverty. In their view, poverty is measured directly through consumption and nutrition outcomes.[66]

In a broader recognition, the World Bank points out that poverty has many faces, changing from one place to another and overtime. It is described in many different ways. Due to the various dimensions of poverty, it is indispensable to look at it through a variety of indicators - levels of income and consumption, social indicators, and now increasingly indicators of vulnerability to risks and of socio-political access. The World Bank then comes to the conclusion that "poverty is a call to action - for the poor and the wealthy alike - a call to change the world so that many more may have enough to eat, adequate shelter, access to education and health, protection from violence, and a voice in what happens in their communities."[67] The eradication of extreme poverty and

---

[63] Joachim Von Braun (1999). "Food Security - A Concept Basis". In: Uwe Kracht and Manfred Schulz (eds.) (1999), *Food Security and Nutrition: The Global Challenge*. Münster: LIT VERLAG: 42.

[64] Craig Calhoun (2002). *Dictionary of the social science*. Oxford: Oxford University Press: 376-377.

[65] Robert Chambers and Melissa Leach (1989). "Trees as Savings and Security for The Rural Poor". *World Development* 17 (3): 329.

[66] Joachim Von Braun and Rajul Pandya-Lorch (1992). "Income Source and Diversification Strategies of the Malnourished Rural Poor": 36.

[67] WB (2003b). *Understanding and Responding to Poverty - World Bank Poverty Net*. Available at http://www.worldbank.org/poverty/mission/up1.htm .

hunger is therefore one of the eight important goals of the Millennium Development Goals (MDGs) established by the United Nations.[68] Therefore, it is found that poverty is the situation that a group of people have no benefit and do not satisfy the human basic needs recognized by the society depending on the socio-economic development and customs and habits of the community.

Both conceptions of food security and poverty are vulnerable. In previous studies, the vulnerability of these conceptions is frequently overlooked. Recently, thanks to some lessons learned of food insecurity, some researchers pay more attention to critique of the vulnerability of conceptions of food security and poverty. According to these researchers, this vulnerability influences strongly and directly on the life of rural people, especially the poor households.[69]

Food scarcity is considered as one of the main aspects of food insecurity. Many rural people in developing countries have to face food scarcity, especially in between-harvest periods. At that time, food prices go up. The poor cannot afford it; therefore, they accumulate experience of how to confront seasonal food scarcity. They try to store some amounts of food for the household during this period. Helen Young refers that there are two main reasons for seasonal food scarcity. They are: 1) war, insecurity and armed conflict, and 2) drought, floods, pests or crop disease.[70] The first reason is completely correct for the problem of food security in many countries of Africa. Wars and armed conflicts, both domestic and international, with their consequences, unfortunately, remain in some other countries such as in Palestine, Afghanistan, and recently in Iraq. Victims are finally innocent citizens. They live in a state of insecurity during and after such wars and conflicts. To them, famine is a reality. This is seemingly appropriate for Vietnam before the period of the Vietnamese Revolution. A terrible famine in Vietnam in 1945 that caused the death of two million people is convincing evidence of extreme and profound food scarcity and food insecurity. Similarly, many thousands of people in the Wollo Region of Ethiopia died in a famine in 1984.[71] They are the consequence of unchecked or uncontrolled long-term food scarcity.

According to Young, the impact of food scarcity varies and depends on human sources and their adaptation. If food scarcity happens in a short time while the people have many sources, they can supplement this scarcity by exploiting available sources or changing their traditional way of life. However,

[68] According to Kevin Cleaver, in addition to the eradication of extreme poverty and hunger, the other seven goals of MDGs include: 1) Achieve universal primary education; 2) Promote gender equality and empower women; 3) Reduce child mortality; 4) Improve material health; 5) Combat HIV/ AIDS, malaria and other diseases; 6) Ensure environmental sustainability, and 7) Develop a Global Partnership for Development. See: Kevin Cleaver (2002). "Issues confronting the 2002 rural development strategy of the World Bank". Unpublished paper: 2.

[69] Robert Chambers and Melissa Leach (1989). "Trees as Savings and Security for The Rural Poor". *World Development* 17 (3): 329-342.

- Maxx Dilley and Tanya E. Boudreau (2001). "Coming to terms with vulnerability: a critique of the food security definition". *Food Policy*, Volume 26: 229-247.

[70] Helen Young (1992). *Food Scarcity and Famine: Assessment and Response*. Oxford: Oxfam Practical Health No. 7: 3.

[71] Helen Young (1992). *ibid*: 3.

if food scarcity is not quickly controlled, it will erode human livelihoods. Therefore, famine is an automatic consequence. Famine thus refers to the later stages of food scarcity when people become destitute and many of them more than normal die due to the conditions produced by famines, which encourage the spread of disease.[72] It is evident that the human livelihood sources are indispensable for the people to get food (both staple-food and supplemental food). Available natural source-based livelihoods contribute considerably to supplementing food shortage of the people, especially, in the between-crops season or in a lean year caused by a natural catastrophe and other factors. However, these sources will erode steadily caused by the quick and uncontrolled population growth as well as by unplanned natural resource management.

Derived from the definition of food security and poverty, food security is thus related to various factors. The determination of criterions of poverty line calculation, the development strategies are accounted partly for the solution of food problems. Policies about food security, hunger elimination and poverty reduction are different from country to country. In Africa, food security depends on entitlement to access to food through a variety of means: on-farm production, market exchange and donations. Therefore, the potential strategies for enhancing food security are distinguished by the realm of food entitlement and the role of the coping strategy within the household budget. Similarly, according to Akhter, in Bangladesh, food security tends to be involved in sustainable multi-livelihoods.[73]

In a specific view, J. A. Ekpere (2001) argues that biodiversity, including agro-biodiversity, is the essential basis of food security and food autonomy for households.[74] According to him, the livelihoods of farmers, fishermen and healers of the local communities still depend almost exclusively on biological resources, innovations, technologies, and practices.[75] Similarly, in reference to the importance of sustainability, Shiva shows that sustainability requires the protection of all species and all people and the recognition that diverse species and diverse people play an essential role in maintaining ecosystems and ecological processes.[76]

The FAO's and World Bank's literature on poverty and food security points out that agricultural growth is essential to income growth in most low-income countries because agricultural output constitutes such a large percentage of total output (24 percent of total output comes from agriculture for all low-income

[72] Helen Young (1992). *ibid*: 3-4.

[73] Farida Akhter (2001). "Resisting "Technology" and Defending Subsistence in Bangladesh: Nayakrishi Andolon and the Movement for a Happy Life". In: *There is an alternative: subsistence and worldwide resistance to corporate globalization*, edited by Veronika Bennholdt - Thomsen, Nicholas Faraclas, and Claudia von Werlhof, North Melbourne. Victoria: Spinifex Press.

[74] J. A. Ekpere (Project Coordinator). "The OAU's Model Law: The Protection of the Rights of Local Communities, Farmers and Breeders, and for the Regulation of Access to Biological Resources (An Explanatory Booklet)". *Organization of African Unity*. Scientific, Technical and Research Commission, P.M.B. 2359 Lagos, Nigeria: 10.

[75] J. A. Ekpere (Project Coordinator). *ibid*: 4.

[76] Vandana Shiva (2001). "Globalization and Poverty". In: Veronika Bennholdt-Thomsen, Nicholas G. Faraclas and Claudia von Werlhof (eds.), *There is an Alternative: Subsistence and Worldwide Resistance to Corporate Globalization.* Victoria: Spinifex Press: 64.

countries). Similarly, in a study by Vandana Shiva (2002), farming systems play a dominant role in food security and nutrition of the people. Moreover, she points out that food security lies in ecologically resilient and economically efficient farming systems, which provide a livelihood to farmers and sufficiency in food for the household, community, regional and national levels, and which are providing safe and nutritious food to consumers.[77] Therefore, ecosystem and farming system have a close and mutual interaction. Both systems are influenced by farmers, and vice versa. In this case, her point of view coincides with the perspective of "human ecology."

"Human ecology" provides the holism needed to comprehend interactions between agroecosystems and human social systems. Among those, agricultural sectors are ecosystem (the so-called agroecosystems) with the large number of interacting and interdependent physical and biological components.[78] Farmers are considered as part of a human social system. Agroecosystems interact with adjoining ecosystems and with the social systems of the people who farm them. These interactions involve exchanges of energy, materials, and information within and between the two systems (Figure 2.1).[79] Agroecosystems and social systems can interact in a range of scales. A few square meters of farmland are an ecosystem, and so is entire continent. Human social systems can be households, villages, ethnic groups, nations, and the international community of nations.[80]

---

[77] Vandana Shiva (2002). "Globalisation of Agriculture, Food Security and Sustainability". In: Vandana Shiva and Gitanjali Bedi (eds.), *Sustainable Agriculture and Food Security: The Impact of Globalisation*. New Delhi: Sage Publications: 24.

[78] One of the main characteristics distinguishing agricultural ecosystems from natural ecosystems is the primary role that human activities have in shaping the structure and function of agroecosystems with the aim of providing desired goods and services. See more: Gerald G. Marten and Daniel M. Saltman (1986). "The Human Ecology Perspective". In: Gerald G. Marten (ed.) (1986), *Traditional Agriculture in Southeast Asia*. Boulder and London: Westview Press: 24.

[79] Gerald G. Marten and Daniel M. Saltman (1986). "The Human Ecology Perspective". In: Gerald G. Marten (ed.) (1986), *Traditional Agriculture in Southeast Asia*. Boulder and London: Westview Press: 20.

[80] Gerald G. Marten and Daniel M. Saltman (1986). *ibid*: 22.

Figure 2.1. Interactions between Agroecosystems and the Human Social Systems

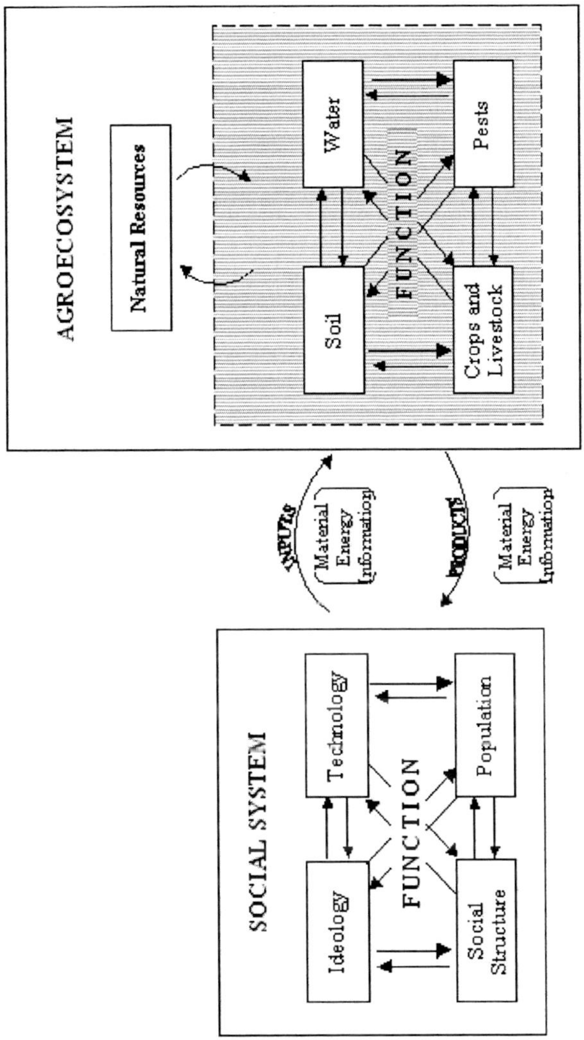

Source: Rambo 1982, modified by Gerald G. Marten and Daniel M. Saltman (1986): 21.

Similarly, Daniel Maxwell and Keith Wiebe (1998) suggest that food security of the non-urban people is closely related to land property and entitlement to natural resources.[1] This is also important factors of the sustainable agriculture which is based on the sustainable use of natural sources - land, water and agricultural biodiversity.[2] Joachim von Braun (1999) also emphasizes importance of land as one of the main productive sources and of the livelihoods for the rural people. He argues that the prevalence of food insecurity tends to be higher among landless or quasi-landless households, which are much more dependent on less reliable sources of income than farm income and on the diversification of the rural economy.[3] It is found that in agrarian countries, agriculture has direct linkages to food security at the local level. Land is one of the most crucial productive sources in these countries. Therefore, land use and land tenure have direct impacts on food security. In addition, their impacts on food security and natural resource management are complex. This is also appropriate for an agrarian country like Vietnam, where ¾ of the country area is hilly and mountainous and about 80 percent of the total population is farmers.

2.2.3 Food security in Vietnam

The empirical evidence of poverty trends is that the part of the population living in the towns tends to be wealthier than before. The rest who mainly live in remote and mountainous areas are driven into poverty. In some remote areas, their seasonal food scarcity lasts from May to October every year. Therefore, the problem of food security is always a regular concern of rural mountain people. However, the levels of poverty of ethnic minorities are different depending on each regional economy, educational knowledge and living standard of each ethnic group. It is clear that the income of a certain area is maybe considered as enough to live, but not acceptable in another area due to the high expense there.

As another understanding of the term "food security", the poverty line can be calculated in different ways depending on each country and each agency. The methodology of identification and determination of poverty line used is a source of regular controversy. In many developed countries, criterion of poverty is normally based on cash income. In comparison, in the developing countries, especially in agrarian countries, food and food consumption are normally used as criteria of poverty determination.

In Vietnam, the concept of food security and its indicators are closely related to the concept and indicators of poverty. There are two different poverty lines: one from the Program on Hunger Eradication and Poverty Reduction of the Ministry of Labor, Invalids and Social Affairs and the other from the results

---

[1] Daniel Maxwell and Keith Wiebe (1998). "Land Tenure and Food Security: A Review of Concepts, Evidence and Methods". Madison: *Land Tenure Center*, No. 129.

[2] Vandana Shiva (2002). "Globalisation of Agriculture, Food Security and Sustainability". In: Vandana Shiva and Gitanjali Bedi (eds.), *Sustainable Agriculture and Food Security: The Impact of Globalisation*. New Delhi: Sage Publications: 11.

[3] Joachim von Braun (1999). "Food Security - A Concept Basis". In: Uwe Kracht and Manfred Schulz (eds.) (1999), *Food Security and Nutrition: The Global Challenge*. Münster: LIT VERLAG: 48.

of the Vietnam Household Living Standard Surveys jointly conducted by the Vietnam General Statistics Office and the World Bank.

The Vietnamese government (with its representative of Ministry of Labour, War Invalids and Social Affairs - MOLISA) determines the poverty line based on the income of food, rice, or equivalent cash that is enough to buy such an amount of food. The poverty criteria have changed across time and depend on the standard of national income. The poverty indicator set by the National Program for the 1996-2000 period was a household whose average per capita income is less than 13 kg of rice per month, and this indicator is applied for to regions of Vietnam. For mountainous areas and islands, the indicator for poverty is a household whose average income is less than 15 kg of rice per capita per month (equal to 55,000 VND). The indicator utilized during the 2001-2005 period was 80,000 VND per household per month for mountainous areas and islands; and 100,000 VND for rural areas in the plains. The indicator used from the year 2005 and thereafter is 200,000 VND per household per month for mountainous areas and islands, and 260,000 VND for rural areas in the plains. Meanwhile, the Vietnam General Statistics Office's definition of "poverty" is households having an income lower than the minimum income needed to cover essential needs of food, clothing, housing, healthcare, and education. This income bracket is defined as "hunger" (or food shortage) to differentiate between the "poor" and "very poor" populations.

However, these criteria seem to be appropriate for the Kinh people, who live mostly in the lowland and in the delta, where the living conditions and the public services of the regions differ unremarkably.[1] Meanwhile, in the uplands of Vietnam, the terrains, living conditions and services are different from one area to another. Therefore, the principle of poverty line based on the food income cannot reflect fully the poverty characteristics among the ethnic minority people in Vietnam. To determine correctly and fully the poverty of ethnic minorities, therefore, it is important to combine the criterion of food income with other criteria such as the quantity of the area of cultivable land, the reduction of natural resource-based economy, and the mode of natural resource exploitation, etc. It is found that food of the mountain people will be insecure when the natural resources in their communities are rapidly eroded and degraded.

Different from the poverty determination by the government, ethnic groups have their own criteria of determination of poverty. These criteria are different from region to region and from one ethnic group to another. Many ethnic groups in the North of Vietnam consider that poverty means lack of wet-rice cultivated land, of food and no silver. The wealth is perceived contrarily. In comparison, the ethnic groups in the Central Highlands think that poverty has the same meaning as lack of food to eat in the between-crops period, no property which can be used for the equivalent barter for food (such as buffalo, cow, and gong, etc.). Additionally, the differentiation between the poor and the rich is explained

---

[1] Bui Minh Dao (ed.) (2003). *Some issues of poverty reduction among ethnic minorities in Vietnam*. A textbook. Hanoi: Social Science Publishing House: 72-73.

spiritually. Being poor means lack of the support of the spirits; and being rich is the opposite.

The household and even regional economic developments are very important to improve the living standard of the people. However, many developing countries make a mistake that creates a contradiction between economic development and environmental protection leading serious ecological and economic consequences. Therefore, the economic development has to be carried out parallel with the environmental protection. It is a principle that leads a sustainable life for the local people, especially for those who live in the uplands and who are perceived to be vulnerable.[1] This coincides with the emotional achievement of a "happy life" of the people in Bangladesh referred by Farida Akhter where farmers want to develop their household economy in combination with the environmental protection by refusing modern fertilizers.[2] Therefore, the solution of hunger elimination and poverty reduction in Vietnam is to encourage the development of agroforestry; apply the incentive credit; make the public traffic system convenient; hand over the land and the forest to households; transmit modern technology; and transfer the structure of production. Additionally, it is necessary to have the social policies of health, education, help in social affairs, and prevent social evil as well as build up the civilized way of life.[3] In another source, the key to food security in the past years in Vietnam had been through a thrust in land policy.[4] The fact is that many land policies of the Vietnamese government have been implemented in the highlands to improve the living standard of ethnic minorities.

In my view, criteria of poverty and food security in Vietnam manifest themselves in the objectives of the development strategies in the different periods. Among those, in general, the cash income and the accessibility to jobs are considered the important criteria to assess food security and poverty in the urban areas, particularly in the large cities. In comparison, in the rural and mountainous areas, it is crucial to develop the socio-economic situation of these regions based primarily on the traditional economy. Particularly, it is essential to combine agriculture with traditional professions to develop the household economy. Different from the lowland areas, it is indispensable to develop the agro-forestry in combination with the expansion of traditional professions in the mountainous regions. However, this combination is different from region to region and from community to community.

---

[1] Ha Que Lam (2002). *Hunger elimination and poverty reduction in the region of ethnic minorities in our country nowadays - current situation and solution*. A documentary book. Hanoi: National Politics Publishing House: 150.

[2] Farida Akhter (2001). "Resisting "Technology" and Defending Subsistence in Bangladesh: Nayakrishi Andolon and the Movement for a Happy Life". In: *There is an alternative: subsistence and worldwide resistance to corporate globalization*, edited by Veronika Bennholdt - Thomsen, Nicholas Faraclas, and Claudia von Werlhof, North Melbourne. Victoria: Spinifex Press.

[3] Ha Que Lam (2002). *ibid*: 150.

[4] *Food Security in Asia and the Pacific* (2000), Asian Productivity Organization, Tokyo.

2.2.4 Levels and approaches of food security

Level and approach of food security vary. Maxwell (1996: 156) shows that over the past four decades, the perception of food security has shifted through three paradigms: 1) from global and national level to household and individual level; 2) from food security to livelihood perspective, or from food security to sustainable livelihoods; and 3) from objective indicators to subjective perceptions.[1] Some other scholars divide conceptual levels of food security into four different levels. They are food security at the household, community, regional and national levels or at the individuals, households, countries and regions.[2]

Hans Lofgren and Alan Richards extend this and argue that there are two levels of food security analysis: macro and micro. On the macro level, if food production in the region as a whole (and most of its countries) falls far short of food requirements, then it is necessary for most countries to turn to imports for a large share of domestic food consumption. On the micro level, food security depends on the ability of individual households to meet their food requirements.[3] According to Joachim von Braun (1999), food security is studied at three different levels: national, household, and socio-economic and demographic. Food security at the national level (the ability to obtain sufficient food to meet the needs of all citizens) can, to some extent, be monitored in terms of need and supply indicators; that is, the quantities of available food versus needs. Food security at the household level may be measured by direct surveys of dietary intake (in comparison with appropriate adequacy norms). These data are costly due to the considerable time required for its collection and processing. If properly analyzed, the level of, and changes in, socio-economic and demographic variables such as real wage rates, employment, price ratios and migration can serve as proxies to indicate the status of, in changes in, food security.[4]

In short, based on all above arguments, I suggest that there are several levels of and approaches to food security. However, in general, there are three major levels of food security: macro level (nationally), meso level (regionally), and micro level (individual household, village, and small-scale community). The approach of food security is different from profession to profession, from one agency to another, and from country to country.

---

[1] Cited in Vuong Xuan Tinh (2003). "Food system of the Hmong in food security perspective". Hanoi: *Ethnology Review*, No. 1.

[2] Vandana Shiva (2002). "Globalisation of Agriculture, Food Security and Sustainability". In: Vandana Shiva and Gitanjali Bedi (eds.), *Sustainable Agriculture and Food Security: The Impact of Globalisation*. New Delhi: Sage Publications: 24.
- Hans Lofgren and Alan Richards (2003). "Food security, poverty, and economic policy in the Middle East and North Africa". In: Hans Lofgren (ed.), *Food, Agriculture, and Economic Policy in the Middle East and North Africa*. Research in Middle East Economics, Volume 5. Amsterdam: JAI Press/ Elsevier: 1.

[3] Hans Lofgren and Alan Richards (2003). *ibid*: 1.

[4] Joachim von Braun (1999). "Food Security - A Concept Basis". In: Uwe Kracht and Manfred Schulz (eds.) (1999), *Food Security and Nutrition: The Global Challenge*. Münster: LIT VERLAG: 47.

2.3 Relationship between local knowledge and food security

In relation to food security and nutrition, according to Joachim von Braun (1999), it is important to refer to behaviour and knowledge "which under certain conditions of availability and access predispose people to buy specific food or to grow them for home consumption, which influence the preparation and distribution of food among household members, including the meeting of special feeding needs, for example, of young children, and which affect breast feeding and general aspects of care."[1] This more or less refers to different ways of the people to access to food and food safety. In addition, suggested by Kate Young (1992), understanding people's way of living and of acquiring food is very important in accessing a food scarcity problem and in deciding on an appropriate response.[2] In the case of Vietnam, as a fundamental awareness of the socio-economic development in the uplands of Vietnam, the most important work is to use potentials of labour forces, land and professions successfully.[3] It is evident that food is an important requirement to turn these potentials into the economic strength at the local level.[4] To do this, it is essential to start from the traditional economy of local communities which mainly manifests itself in the agro-forestry and partly in the forage economy. In this case, food security of the mountain people, including the Yao people, lies in these economic sectors. Therefore, to study the uplanders' knowledge of food security, it is indispensable to focus on the application of frameworks of "human and cultural ecology" and "ethnoecology" to this study.

A fact proves that a hasty breakthrough of traditional economic factors leads many harmful effects. However, it is necessary to avoid repeating old procedures of the traditional production which are inappropriate to the changing socio-economic situation. Moreover, it is important to combine advantages of the farmers' knowledge with the strength of modern technology in addition to rearrangement of the appropriate mode of production for desired results. The inheritance of the traditional economy is not a sufficient condition for the development, but a necessary condition. Therefore, this production cannot overcome its small-scale and the low labour productivity without application of advantages of the modern technology to the production.

There will be remarkable shortcomings to study local knowledge without "gender studies" because this kind of knowledge is different from women and men. In addition, the contributions of women and men to food production are also different. Yearly data obtained from FAO show that both men and women play critical roles in agriculture throughout the world. However, the rural

---

[1] Joachim von Braun (1999). *ibid*: 45.

[2] Kate Young (1992). "Household resource management". In: Lisa Ostergaard (ed.), *Gender and Development: A Practical Guide*. London and New York: 4.

[3] Be Viet Dang (1985). "Some issues of the socio-economic development in the Northern mountain provinces". Hanoi: *Ethnology Review*, No. 1: 13.

- Nguyen Kim Lai (1993). "Private ownership in agriculture and its potentials in our country nowadays". Hanoi: *Philosophy Review*, No. 3: 37.

[4] Be Viet Dang (1985). *ibid*: 15.

women in many developing countries play a dominant role in producing food and in supporting labour required for food production. In Sub-Saharan Africa, women contribute 60-80% of the labour required for food production both for household consumption and for sale. In Asia, women make up 50% of food production. The similar situation exists in Pacific, in Latin America. In a study by Vandana Shiva (2001), to answer a question of who feeds the world, she enumerates contributions of small farmers in the Third World, particularly of women farmers, to food production, to the maintenance of local crops contributing to ensuring the agro-biodiversity.[1] Many other researchers also highlight the key role of women farmers in biodiversity conservation as the important basis of household food security.[2] Nevertheless, a title of "*Women Feed the World*" by FAO in 1998 is considered an evidence to affirm the domination of women in feeding the world as the world's primary and principle food producers.[3]

Despite their significant contributions to global food security, women farmers are frequently underestimated and overlooked in the development strategies. They are even considered "non-productive" and "economically inactive."[4] Vandana Shiva (2001) points out reasons for the devaluation of the role of women are that "much of their work in rural and indigenous communities is undertaken in co-operation with nature, and is often contradictory to the dominant market-driven "development" and trade policies", and "work that satisfies needs and ensures sustenance is devalued in general, there is less nurturing of life and life-support systems."[5] Thanks to the gender inequality, feminist movements have developed since the 1980s to gain rights for women to be "visible" in the development. This aim has been continuously addressed by many agencies and organizations in the world.

In summary, it is necessary to have the sound and systematic development strategies that both develop the household economy and protect the environment to

[1] Vandana Shiva (2001). "Globalization and Poverty". In: Veronika Bennholdt-Thomsen, Nicholas G. Faraclas and Claudia von Werlhof (eds.), *There is an Alternative: Subsistence and Worldwide Resistance to Corporate Globalization*. Victoria: Spinifex Press: 57-58.

[2] J. A. Ekpere (Project Coordinator). "The OAU's Model Law: The Protection of the Rights of Local Communities, Farmers and Breeders, and for the Regulation of Access to Biological Resources (An Explanatory Booklet)". *Organization of African Unity*. Scientific, Technical and Research Commission, P.M.B.2359 Lagos, Nigeria: 22.

- J. W. Watson and P. B. Eyzaguirre (eds.) (2002). "Home garden and in situ conservation of plant genetic resources in farming systems", *Proceedings of the Second International Home Gardens Workshop*, 17-19 July 2001, Witzhausen. Federal Republic of Germany, International Plant Genetic Resources Institute (IPGRI), Rome.

- Christina H. Gladwin, Anne M. Thomson, Jennifer S. Peterson, and Andrea S. Anderson (2001). "Addressing food security in Africa via multiple livelihood strategies of women farmers". *Food Policy*, Volume 26, Number 2: 181.

- Kate Young (1992). "Household resource management". In: Lisa Ostergaard (ed.) (1992), *Gender and Development: A Practical Guide*. London and New York

[3] FAO (1998). *Women Feed the World*, World Food Day, Rome, 16 October.

[4] Vandana Shiva (2001). "Globalization and Poverty". In: Veronika Bennholdt-Thomsen, Nicholas G. Faraclas and Claudia von Werlhof (eds.), *There is an Alternative: Subsistence and Worldwide Resistance to Corporate Globalization*. Victoria: Spinifex Press: 60.

[5] Vandana Shiva (2001). *ibid*: 60.

achieve sustainable development, especially for the ethnic minority people in the uplands. To do this, first, in my view, it is very important to maintain and reinforce the sustainable multi-livelihoods for local people. They are the first people who know what they should do with their available resources and how to adapt to the environment in order to access to food and maintain their lives. In the uplands of Vietnam, the combination of agro-forestry and natural resource management is very important to solve dominantly food problems among ethnic minorities. The local people also accumulate a lot of knowledge and experience in these realms. Therefore, in this study, I refer to the farmers' knowledge regarding agro-forestry and the natural resource management (including their knowledge of gathering, hunting and fishing). This also means to learn about their different ways of accessing to food, including their ways of producing food, of using and managing the available livelihoods in their communities. Among those, their knowledge is referred to as one of the most important human sources for them to survive and develop.

Chapter 3
PROCEDURES AND METHODOLOGY

3.1 Procedures

The fieldwork data were indispensable for my study. My fieldwork was divided into two phases. The first phase took place in the dry season which was considered an ideal fieldwork period in Vietnam because it coincided with the farmer's agricultural leisure that created a good condition for research surveys and interviews. The second fieldwork coincided with the farmers' cultivating season. Therefore, I could witness their agricultural activities which I could not do in the first fieldwork. Additionally, I could compare a difference of what the farmers said and what they did.

The research areas are separate and distant from each other. It was not hard for me to reach to Tả Phìn commune because motorbike drivers were always available in the Sa Pa town. In addition, thanks to the tourist resort, the road from the town to this commune was relatively good. On the contrary, the road to Bản Khoang commune is very bad. Even, although both the driver and I had to go by foot in some pieces of road, small accidents occurred because of the slippery and unsafe road, especially in rainy season. To get to Nậm Cang commune, it was much harder and more time-consuming than to reach the two other research communes because the road there was being upgraded and enlarged.

In the regard to food and accommodation, while I conducted my fieldwork, I did not have to pay for my accommodation. However, when I stayed in Tả Phìn commune, I normally bought some foodstuffs (such as pig meat, tofu and some different kinds of vegetable) for our meals because the local people have a shortage of these foodstuffs. When I stayed in the two other research communes, I rarely bought foodstuffs for our meals because they are normally available in the villagers' household. Moreover, I spent an amount of money on buying sweets for the children and for our talk and discussions. In addition, sometimes, I shared with the local people some domestic chores (such as slicing vegetables for pigs, cooking, or embroidering) leading to an intimate atmosphere in my communication with the villagers. This helped me to restrict a gap between the villagers as insiders and me as an outsider in order to get as much valuable information as possible.

3.2 Methodology

This study is analyzed based on the two main following documentary sources: the literature source gathered from the available documentation and the data collected in the research areas. In order to collect the data in the research areas, I applied the following methods.

3.2.1 Participant observation

During my stay in the Sa Pa district, *participant observation* was one of my most important methods used to collect data. I made direct contact with the local people while they were proceeding with their daily work. I completely abided by the principle of "share of three things with the local people" while I was carrying out my fieldwork. I was eating, staying and working with the villagers to get to know how they perceive the world and how they behave in it. I wanted to find out what happened in their villages and what is happening with them. Staying with them, sleeping on their bed and even sleeping with their daughters; eating their ample meals for a guest, or partaking in their daily meal, and sharing in the domestic work brought me esteem from them. By doing this, they were willing to spend hours telling me their historical stories, their spiritual beliefs and many other stories. Based on that, I could develop new ideas about their culture.

It was hard for me to write the information down in a notebook while I was talking to the farmers in their fields; therefore, I used a camera and a tape recorder to take and keep documentary pictures and record their sayings. In some cases, some women were shy talking with me when I was using the tape recorder. In these cases, using a notebook was the best way. I also met some of them again in their houses, if necessary.

In general, by participant observation, I could interpret what the local people said and did. In addition, I could understand their comprehensive views of culture and their living situation.

3.2.2 In-depth interview

Using the *in-depth interview* method provided me with valuable qualitative information. I chose some key informants because they know more than the others do. Some of them have specialized knowledge. This does not mean that a good key informant who was experienced in the village could understand fully and thoroughly every aspect of the community; therefore, I chose the key interviewees and informants appropriate to each research objective and question. In addition, I asked the informants a series of pre-arranged questions based on pre-selected topics. Sometimes I involved them in a free-ranging interview.

To get information regarding the farmers' perception of the spiritual world and their religion, my key interviewees were village shamans. In order to get the information of the village history, the process of emigration and immigration, the indigenous experience of agricultural practice, the village patriarchs and elders are ideal key informants. They have witnessed the village vicissitudes in their lives as well as have heard something told by their ancestors. Therefore, they told me their own previous lives and the history of their community thoroughly and elaborately better than anybody else did. Female villagers, through individual interviews, gave me much information of their experience in practicing agriculture (especially in keeping their traditional crops for seeds), in gathering wild plants in the forest and in processing food for people and domestic animals. However, in some cases, some of my female informants could not speak Vietnamese or they were not fluent in Vietnamese. Therefore, I needed the help of a translator. The chosen translator was a Yao woman in their village or their female neighbour who was fluent in Vietnamese. To know the experience in timbering, in ploughing and raking fields, male villagers are obviously chosen as the first important interviewees. Different from the case of interviewing women, all Yao men can speak Vietnamese well so that I needed no native translator.

In-depth interviews additionally helped me to crosscheck the field data and to add some information lacked by using other research methods. As an example, by using a set of questionnaire only, I could not gather information about villagers' beliefs in rice spirits. They maintained spiritual ceremonies relating to the agricultural activity every year with the aim of expecting good harvests. Only by the participant observation, I did not get the information about the farmers' ways of cultivating because my first fieldwork did not coincide with the sowing and planting season. Therefore, the individual or in-depth interviews helped me to improve these shortcomings.

3.2.3 Informal interviews

I used *informal interviews* to collect data from the villagers whom I met suddenly in the village path while they were following tourists to sell to them their handicraft products or who were embroidering their clothes and bags by the side of road. This method allowed me to gain more information about what I have already learned from other villagers and what I have never heard about before. In general, I normally tried to assemble a mix of informal interviews and individual interviews.

3.2.4 Surveys

Different types of surveys were useful tools for me to collect statistical information on events and points of view of some certain informants. By using the *respondent survey*, I learned the activities and roles of political and social organizations in the community. To do it, I involved local administrators and leaders of the different Unions (such as the head of Peasants' Association, of Veterans' Organization, of Woman's Association and of Youth Union) in the separately specific surveys. Issues raised in these surveys were their responsibilities, benefits and the work that they have already done and not completed yet, advantages and difficulties that they have met to introduce governmental policies and modern technologies to the local people. Based on that, I could also get information about how the local people had responded to the government's policies and to the introduction of new varieties and new agricultural techniques to their community. Each administrator had his or her own opinion and own ways of communicating with the local people. Therefore, by this method, I understand their terms and connections with the people.

To get information about household composition, I came to visit the head of households and asked them for the related questions. In the village level, I visited the head of villages to ask them a series of questions about the number of the people in their villages counting towards ethnic groups. Based on that, the village composition was analysed. This analysis contributed to learning about a relation of ethnic groups in the same village and community.

In order to know the number of people who were involved in the village market, I met the head of the village and the head of the Woman's Association. In these meetings, I applied the *personal surveys* to count these items. In some communes, there were some clubs of making handicraft. The participants came from different villages and belonged to different ethnic groups. The head of

Woman's Association normally managed these clubs. She knew the quantity of participants and their working quality.

3.2.5 Participatory rural appraisal (PRA)

This is a common method applied to different development projects, including projects of hunger eradication and poverty reduction. I used some tools of this method to collect data in the research sites.

- *Group discussion* was divided based on different research criteria.

Villagers were grouped to discuss about their skills in agricultural practice and in natural resource management, their advantages and disadvantages of food production and of their lives. However, depending on each research question and objective, these groups were also divided into sub-groups representing different groups of people in their village.

For example, to learn about the farmers' experience of choosing, categorizing and preparing the cultivable land, the village elders and the middle-age men were firstly involved in discussion groups because they were mainly responsible for this step of the production process. Women groups focused mainly on discussions of female experience in practicing agriculture (mainly in sowing and planting plants as well as in feeding and caring for domestic animals) and in gathering wild vegetation in the forest. In addition, these groups gave me much information about gender roles and labour division in their family. Another main issue discussed in their groups was the position of woman in the family, their educational level, their communication situation, and their ways of taking care of children. Issues of assessment and application of new and modern techniques as well as impacts of the education were raised in the discussion groups of both men and women. My male colleague, Doan Viet who works in the Institute of Anthropology in Hanoi, Vietnam, facilitated the male group discussions. Meanwhile, I facilitated group discussions of both men and women. Many Yao women were very shy of communicating with outsiders. Therefore, it was not ideal for my male colleague to facilitate group discussions of women. To investigate villagers' beliefs and ritual ceremonies referring to procedures of agricultural practice and natural resource management, groups for village shamans were established. However, the information relating to the secret profession of the shaman (such as some fortune telling and some procedures of organizing and praying in the "great" worships) could not be collected in the discussion group.

- *Drawing the topographic short cut*

I guided and encouraged villagers to draw village diagrams with the distribution of houses, trees and kinds of crops in the sloping measure of topography. Based on that, I primarily recognized the distribution of their cultivated crops and plants appropriate to slopes of the soil. This also presents the farmers' knowledge of their traditional land classification and their selection of plants appropriate to each kind of soil in order to use soils effectively and to increase their crop output.

- *Tabulating the crop calendar*

I used this tool to find out seasonal calendars of different cultivated crops, mainly staple crops and cash crops, by the villagers. The calendars were based on the lunar calendar appropriate to the cultivating calendar of the local farmers.

In short, the PRA application was carried out in a group of the people who speak Vietnamese proficiently and who have many and easier opportunities than the others to communicate with the outside world, normally the male groups.

3.2.6 Questionnaire

I designed a questionnaire consisting of 64 questions relating to my research objectives. It included three parts. The first part comprised nine demographic questions of informant's personal information such as: name, age, ethnic group, sex, education level, language used while answering questions, all social activities that the informant took and has taken part in and informant's profession. The second one asked for information about informant's family, labour in the family (staple food-winner and assistant labour), current house situation, and process of emigration (if yes). Information about the household economy, the last one, was the most important part of this questionnaire consisting of 48 questions. Data collected in this part told me their family income sources, daily meals and nutrition, the vicissitudes of the family (poor or rich harvest, poverty, etc.) and allocated land. My colleague helped me to inquire about questionnaire.

In general, I could gather different kinds of information and the data in the villages by combining various research methods. Afterwards, I analyzed them, both qualitatively and quantitatively. In addition, this is also a historical and contemporary research.

Chapter 4
RED YAO PEOPLE AND SOCIO-ECONOMIC CONDITIONS OF THE RESEARCH AREAS

4.1 The Red Yao people in the ethnic structure of Vietnam and research areas

4.1.1 Population, habitation and origin of the Yao in Vietnam

Vietnam is a multi-ethnic country. Its total population is 76,324,753 people (according to the Vietnam general population census dated on 1st April 1999) belonging to 54 ethnic groups. There is a relatively great disparity in the population distribution of the country. This situation is widespread from the North to the South, from the delta region to the upcountry area, from the urban to the rural regions, from the lowlands to the uplands. Although the delta makes up only one-fourth of the whole area of Vietnam, more than three-fourth of the population of the entire country is concentrated there. In comparison, the mountainous areas account for three-fourth of the total area, but has less than one-fourth of the Vietnamese population. Among 54 ethnic groups in Vietnam, the Kinh people (the majority group in this country), the Hoa, the Khmer and the Cham reside mainly in the delta, the littoral and in the midlands. They have settled and mainly farmed. The rest of the people live mostly in the mountainous areas. Of these, many ethnic minorities practice slash-and-burn cultivation.[1]

The Yao are an ethnic minority in Vietnam. This group originates from China. The Yao people came to Vietnam long ago, as early as the beginning of the thirteenth century and as late as the beginning of the twentieth century) and in different ways.[2] The myth of their origin from China is written in many books on *Bảng văn*, *Quế hải ngu hành chí*, *Thuyết man*, *Sưu thần ký*, *Quảng Đông tân ngữ* and even in magic manuals of the Yao shamans. Their myths today remain in different Yao sub-ethnic groups.[3] In some cases, they have maintained their old convention, which is to usher the soul of dead people back to Duong Chau (Giang To, China).[4] Therefore, they have taken with them many factors and characteristics of the Chinese.

They have various sub-ethnic groups depending on criteria of classification. Based on their cognomina and other names called by other ethnic groups, there are more than 30 Yao sub-ethnic groups. Based on their cultural characteristics, as reflected mostly by the clothes of Yao women, there are seven

---

[1] Khong Dien (1995). *Population and ethnic population in Vietnam.* Hanoi: Social Science Publishing House: 78-81.

[2] Another argument is that the Yao may have been present in Vietnam in the eleventh century, but their emigration processes to their current habitats happened mainly from the thirteenth century to the 1940s. See: Institute of Ethnology (1978). *Ethnic minorities in Vietnam (in the Northern provinces).* Hanoi: Social Science Publishing House.

- Be Viet Dang, Nguyen Khac Tung, Nong Trung, and Nguyen Nam Tien (1971). *The Yao in Vietnam.* Hanoi: Social Science Publishing House: 18-23.

[3] Jess G. Pourret (2002). *The Yao - The Mien and Mun Yao in China, Vietnam, Laos and Thailand.* London: Thames & Hudson: 18.

[4] Institute of Ethnology (1978). *ibid*: 25.

Yao sub-ethnic groups. Based on the language, there are two Yao branches of *Kềm Miền* and *Kìm Mùn*.[1]

This ethnic group ranks ninth in population compared with the others. Their population has increased gradually (Table 4.1).

Table 4.1. Population of the Yao people (1963-1999)

Years	Total	Of which		Proportion compared to the whole population in Vietnam (%)
		Male	Female	
1963[2]	168,071	72,373	93,698	1.2
1974[3]	290,792	144,178	146,614	1.29
1979[4]	345,735	171,560	174,175	0.66
1989[5]	437,945	236,991	236,954	
1999[6]	620,538			0.8

Before 1975, the year of the Vietnamese Unity, the Yao people lived in 16 provinces. However, they were concentrated in 7 provinces, 86 districts, and 165 communes of the uplands and the midlands in the North.[7] In later decades, a number of the Yao people emigrate to the Southern provinces and are concentrated mainly in the three provinces of Dak Lak, Dong Nai and Lam Dong. However, the mountainous areas in the Northern Vietnam are still their main residences. Nowadays, members of this ethnic group reside in 39 provinces and cities belonging to 1,035 communes throughout the country.[8]

4.1.2 Population and distribution of the Yao in the research areas

Lao Cai province is a frontier province in the North Mountains. It shares the border with Van Nam province of the People's Republic of China to the North, with a border length of 203.5 km and border towns at: Lao Cai, Muong Khuong and Bat Xat, with Yen Bai to the South, with Ha Giang to the East, and with Son La and Lai Chau to the West. Lao Cai province was re-established in 1991 after the separation from the old Hoang Lien Son province. There are nine districts and one provincial town including 180 communes and urban areas.

[1] Be Viet Dang, Nguyen Khac Tung, Nong Trung, and Nguyen Nam Tien (1971). *ibid*: 30-32.
- Nguyen Khac Tung (1997). "Return to the classification of Yao sub-ethnic groups in Vietnam". *Ethnology Review*, No. 3: 30-37.

[2] General Statistics Office (1962). *Population in the North of Vietnam*. Hanoi.

[3] General Statistics Office (1976). Quoted in Khong Dien (1995), *Population and ethnic population in Vietnam*. Hanoi: Social Science Publishing House: 298.

[4] General Statistics Office (1979). *Vietnam population* (Vietnam general population survey dated 01/10/1979). Hanoi.

[5] General Statistics Office (1991). *1991 Vietnam general population census - Result of exhaustive census, Volume I)*. Hanoi: Statistical Publishing House: 66.

[6] General Statistics Office (2001). *1999 Vietnam general population and houses census*. Hanoi: Statistical Publishing House: 21-46.

[7] Be Viet Dang (1998). "The Yao in Vietnam - Traditions in the contemporary period". In: *The cultural and social development of Yao people: Present and Future". Proceedings of an international workshop on the Yao held in Thai Nguyen province in December 1995*. Hanoi: 17-30.

[8] Khong Dien (1995). *Population and ethnic population in Vietnam*. Hanoi: Social Science Publishing House: 121.
- Pham Quang Hoan and Hung Dinh Quy (eds.) (1999). *Traditional culture among the Yao in Ha Giang province*. Hanoi: National Culture Publishing House: 13.

Among those, 138 communes have been identified as extremely poor communes belonging to 152 remote communes, and making up more than 76% of all communes and urban areas of Lao Cai province.[1]

According to the general population census of Lao Cai province dated on 1st April 1999, the Yao people make up 12.49% of the whole provincial population, ranking third among the ethnic minorities and making up a relatively high population rate in this region (after the Hmong people of 20.83% and the Tay of 13.74%). Therefore, compared to the general population survey of Lao Cai province dated 1st April 1989, the Yao population had increased by 0.17%.[2]

The Yao people here are categorized into three different sub-ethnic groups: the Red Yao, the Yao Ho and the Yao Tuyen. Among those, the Red Yao account for 66.7% of the total Yao population in Lao Cai province. They reside mainly in the highland communes of Sa Pa, Bat Xat, Van Ban, Than Uyen, Bao Yen, Bac Ha, and Bao Thang districts.[3] The Yao communes have gradually increased in number, from 72 communes (in 1960) up to 110 communes (in 1979) and to 114 communes (in 1989).[4]

Sa Pa is one of Vietnam's major tourist resorts thanks to its natural beauty and the vivid presence of ethnic groups. The total area of Sa Pa consists of 678.64 km^2.[5] Besides the Sa Pa town, there are 17 communes, 86 villages and 14 residential groups.[6] Nine ethnic groups live in this district. Among them, the Yao people account for 25.5% of the total population, ranking 2nd after the Hmong. They live in the township and 12 communes of Sa Pa district (Figure 4.1).

---

[1] Lao Cai People's Committee (2002). *Report on the result of work of the hunger elimination and poverty reduction in 2002 - Tendency and solution of hunger elimination and poverty reduction from 2002 to 2003.* Report No. 21/BC-UB dated 26th March 2002: 1.
- Lao Cai People's Committee (2003). *The comprehensive poverty reduction and growth strategy in the period 2004 - 2010.* Lao Cai: October 2003: 3.

[2] Lao Cai Statistics Office (2001). *Basic statistical data of Lao Cai province during the 10-year-old reestablishment from 1991 to 2001.* Hanoi: Statistical Publishing House: 22.

[3] Tran Huu Son (1999). *Proverb and riddle of the Yao.* Hanoi: National Culture Publishing House: 5.

[4] Khong Dien (1995). *Population and ethnic population in Vietnam.* Hanoi: Social Science Publishing House: 191.

[5] Lao Cai Statistics Office (2001). *Basic statistical data of Lao Cai province during the 10-year-old reestablishment from 1991 to 2001.* Hanoi: Statistical Publishing House: 7.

[6] Besides Sa Pa town, Sa Pa district has 17 communes: Tả Giàng Phình, Hầu Thào, Tả Van, Bản Phùng, Trung Trải, Thanh Kim, San Sả Hồ, Sử Pán, Bản Hồ, Bản Khoang, Nậm Sài, Suối Thầu, Nậm Cang, Lao Chải, Tả Phìn, Thanh Phú and Sa Pa.

Figure 4.1. Population and distribution of the Yao in some communes of Sa Pa district in comparison to other ethnic groups.[1]

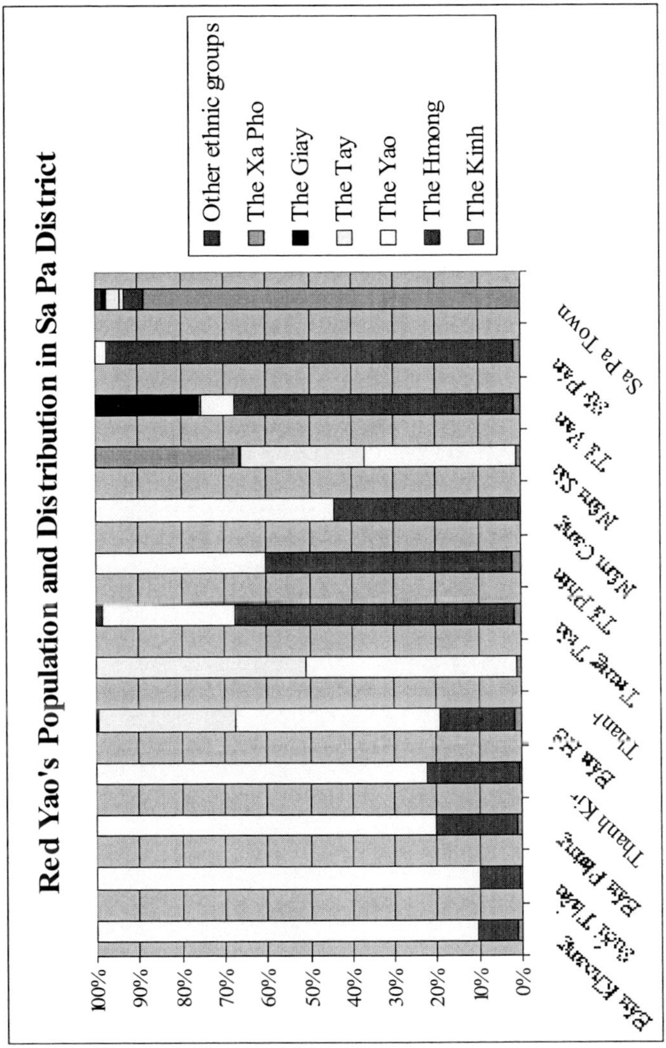

Sources: 1) Report on initial results of the 1999 census in Sa Pa district; 2) Initial results of Sa Pa population census dated 1.4.1999.

[1] To facilitate the observation of Yao population and their distribution, I classified this list in ascending number of Yao population in communes of Sa Pa district.

There are three ethnic groups in Tả Phìn commune: the Hmong (representing 57.56% of the total population), the Yao (40.15%), and the Kinh (2.29%). All Yao people in this commune belong to the Red Yao. Their population increases gradually. In 2003, the Yao people make up 41.3% of the communal population (increasing 1.2% compared to the year of 1999), ranking second in population of the total ethnic groups in this area.

Compared to Tả Phìn commune, the inhabitants of Bản Khoang commune include the Yao (with 89.45% of the communal population), the Hmong (9.58%), the Kinh (0.79%), the Tay and some other ethnic minorities (making up a small part of population) (in 1999). However, they contribute to diversifying the ethnic groups in this area. There are 10 villages in this commune.[1] Among them, six villages belong purely to the Yao: the villages of Can Hồ B, Suối Thầu, Da Khấu, Kìm Ngan, Sa Chải and Sín Chải. A pure Hmong village is named Can Hồ Hmong. The rest of the villages include some different ethnic groups living together, for example, the Yao with the Kinh or the Yao with the Hmong. However, the Yao are in the majority.

As at Tả Phìn commune, there are three ethnic groups in Nậm Cang commune: the Yao, the Hmong and the Kinh. The Yao and the Hmong live in the two separate hamlets. Nậm Cang hamlet is a residence of the Yao people. The Hmong reside in Nậm Than hamlet. The Kinh live in both of these hamlets. Among them, the Yao people make up the majority (55.91% of the total communal population). The second densely populated people are the Hmong, accounting for 43.44%. The rest are the Kinh people (0.65%).

It is found that the population of the Yao in all research areas, like those of other ethnic groups in Sa Pa district, increases gradually through both the natural population growth and immigration. The total population of this district is still increasing, although the rate of population growth decreases yearly (Figure 4.2 and Figure 4.3). These figures reveal the higher population growth of this area in comparison with the average national rate. In addition, population density in this district is also different from commune to commune (Figure 4.4).

---

[1] Ten villages of Bản Khoang communes include Can Hồ A, Can Hồ B, Can Hồ Hmông, Phìn Hồ, Lủ Khấu, Suối Thầu, Da Khấu, Kìm Ngan, Sa Chải and Sín Chải villages.

Figure 4.2. Population growth in different areas of Sa Pa district (1990-2005)

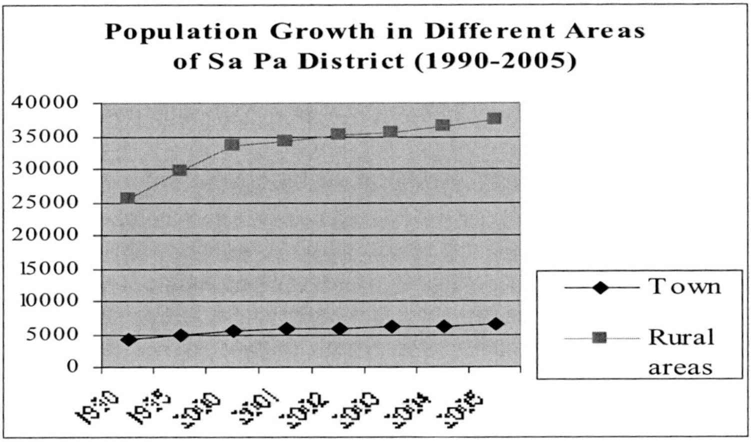

Source: 1) Statistical Yearbook of Sa Pa district, Lao Cai province. 2003;[1]
2) Sa Pa District People's Committee. 2004.[2]

Figure 4.3. Rate of population growth in Sa Pa district (1990-2005)

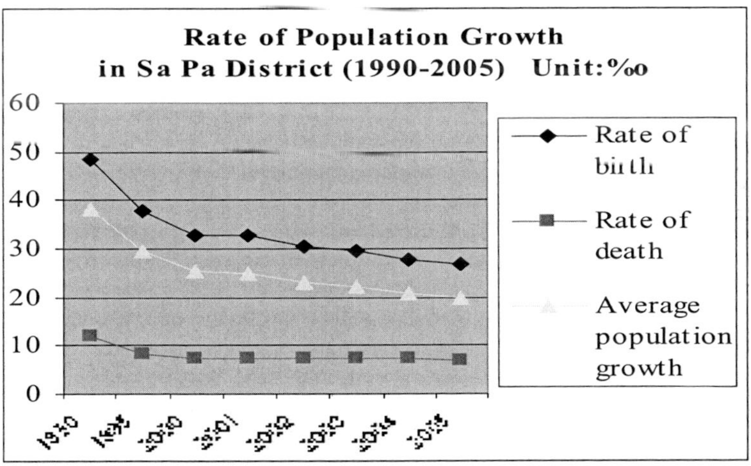

Source: 1) Statistical Yearbook of Sa Pa district, Lao Cai province. 2003. ibid.;
2) Sa Pa District People's Committee. 2004. ibid.

[1] Department of Statistics and Planning of Sa Pa district (2003). *Statistical Yearbook of Sa Pa district, Lao Cai province*.

[2] Sa Pa District People's Committee (2004). *Report on socio-economic situation in Sa Pa district in the period of 2000-2005*, Sa Pa: 12/2004.

Figure 4.4. Population density in Sa Pa district in 2004.[1]

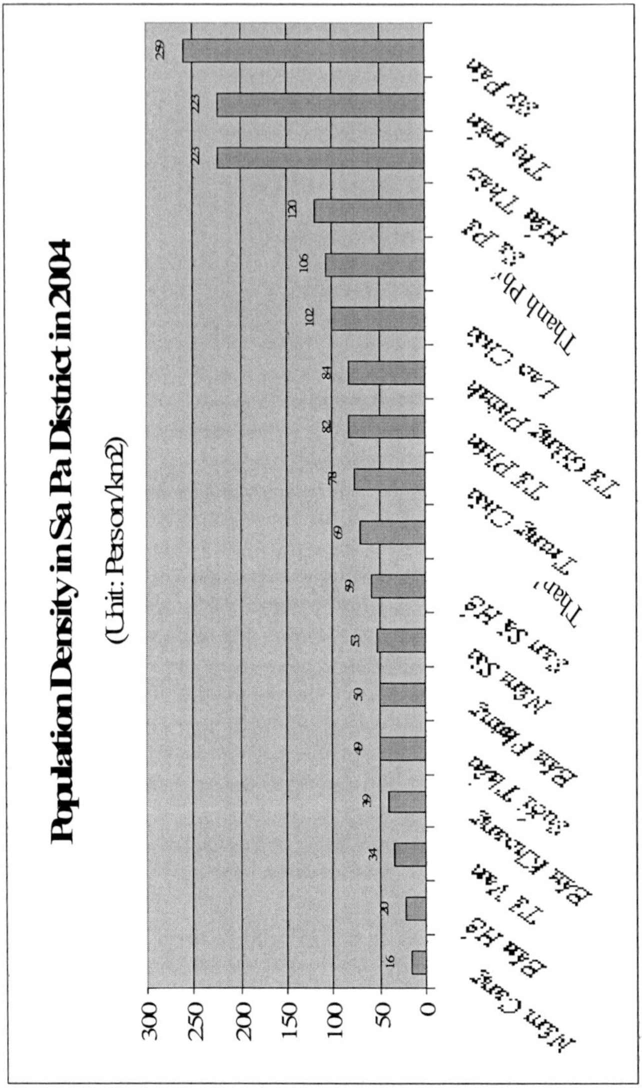

Source: Sa Pa District People's Committee. 2004. ibid.

[1] The population density of communes in this figure has been arranged in ascending order.

The massive birth rate decreases shown above compared remarkably with the natal proportion of all of Northern Vietnam in 1936 (48‰) and in 1960 (46‰), but is still much higher than the average natal rate of developed countries in the period of 1980 - 1985 (15.5‰).[1] Belief that "the more children we have, the more fortune we own", "God generates elephant, afterwards certainly grass as well", and "the more children we have, the more labour we have" make the natural growth rate of the mountain people higher than that of the lowlanders. This increasing population growth of the Yao people and that of other groups puts strong pressure on the natural resources in their regions, particularly on their productive sources (land, water source, and biodiversity, etc.) as one of their important livelihoods.

4.2Natural conditions

4.2.1 Terrain

A typical physical characteristic of this region is that its terrain is strongly partitioned resulted by only a part of its alternation of high mountains and hills. This partition generates various big and small valleys along the Red River. Lao Cai's topography has sharp slope. The lowest area is 80m above sea level. The highest peak in this province, also in Vietnam, is Fansipan (3,143m in height) belonging to the Hoang Lien Son chain, composed largely of fine crystallized rocks such as ryholite. Those areas are characterized by high mountains with a distinctive conical form and steep slopes.[2] Mountain Ta Giang Phinh is 3,090m in height, and Mountain Pu Luong is 2,938m, respectively. Based on its height, Lao Cai's topography is divided into 7 main steps: 100-150m; 300-500m; 600-1,000m; 1,300-1,400m; 1,700-1,800m; 2,100-2,200m and 2,800-2,900m. The area with greater than 25-degree slopes in this region accounts for 80% of the total area of this province.[3] The partition of the terrain makes the cultivable land disperse, formless and uneven.

4.2.2 Climate

4.2.2.1 Temperature

As in other districts of Lao Cai province, Sa Pa district has a tropical climate, with an average temperature from 15^0C-16^0C. Especially, in winter, Sa Pa's temperature is sometimes below 0^0C. In a study by Le Ba Thao (2002), he shows that it is colder in the high mountain range of Fansipan than in other mountainous areas of Trung Khanh (-3^0C), Lang Son (-2,1^0C), Cao Bang, Dien Bien and Lai Chau (-0,8^0C). Snow exists in Sa Pa at the altitude of 1,571m.[4] Thus, in winter, people cannot cultivate rice and other staple food crops, except some kinds of vegetable and spices.

---

[1] Khong Dien (1995). *Population and ethnic population in Vietnam.* Hanoi: Social Science Publishing House: 230, 285.

[2] Epprecht M. and Heinimann A. (eds.) (2004). *Socioeconomic Atlas of Vietnam. A Depiction of the 1999 Population and Housing Census.* Swiss National Centre of Competence in Research (NCCR) North-South, University of Berne. Berne: 40.

[3] Lao Cai People's Committee (2003). *ibid*: 3.

[4] Le Ba Thao (2002). *Vietnam - territory and geographic regions.* Second Edition. Hanoi: The Gioi (the World) Publishing House: 71.

4.2.2.2 Rainfall

The average rainfall is 2000-2500 mm/year, which is much higher than that of the other northern provinces of Vietnam (about 1,700 mm/year). However, the rainfall is different from month to month (Figure 4.5).

Figure 4.5. Rainfall in Sa Pa District in 2003

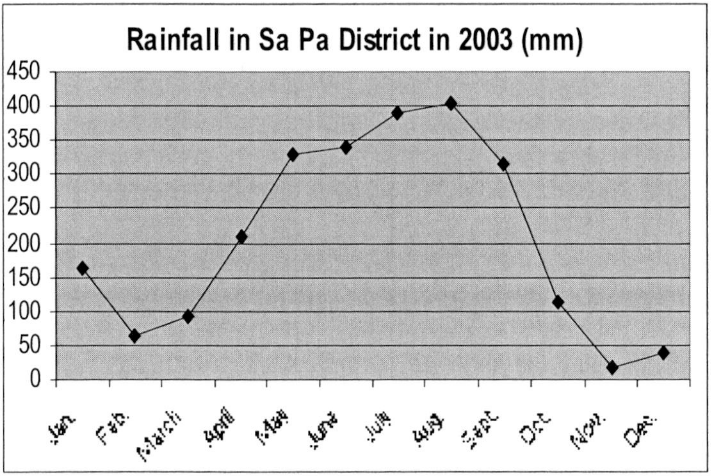

Source: Sa Pa District People's Committee 2004. ibid.

The above figure shows that the rainy season lasts from April to September. Therefore, this period is favourable for cultivation because the people have enough water for their rice fields and some soil plots of vegetables. However, in years, there have been floods in the rainy season, especially from June to the beginning of September, because the total water quantity in this period accounts for from 70% to 80% of the total yearly water quantities.

The dry season starts in October and continues through March of the next year. In this time, the land is hard and dry. In some months, rainfall is only between 16 mm to 40 mm. The dry season, therefore, is called the mild season. The yearly rainfall in this season makes up only from 20% to 30% of the total yearly water occurrences. Therefore, the local people practise only single-crop of rice in the rainy season.

4.2.3 Water sources

There are four main rivers in Lao Cai province: the Red River, Chay River, Nam Mu River and Ngoi Nhu River. Additionally, there are more than 100 springs and thousands of rivulets and channels running throughout communes and districts of Lao Cai. However, the number of rivers and springs differs depending on the district and commune. In Sa Pa district, there are two tributaries of the Red River, the Ngoi Bo and Ngoi Dum. Their water comprises about 9.5 billion m^3; however, only 2.25% of this potential is developed and used. The water content is unequal in terms of both place and time. Although the underground water content consists of 30 million m^3, it is very rare in the rocky mountains, especially in the dry season.[1] The quantity of water in all rivers and springs depends mainly on the rainfall and strongly influences local cultivation. Therefore, in addition to the coldness, lack of water in the dry season makes it impossible for the people to cultivate rice in this period.

4.2.4 Soils and forests

4.2.4.1 Soils

The total area of this province consists of 8,057.08 km^2. The agricultural area includes 920 km^2 (accounting for 11.5% of the total provincial areas); the forest land makes up 2,886.78 km^2 (35.8%); and the unutilized area comprises 4,043.7 km^2 (50.6%). The soil in Lao Cai province is relatively fertile including 10 groups with 30 main kinds of soil favourable for various crops.[2] However, soils differ from district to district.

In Sa Pa district there are four major types of soil. They are high mountain alit humus soils, high mountain yellow-red humus soils, feralitic soils developed on sandstone and feralitic soils formed by cultivation of wet rice (Table 4.2).[3]

---

[1] Lao Cai People's Committee (2003). *The comprehensive poverty reduction and growth strategy in the period of 2004 - 2010*. Lao Cai: October 2003: 5.

[2] Lao Cai People's Committee (2003). *ibid*: 3.

[3] According to Le Ba Thao (2002), feralitic soils contain less protoplastic minerals, a lot of ferric sesquioxide and aluminium. Additionally, it includes titanium oxide and manganese. This is very favourable to plant growth. See more: Le Ba Thao (2002). *Vietnam - territory and geographic regions*. Second Edition. Hanoi: The Gioi (the World) Publishing House: 85.

Table 4.2. Soil types in Sa Pa district

Name of soil	Nature of soil and appropriate plants	Elevation (m)	Distribution in communes	%
High mountain alit humus soils	Litter layer is not completely decomposed, sometimes up to 80 cm thick; low potential for cultivated crops, but some medicinal herbs	Over 1,700	Bản Khoang, Tả Giàng Phình, San Sả Hồ, Lao Chải, Tả Van	18.0
High mountain yellow-red humus soils	Soil stratum is medium, with light sandy clay loam; appropriate for many forest trees, industrial trees, fruit trees and medicinal herbs	700-1,700	Tả Phìn, Bản Khoang, Hầu Thào, Tả Van, Lao Chải, Trung Chải, Sa Pả, San Sả Hồ, Tả Giàng Phình, Sa Pa town	65.3
Feralitic soils developed on sandstone	Soil contains less protoplastic minerals, much ferric sesquioxide and aluminium, titanium oxide and manganese; favourable to different crops	400-700	Nậm Cang, Nậm Sài, Bản Hồ, Sử Pán, Thanh Kim, Bản Phùng, Thanh Phú, Suối Thầu	5.2
Feralitic soils formed by cultivation of wet rice	The soil is acid, but still rich; favourable for wet-rice crops		Most communes, except Sa Pa town	2.0
Others				9.5

4.2.4.2 Forests

Based on the terrain altitude identified by Le Ba Thao (2002), there are three kinds of forests in Lao Cai province. They are *humid subtropical jungles with the yearly green trees* (a kind of chestnut and bamboo forest), *mixed humid subtropical jungles* (normally coniferous forests grown with small clusters of chestnut, bamboo, rhododendron, and the solid coniferous in the underbrush) and d*warf forest in the high mountains* (commonly with bamboo and the bamboo-like phyllostachys only 0.20m-0.40m to 2m-3m in height).[1] The total forest area of this region in 2002 is 260,400 ha (equalling 2,604 km^2), making up about 2.3% of the total forest land of Vietnam. Among those, the natural forest comprises 213,000 ha (equalling 2,130 km^2) accounting for 2.2% of the total natural forests of Vietnam, and reforested areas encompass 47,400 ha (equalling 474 km^2) (making up 2.4% of the completely reforested areas of Vietnam).[2]

Sa Pa district has a total area of 678.64 km^2.[3] Among those, the forest area of the whole district makes up about 75% of the total areas of the province. However, the forest cover of this district accounts for 48.5%. This district includes two kinds of forestland: that covered by trees (encompassing both natural and planted forests) and the bare land. Of those, the forestland covered by trees consists of 64.6% of the total forest land of this district whereas the bare land comprises 35.4%. Below is a list of classification of the land and the forest cover in Sa Pa district in 2003 (Table 4.3).

[1] Le Ba Thao (2002). *Vietnam - territory and geographic regions.* Second Edition. Hanoi: The Gioi (the World) Publishing House: 91.

[2] General Statistics Office (2003). *2002 Vietnam Statistical Yearbook.* Hanoi: Statistical Publishing House: 156.

[3] Lao Cai Statistics Office (2001). *Basic statistical data of Lao Cai province during the 10-year-old reestablishment from 1991 to 2001*. Hanoi: Statistical Publishing House: 7.

Table 4.3. Current use of the land and the forest cover in 2003 in Sa Pa district, Lao Cai province (Unit: ha).[1]

Communes	Total area	Forest land area	Of which				Other lands	Forest cover (%)
			Forest land covered by trees			Bare land		
			Total	Natural forest	Reforestation			
Bản Hồ	11 439	6 443.9	4 667.8	4 439.7	228.1	1 776.1	4 995.1	40.8
Nậm Cang	7 068	5 423.8	4 697.1	4 697.1	0	726.7	1 644.2	66.5
Tả Van	6 759	5 101.6	4 680.9	4 519.3	161.6	420.7	1 657.4	69.3
San Sả Hồ	5 763	4 808.5	4 547.3	4 163.3	384.0	261.2	954.5	78.9
Bản Khoang	5 663	4 111.1	1 784.2	1 519.4	264.8	2 326.9	1 551.9	31.5
Trung Chải	4 000	3 526.5	2 340.4	1 363.5	976.9	1 186.1	473.5	58.5
Bản Phùng	3 017	2 694.1	932.9	932.9	0	1 761.2	322.9	30.9
Suối Thầu	2 992	2 532.6	1 052.7	924.2	128.5	1 479.9	459.4	35.2
Lao Chải	2 828	2 302.5	1 741.9	1 520.8	221.1	560.6	525.5	61.6
Tả Phìn	2 725	1 865.7	1 044.1	939.2	104.9	821.6	859.3	38.3
Nậm Sài	2 470	2 093.3	786.7	634.8	151.9	1 306.6	376.7	31.9
Tả Giàng Phình	2 423	2 129.9	1 001.2	894.1	107.1	1 128.7	293.1	41.3
Sa Pa Town	2 409	1 929.4	1 050.0	96.2	953.8	879.4	479.6	43.6
Sa Pả	2 334	1 809.9	1 079.7	289.7	790.0	730.2	524.1	46.3
Thanh Kim	2 071	1 600.5	508.4	472.2	36.2	1 092.1	470.5	24.5
Thanh Phú	2 063	1 613.6	491.7	265.5	226.2	1 121.9	449.4	23.8
Sử Pán	933	365.4	192.4	177.8	14.6	173.0	567.6	20.6
Hầu Thào	907	531.9	285.8	260.6	25.2	246.1	375.1	31.5
Total	**67 864**	**50 884.2**	**32 885.2**	**28 110.3**	**4 774.9**	**17 999.0**	**16 979.8**	**48.5**

[1] Villages are listed by the author in the ascending order of the total area.

Based on this table, the forest cover of this district is relatively high. However, this forest cover is very different from commune to commune. Communes with abundant forest cover include San Sả Hồ, Tả Van, Nậm Cang and Lao Chải communes (occupying more than 60% of the forest cover). The least forest cover exists in the communes of Sử Pán, Thanh Phú, and Thanh Kim (fewer than 25%). Therefore, there is a big disproportion in forest cover in different communes. Inhabitants in the communes with more forest area have more opportunities to benefit from the forest than do people in the other communes with less forest land. Additionally, in many cases, the more forest land the people have, the more income they earn in these areas of forest by planting *thảo quả*. However, this seems more appropriate to the Red Yao people because they work much harder and are better educated than other ethnic minorities in the same region. It is found that the people and the forest have a close relation with each other. The Yao names of *Dìu miền*, *Kiềm miền*, and *Kìm mùn* themselves express their close relationship with the forest and the environment, as the people who live in the forest or near the forest.

The terrain of highland mountains, the impacts of tropical climate and the different kinds of soil create an extremely diverse natural environment in this region. This leads to an abundant fauna and flora with many valuable and rare genes favourable for the development of agro-forestry and tourism. However, the strongly partitioned terrain with high sloping land and the some complicated aspects of the climate accompanied sometimes by the hoarfrost and long cold periods are some of main challenges for the inhabitants to expand their agriculture on a larger-scale.

4.3 Political development and institutional arrangements

Although French colonialists invaded Vietnam in 1859, the French established their control over the northern mountain of this country very late in the colonial era. They achieved relatively full "pacification" of this region only after the turn of the century. However, even before the French conquest the highlands had been in continuous turmoil for several generations, as Vietnamese rebel forces, Chinese armies and paramilitary forces (the infamous "Black Flags" and "Yellow Flags") and ordinary bandit gangs contested with the colonial forces and each other for control of territory, people and trade, especially that of opium. Lao Cai province, as an important point for cross-border trade with China, was the major base for the Black Flag paramilitary forces of Liu Yung-fu, until they were recalled to China in 1885.[1]

Before the Vietnamese August Revolution, the Yao society was colonial and semi-feudal as was characteristic of Vietnamese society as a whole. The ethnic minorities in northern Vietnam, including the Yao community, were governed by two different social systems. The first was a colonial and semi-feudal relation, which dominated the whole country. The second was an internal relation

[1] McAleavy (1968), cited in A. Terry Rambo (1997). "Development trends in Vietnam's northern mountain region". In: Deanna Donovan, A. Terry Rambo, Jefferson Fox, Le Trong Cuc and Tran Duc Vien (1997), *Development Trends in Vietnam's Northern Mountain Region*. Honolulu: East-West Center, and Hanoi: National Politics Publishing House: 11.

of each location and each ethnic group depending on their range of social progress.[1] To better control the ethnic minorities, French governors divided Vietnam into three separate parts: the North, the Middle and the South. Among those, residences of the Yao ethnic group belong to the North. Each section was considered to be a part of Indo-China. In the Yao habitats, there were administrative systems of mandarins, ruling classes, "*lang đạo*", governors and land proprietors. Most of the staff in the French Colonial Office was the upper class of the community, the head of the clan, or the locally prestigious head of the commune.[2]

In addition to the economically hard policies of exploitation, the French colonists paid attention to the implementation of "divide and conquer" in the mountainous areas. However, the Yao and Hmong shifting cultivators of the higher elevations remained largely outside the reach of the French administration except through its collection of head taxes and enforced purchase of their opium by the colonial monopoly.[3] Bonifaxi, a French military officer, stated that the multi-ethnic abundance in the Yao habitats made the functions of ruling lieges complicated, but facilitated French domination because it was very hard for these people to cooperate with each other to turn against the French "divide and conquer" dominion.[4]

Since 1954, after the capitulation of the French colonial army at Dien Bien Phu, the northern provinces of Vietnam have started a new phase of their development. In addition, from this period, the history of Vietnam is punctuated by two other key dates: 1) the so-called Vietnam War against the American Army ended in 1975 with the reunification of the country; 2) since 1986, many incremental economic reforms towards a market-oriented economy, primarily the "Doi Moi" policy of the central government, have been implemented in Vietnam. Since 1954, the government rapidly attempted to introduce many socio-economic changes in the mountainous regions. Although, the war of the Vietnamese against Chinese army occurred in 1979 in some frontier provinces of the Northern Vietnam, including Lao Cai province, the government's policies continued to be implemented in the mountains to try to achieve their objectives.

The administrative regime was re-established, including both the macro level (including various ministries, offices and organisations) to the micro level (comprising provinces, districts, communes and villages). At the communal level, there is the Communal People's Committee. It includes various departments, such as the communal people's council, the department of settlement, farmer's association (with its representative of department of

[1] Institute of Ethnology (1978). *Ethnic minorities in Vietnam (in the Northern provinces)*. Hanoi: Social Science Publishing House: 46.

[2] Be Viet Dang, Nguyen Khac Tung, Nong Trung, and Nguyen Nam Tien (1971). *The Yao in Vietnam*. Hanoi: Social Science Publishing House: 180-181.

[3] A. Terry Rambo (1997). "Development trends in Vietnam's northern mountain region". In: Deanna Donovan, A. Terry Rambo, Jefferson Fox, Le Trong Cuc and Tran Duc Vien (1997), *Development Trends in Vietnam's Northern Mountain Region*. Honolulu: East-West Center, and Hanoi: National Politics Publishing House: 11.

[4] Be Viet Dang, Nguyen Khac Tung, Nong Trung, and Nguyen Nam Tien (1971). *ibid*: 182.

agricultural expansion), woman association, youth union, etc. All these departments play an important role in introducing the government's policies to the local people and implementing these policies with the cooperation of the people at the local level.

The government has made and issued many policies regarding agriculture, particularly land use, and the forest protection and development as the basic livelihoods of the farmers and the mountain people. These policies are described in detail in the following chapters of this thesis because they are closely related to the farmers' food production and their access to food.

In addition to the strategic policies implemented in the whole country, the government also issued some specific policies and programmes for the mountainous and remote areas. Among those, one of the policies that has had the most remarkable and strongest impact on the ethnic minority people, is the policy of Cabinet Council's sedentarization and fixed cultivation in 1968.[1] As a result of the campaigns for sedentarization and fixed cultivation, many ethnic minorities have come down from the mountains and now reside in the valleys. However, these campaigns have progressed slowly because it is difficult for the uplanders to adapt to the new environment, which is different from their old residence in the higher areas.

According to Be Viet Dang (1985), until the beginning of the 1980s, about 1 million people in the northern region still lived in impermanent settlements with shifting cultivations.[2] In Sa Pa district, the plan for arranging stable accommodations for the people was very important and involved production development and campaigns for sedentarization and fixed cultivation. From 1999 to 2005, the government continuously invested in arranging stable residences for poorest communes in the whole district. As a result, in this period, 933 households reside in fixed accommodations. To help them overcome some difficulties in their new residences, the government supported some water constructions for them, which are described in detail in the fifth chapter.[3] These created favourable conditions for the people, allowing them to stabilize their residences and develop their production. In addition, it also helps the local administrators to keep public order, protect the people from social evils, propagandize policies of the government for the people and contribute to eradication of hunger and reduction of poverty at community and village levels.

In addition, it is also important that two programmes were launched recently with targeted assistance for poor communes. The first programme is the

---

[1] Cabinet Council (1968). "Resolution 38/CP of The Cabinet Council dated 12th March 1968 about the work of a crusade in favour of settled agriculture and the settlement in combination with the collectives applied to the people who still live in the nomadic life". In: Parliament Council of Ethnic Groups. Session X.(2000), *The policy and law of ethnic groups of the Vietnam Communist Party and the government*. Hanoi: National Culture Publishing House: 338-348.

[2] Be Viet Dang (1985). "Some issues of the socio-economic development in the Northern mountain provinces". Hanoi: *Ethnology Review*, No. 1: 16.

[3] Sa Pa District People's Committee (2005). *Report on results of effectuation of the Programme 135 in the period of 1999-2005 in Sa Pa district*: 4.

national target programme on hunger eradication and poverty reduction for the period of 1998-2000, which is under the Ministry of Labour, Invalids and Social Affairs (MOLISA), but also involves other Ministries, and targets the poorest segments of the population in rural and urban areas. The second programme is the socio-economic development programme for especially difficult mountainous and remote communes, which is under the Committee for Ethnic Minorities and Mountain Areas (CEMMA), and calls for orchestrated efforts and targeted resource provision in disadvantaged communes (the so-called Programme 135).[1]

These programmes aim at creating good conditions for the people to overcome poverty, backwardness, slow development and, therefore, promote them integration into the development of the whole country. This contributes to ensuring the social order and the national security. To achieve these general aims, the Programme 135 is divided into two phases: 1998-2000 and 2000-2005. This programme was conducted in about 1,000 of the poorest communes, making up about 58.3% of the total poor communes in the whole country. The people who benefit from this programme belong to seven provinces, including Sa Pa district (Lao Cai province).[2] One of the specific objectives of this programme is to decrease the number of poor households and achieve fewer than 25% in 2005 as well as to encourage the farmers' own experience. To do this, it is important to promote internal forces of households in cooperation with their communities. In addition, it is necessary to have the constructive support of the government in order to develop the local strength of land, labour, and the natural and socio-economic situation in their region. Based on that, it creates a new change in production and in the material and spirit life of the local people. In addition, it is necessary to have a systematic solution, particularly to concentrate on developing of agro-forestry, constructing the infrastructure in the rural areas, promoting development in the system of education, public health, culture and society in these regions.

4.4Social conditions

4.4.1 Family and kinship

The Red Yao's kinship system plays an important role in the village. Each village has a major lineage that makes up the majority of the population there. This lineage came to the current villages earlier than the others. Therefore, the people who belong to this lineage normally have occupied and obtained a larger amount of cultivable land than the other inhabitants. In this case, their customary law has

[1] Decision 135/1998/QĐ-TTG dated 31/7/1998 by the Prime Minister. "An approval of the socio-economic development programme for especially difficult mountainous and remote communes". In: Parliament Council of Ethnic Groups. Session X (2000), *The policy and law of ethnic groups of the Vietnam Communist Party and the government*. Hanoi: National Culture Publishing House: 667-677.

- WB (2001). Project appraisal document on a proposed credit in the amount of SDR 87.9 million (US$110 million equivalent) to the Socialist Republic of Vietnam for a northern mountains poverty reduction project. Rural Development and Natural Resources Sector Unit, East Asia and Pacific Region, *Report* No: 21233-VN: 4.

[2] Decision 135/1998/QĐ-TTG dated 31/7/1998 by the Prime Minister. *ibid*: 668, 675.

empowered them to keep this amount of land for their long-term use. In some cases, this creates a conflict with implementation of the government's land law at the local level. As a result, there are some land disputes in the communities.

The Yao patriarchal family is the basic social and economic unit. In the past, all family power belonged to the husband as the family holder. Therefore, he was normally the decision-maker in his family. Women were dependent on their parents, their husbands and their sons. In their small-scale society, they were undervalued and not allowed to participate in any social activity. However, in the present, although the husband's voice is still dominant in the family, he sometimes shares something with his wife and his adult sons. Particularly, in the young families, the trend is towards more equality between the husband and his wife in solving problems of their family, including developing their household economy.

The united coherence of the Yao community and their kinship is expressed visibly. They still rely on mutual help in production and daily life. Their labour exchange in production, derived from the period of the old rural communal association, is still popular and considered a good thing in their community. Family, descent and village are places where the local people maintain and protect their cultural identities, including their local knowledge.

4.4.2 Health care and education

The requirement of improvement of human sources is significant, and referred to in many social policies of the government. One of the most important achievements is that the health and educational level of the uplanders have greatly improved from the implementation of public health and education policies in the mountainous and remote areas.

4.4.2.1 Health care

The people in Sa Pa district benefit from the priority of health care programmes. They are legally allowed to be examined and treated free of charge in the local, regional and national medical stations and hospitals issued by the Decree 95/CP dated 27/8/1994. In Sa Pa district, more than 95% of all children are given complete vaccinations. The rate of malnourished children is below 31%.[1] The health of the people as a quality of labour forces is basically ensured, which is one of the most important conditions for the socio-economic development.

4.4.2.2 Education

Apart from improvements to the health care system, all levels of the government also have paid attention to improving the educational system in different communes. As a result, in Sa Pa district, up to 2005, 97% of the school aged children are attending school. The material facilities of many communes are much better than before, now funded by the Programme 135. In general, the education in the recent years in this area has achieved remarkable results. This situation has gradually improved much more than before (Table 4.4).

---

[1] Sa Pa District People's Committee (2005). *Report on results of effectuation of the Programme 135 in the period of 1999-2005 in Sa Pa district*: 7.

Table 4.4. Education system in Sa Pa district (2000-2006)

	2000-01	2001-02	2002-03	2003-04	2004-05	2005-06
Numbers of schools	**25**	**25**	**27**	**35**	**44**	**46**
Primary school	10	3	4	12	22	24
Primary and junior high school	13	20	21	12	2	-----
Junior high school	1	1	1	10	19	21
High school	1	1	1	1	1	1
Numbers of classrooms	**376**	**427**	**410**	**434**	**465**	**482**
Primary school	134	56	60	228	353	370
Primary and junior high school	222	352	328	175	15	-----
Junior high school	10	11	11	21	85	96
High school	10	8	11	10	12	14
Numbers of classes	**468**	**443**	**491**	**535**	**720**	**770**
Primary school	410	368	398	404	528	540
Junior high school	51	67	84	123	181	217
High school	7	8	9	8	11	13
Numbers of teachers	**518**	**553**	**541**	**607**	**788**	**850**
Primary school	366	372	400	413	499	504
Junior high school	135	163	123	175	266	320
High school	17	18	18	19	23	26
Numbers of pupils	**8524**	**8826**	**8995**	**9229**	**10725**	**11600**
Primary school	7143	7261	6970	6485	6556	6600
Junior high school	1094	1277	1729	2447	3747	4500
High school	287	288	296	297	422	500

Source: Sa Pa District People's Committee 2004.[1]

Moreover, some programmes gave professional refresher courses and continuation education to local cadres in order to improve their professional abilities. Some good farmers were chosen for courses of agricultural and forestry development which were held in the communes, or in the districts, or in the provinces. In the period of 1999-2005, there were 2,921 participants in different short training courses.[2] However, the participants differ in age and profession, thus, their ability to acquire knowledge was limited. Despite this, the professional quality of the local cadres has improved. Through these training courses, the local cadres began to introduce to the peasants different kinds of information relating to agro-forestry development and to modern technology. This partly created favourable conditions for them to develop their household economy and reduce poverty in their communities.

[1] Sa Pa District People's Committee (2004). *Report on socio-economic situation in Sa Pa district in the period of 2000-2005*, Sa Pa: 12/2004.

[2] Sa Pa District People's Committee (2005). *Report on results of effectuation of the Programme 135 in the period of 1999-2005 in Sa Pa district*: 5-6.

4.5Economic conditions

4.5.1 Economic structure in Sa Pa district

In the period of 2000-2005, Sa Pa district obtained an average GDP growth rate per year of 19.65% (Sa Pa District People's Committee 2004).[1] This rate is much higher than that of the country as a whole (7.7% in 2004).[2] Sa Pa district has had the most rapid economic development in comparison with other districts of Lao Cai province and ranks second in this province in annual budget, after Lao Cai Township. There is movement in the economic structure in this district appropriate to the work of the industrialization and modernization in Vietnam (Figure 4.6).

Figure 4.6. Economic structure of Sa Pa district. Unit: %

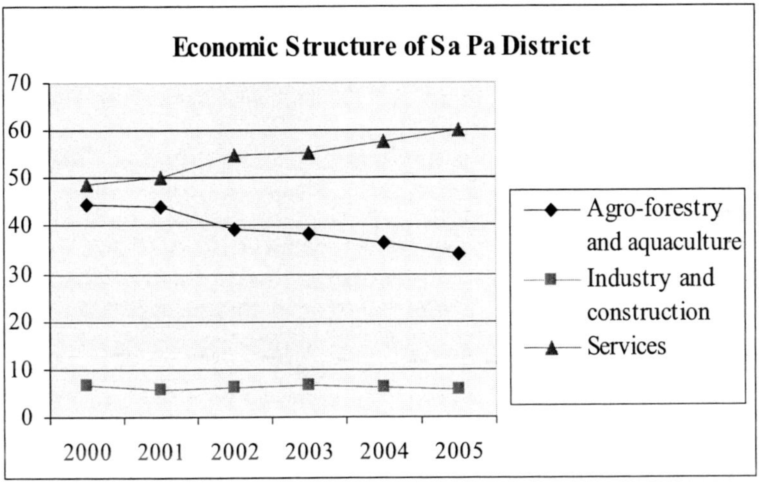

Source: Sa Pa District People's Committee 2004: 29.[3]

The economic structure of this district has shifted in the direction of gradually increasing the development of services and the industrial domain as well as of decreasing the growth rate of the agriculture. The French recognized the tourism potential of this region since the period of their colonialism. According to Reed (1995: 45-46), the French colonial government established hill stations in Sa Pa (excluding Tam Dao and Ba Vi) in the 1890s. These stations were considered necessary to maintain the physical and mental health of long-term European residents in the tropics, especially soldiers.[4] With tourism

---

[1] Sa Pa District People's Committee (2004). *ibid.* It is remarkable that local administrators have estimated results of the year 2005 written in this source.

[2] VNECONOMY updated on 5 January 2005, also available at http://www.vneconomy.com.vn/eng/index.php?param=article&catid=D2&id=050105140117

[3] Sa Pa District People's Committee (2004). *Report on socio-economic situation in Sa Pa district in the period of 2000-2005*. Sa Pa: 12/2004.

[4] Cited in A. Terry Rambo (1997). "Development trends in Vietnam's northern mountain region". In: Deanna Donovan, A. Terry Rambo, Jefferson Fox, Le Trong Cuc and Tran Duc Vien (1997), *Development Trends in Vietnam's Northern Mountain Region*. Honolulu: East-West Center, and Hanoi: National Politics Publishing House: 39.

opening up in 1993, the marketplace suddenly boomed with the display of highland material culture back in favour, resulting in changes in every aspect of the marketplace's appearance and composition, and in the dislodgement of ancient trades and traders to make room for new ones.[1] Nowadays, tourists have gradually increased in number in this region, from 49,322 people in 2000 up to 200,000 people in 2005. Therefore, the income from tourism also increases, at a growth rate of 19.12% per year.[2] However, the people who mainly benefit from tourism are the Kinh people and the traders who invest in hotels and restaurants. In comparison, the accessibility of the ethnic minorities to tourism is less than the Kinh and the traders in the Sa Pa town. Therefore, it is found that most ethnic minorities benefit remarkably from agro-forestry. However, some Yao and Hmong ethnic people can also earn money from selling their traditional handicrafts to tourists.

In addition to the potentials of tourism, this district also has many advantages for development of agro-forestry. In agriculture, cultivation is dominant (Table 4.5). Cultivation developed in the period of 2000-2003, increasing from 77.72% in 2000 up to 81.10% in 2003. However, the rate of growth decreases in the following years, from 79.86% in 2004 to 78.92% in 2005.

Table 4.5. Agricultural structure of Sa Pa district. Unit: %

No.	Agricultural structure	2000	2001	2002	2003	2004	2005
1	**Cultivation**	**77.72**	**79.65**	**79.06**	**81.10**	**79.86**	**78.92**
	- Staple food crops	71.40	66.66	61.57	60.61	61.62	59.56
	- Vegetables and beans	15.76	16.61	14.41	13.26	14.05	14.18
	- Industrial plants	2.07	3.70	2.02	1.81	1.90	1.78
	- Fruit trees	3.87	4.27	4.33	3.21	3.03	3.18
2	**Animal husbandry**	**22.28**	**20.35**	**20.94**	**18.90**	**20.14**	**21.08**
	- Cattle	66.70	67.09	70.41	71.98	73.49	74.44
	- Poultry	15.82	15.77	14.97	14.16	14.04	13.04
	- Others	17.48	17.14	14.61	13.86	12.48	12.52

Source: Sa Pa District People's Committee 2004. ibid.

The local farmers usually give priority to growing food crops, particularly staple food such as rice and maize. In the past six years, their wet-rice productivity gradually has increased in quantity because the peasants have enlarged the area of their terraced fields and applied the hybrid rice to their cultivation. The total area of the rice terraced fields of the whole district increases, from 1,769 ha in 2000 to 2,335 ha in 2005. The other grainy cereal crops also increase in output (Figure 4.7). Therefore, the average cereal output per capital of this district is also increased, from 190.9 kg/person in 2000 to 277.5 kg/person in 2005 (Figure 4.8). As a result of this cereal growth, many people use rice not only for themselves but also for their domestic animals.

[1] Jean Michaud and Sarah Turner (2000). "The Sa Pa marketplace, Lao Cai province, Vietnam". Victoria University of Wellington: *Asia Pacific Viewpoint*, Vol. 41, No. 1: 86.

[2] Sa Pa District People's Committee (2004). *ibid.*

Figure 4.7. Cereal output of Sa Pa district (Unit: ton)

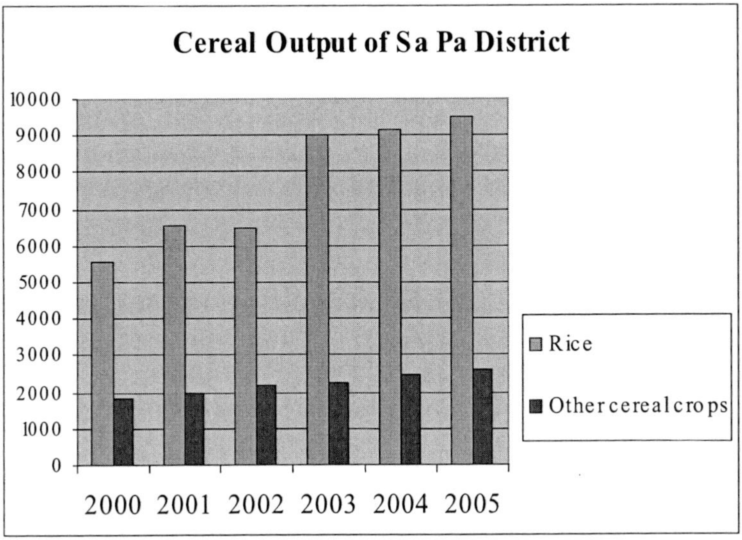

Source: Sa Pa District People's Committee 2004. ibid.

Figure 4.8. Cereal output per capita of Sa Pa (Unit: kg/person)

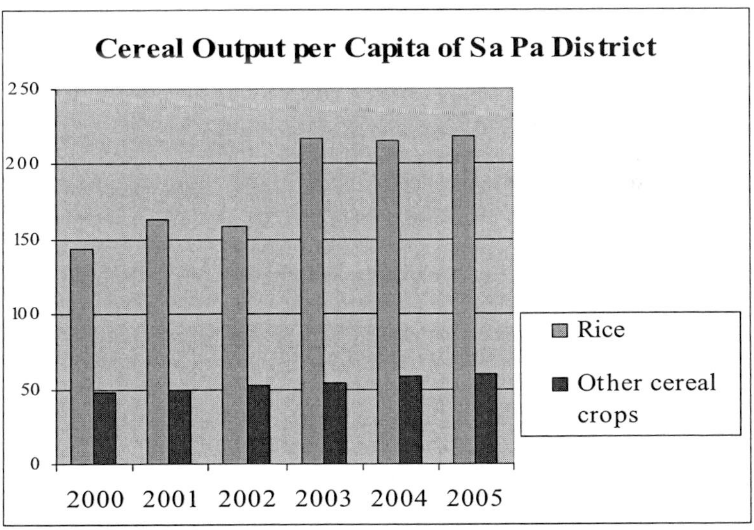

Source: Sa Pa District People's Committee 2004. ibid.

In addition to the cereal crops, the people shift the crop structure appropriate to the natural conditions of each commune. In the upland communes of Sa Pa district, the peasants focus on planting and developing tropical fruit trees, medicinal herbs, different kinds of beans and flowers. The area of fruit trees increases about 80 ha; the area of *thảo quả* is 3,200 ha. In recent years, some people have planted many kinds of valuable imported cash crops such as trees of *lã quan thảo*, Japanese tea, artichoke, mushroom and rose. However, the people near the town mainly plant these trees whereas the ethnic minorities rarely plant them because most of them live far from town. In addition, they also develop special local vegetables. In general, since 2000 the local people have invested remarkably in the development of their own cash crops. This has gradually led an improvement in their living standard.

Apart from cultivation, animal husbandry has also brought remarkable achievements, although this economic sector is less expansive than cultivation. Based on Table 3.5, the number of cattle of the people in Sa Pa district has successively increased in quantity in recent years, from 66.70% of the total growth rate of the animal husbandry in 2000 to 77.44% in 2005. This has resulted from the increasing consumption in the area, particularly from tourist demands. The poultry breeding is declined because of animal diseases and a lack of interest on the part of the local people.

The industry of this district is also developed. The industrial output in 2005 increased 2.4 times over that of 2000. This was concentrated in the development of traditional professions, such as in producing wooden furniture and in making handicrafts and brocade. These products mainly meet the domestic demands of the local people and partly satisfy requirements of the tourism.

4.5.2 Poverty

As a result of the implementation of the Programme 135 and many governmental policies in Sa Pa district, the poverty of this district is below 10% of the total population in comparison with less than 25%, as planned by the Programme 135. However, this poverty varies depending on the communes (Figure 4.9 and Figure 4.10).

Figure 4.9. Communes in Sa Pa district benefiting from the Programme 135 and results of this programme

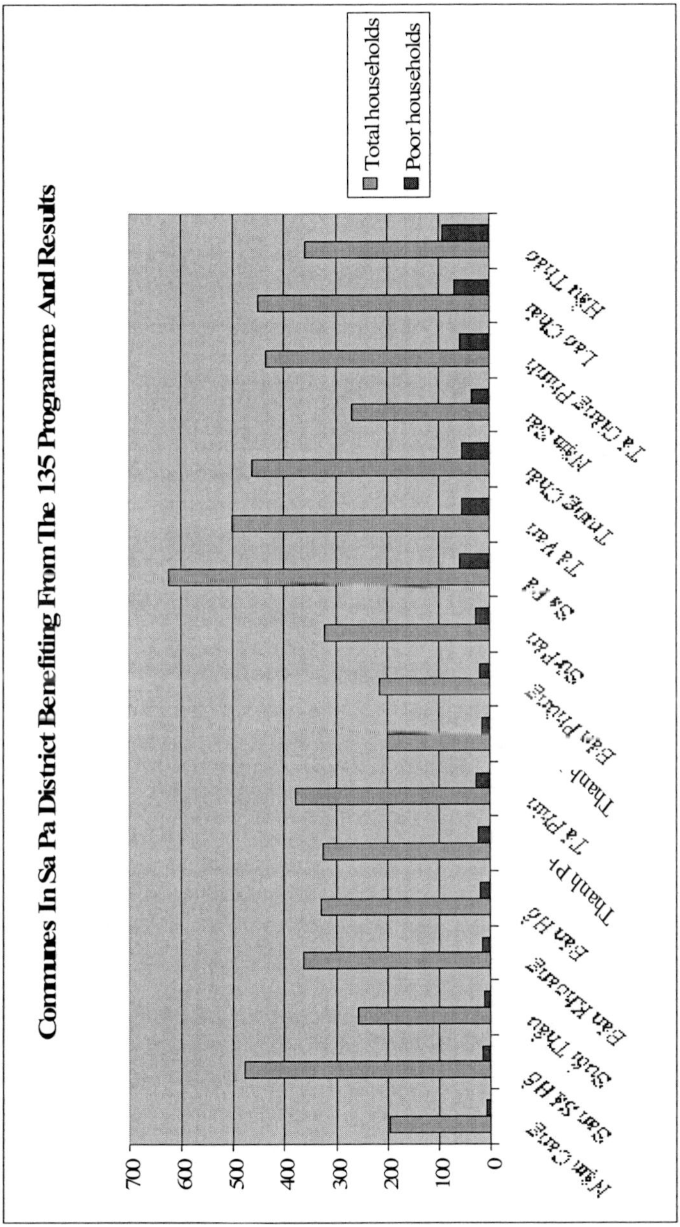

Source: Sa Pa District People's Committee 2005.

Figure 4.10. Ethnic minority people in Sa Pa district benefiting from the Programme 135 and results of this programme

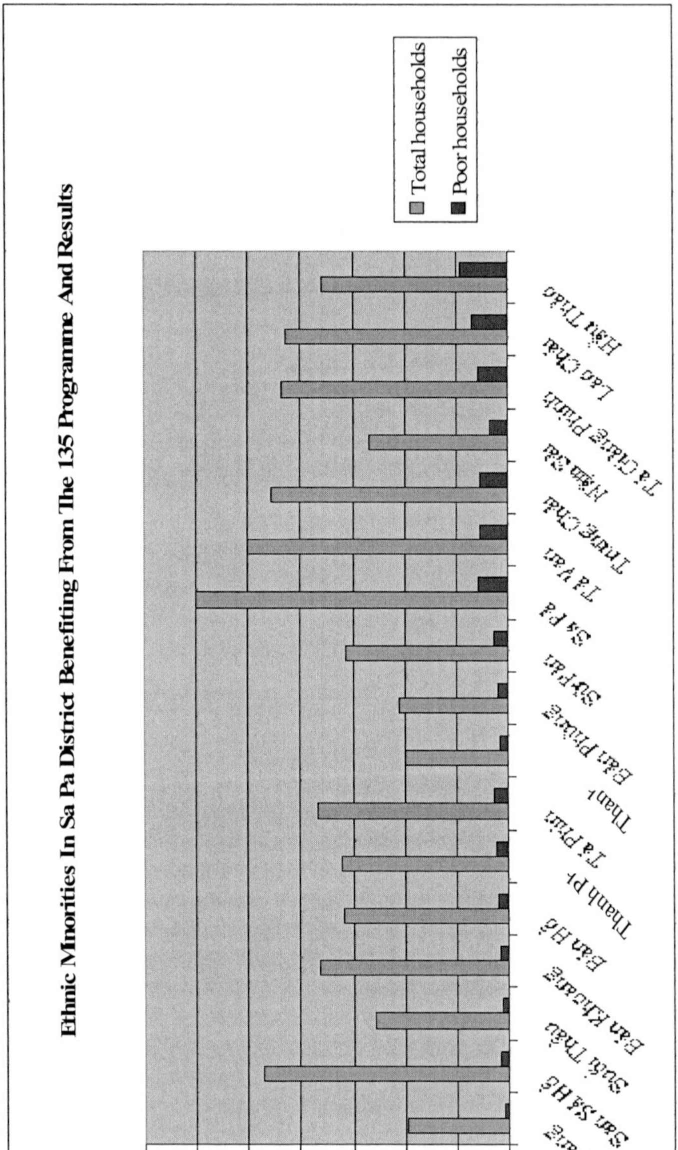

Source: Sa Pa District People's Committee 2005. ibid.

In general, although the economic development of the Sa Pa district marks an obvious advance, poverty remains in all communes of this district. However, the rate of poverty differs from commune to commune. Moreover, it is concentrated in the rural areas and mainly in the communities of the Hmong and of the Xa Pho. In the three research areas, the Nậm Cang commune is in the most remote area. However, the poverty in this commune is lowest. In comparison, the Tả Phìn commune has the highest poverty in spite of its position of a nearest place and of a well-known tourist resort.

However, since 2005 the government has applied the new criteria for poverty in the country. Based on these criteria, poverty rate will be higher than that reflected under the programme 135 (See more: Appendix 1).

4.6Summary

The Yao people have a close relation with their environment and their society, and vice versa. The physical conditions in their communities have strongly influenced their options of tools for production and their traditional agricultural practices. This reflects their adaptation to the natural environment. In addition, the local people cannot live isolated from their own small-scale society. Therefore, they are influenced by the socio-economic conditions of their society.

Policies of different levels of the government play an important role in helping local farmers overcome poverty and improve their living standard. Based on that, their food supply is gradually more secure than before.

Despite all the efforts of governmental policies, the Yao farmers' rapid population growth and the unequal population density of their residences in combination with those of other ethnic groups have put a remarkable pressure on the land, water and other sources as their most important livelihoods. Therefore, food security and ecological security are still problematic in this region.

Chapter 5

LOCAL KNOWLEDGE OF CULTIVATION OF THE YAO PEOPLE

5.1Varied types of cultivation

Like other ethnic minorities living in an agrarian country, the Yao people have a traditional agriculture. In a study by John Dixon, Aidan Gulliver, and David Gibbon (2001), the extensive mixed farming system of highland farmers in eastern Asia and the Pacific region also describes the farming system of the Red Yao in northern Vietnam.[1] This system can be subdivided into permanent and shifting cultivation subtypes. In Sa Pa district (Lao Cai province), cultivation makes up a large proportion of the local economy. The Red Yao engage in the following cultivation types: shifting cultivation, wet-land agriculture and gardening.

5.1.1 Shifting cultivation (đẩy in Yao language*)*

This is an indigenous form of cultivation of many ethnic minorities in the highland of Vietnam, including the Yao people. It is the most complicated cultivation type in the world. It includes diverse cultivation systems. It exists in various ecological conditions, from the upland to the plain, from the forest region to the grassland and in many countries around the world in the last thousand years.[2] This is a slash-and-burn and rotational cultivation system. Planting periods are normally shorter than fallow periods.[3] Traditionally, in the Yao communities in Sa Pa district, the length of fallow periods for forest is 10-15 years and for bush it is 5-7 years. In the five recent years, however, many people have mainly spent 1-3 years for their fallow period because of lack of cultivated land resulting from increasing population growth and high population density. Therefore, their traditional shifting cultivation is no longer an ideal solution for agriculture if they do not apply some new techniques to their cultivation.

Although shifting cultivation is no longer common in many countries due to the application of modern agricultural techniques, it remains in equatorial tropical regions. In Vietnam, some 3 million people live on the swiddening.[4]

---

[1] John Dixon, Aidan Gulliver, and David Gibbon (2001). *Farming Systems and Poverty: Improving Farmers' Livelihoods in a Changing World*. Principal Editor: Malcolm Hall, FAO, Rome, Italy. Also available at: www.fao.org/DOCREP/003/Y1860E/y1860e00.htm

[2] J. E. Spencer (1966). *Shifting cultivation in Southeast Asia*. University of California Publication in Geography, Vol. 19. Berkeley: University of California Press.

- Michael C. Howard (1996). *Contemporary Cultural Anthropology*. Fifth Edition. New York: HarperCollins College Publishers: 85.

[3] H. C. Conklin (1957). "Hanunoo agriculture: A report on an integral system of shifting cultivation in the Philippines". *Forestry Development* Paper 12, FAO, Rome.

- John Clammer (1993). "Fishermen, Forest-eaters, Peddlers, Peasants, and Pastoralists: Economic Anthropology". In: Grant Evans (1993), *Asia's Cultural Mosaic - An anthropological Introduction*. Singapore: Prentice Hall: 159.

[4] Michael C. Howard (1996). *Contemporary Cultural Anthropology*. Fifth Edition. New York: HarperCollins College Publishers: 85.

- Do Dinh Sam (1994). "Shifting Cultivation in Vietnam: Its Social, Economic and Environmental Values Relative to Alternative Land Use". London: International Institute for Environment and Development. *HED Forestry and Land Use* Series No. 3.

Despite different performances, shifting cultivators still observe a close productive cycle: choosing cultivable land, slashing and burning, cropping, harvesting and fallowing. The Yao people in Sa Pa district have accumulated much experience in cultivation on their sloping land, from the choice of cultivable land to the harvest. In principle, their shifting cultivation has two basic stages: removing the old vegetation and managing the new vegetation. This type of cultivation is similar to those of many other uplanders in the Southeast Asia.[1]

5.1.1.1 Choosing land for cultivation

Before 1968, when the Yao people lived in a nomadic life, they moved to the primary forest to find cultivable land and then settled down in this area. Traditionally, the peasants choose varieties appropriate to cultivable land in their own ways (Table 5.1).

Table 5.1. Criteria for choosing crops appropriate to every plot

Criteria for land classification		**Appropriate crop**	**Inappropriate crop**
Nature of land	Wild vegetation		
Umber, less loose and relatively flat plots		Rice	
White soil			Rice
Salty and a little bit austere soil		Rice	
Too austere soil			Rice
Black, humus and thick soil		Maize, sweet potato, soy-bean	
	ghim plants, mugwort (*lay ngoặy*) and *nhài uôm luộm* plants	Maize	
	Nhài uôm luộm plants	Taro	
	Alang grass (Imperata Cylindrica)	Soy-bean	

Fixing a good date for the selection of cultivable land was very important because it determined whether they could find good soils. The Yao choose an auspicious day based on the fortune telling through the shaman's handwriting. A magician is not only responsible for worship in the village, but also helps villagers find an auspicious day for special work and activities. The time for

[1] H. C. Conklin (1957). "Hanunoo agriculture: A report on an integral system of shifting cultivation in the Philippines". *Forestry Development* Paper 12, FAO, Rome.

- R. F. Watters (1960). "The nature of shifting cultivation". *Pacific Viewpoint* 1: 59-99.

- Gerald G. Marten (1986). *Traditional Agriculture in Southeast Asia: A Human Ecology Perspective*. Westview Press/ Boulder and London: East-West Center.

choosing cultivable ground normally coincides with October in the lunar calendar. Nowadays, less attention is paid to this work because extension of cultivated land through clearing the forest by fire is prohibited.

As soon as a farmer has chosen the area for cultivation, he must sign his "ownership" of this plot. He does that in a traditional way, meaning within the customary law. He makes a fissure in a certain tree in the area by his knife, and then crams a stick into this fissure in order to inform the latter that this plot has its owner. This mark is similar to the *Taleo* by the Thai and the Tay in Vietnam or by the Trobrianders in the earliest years of the twentieth century.[1] Afterwards he uses a knife to cut a patch of grass from the bottom of his hill and puts it to a higher part of the area to mark the area that he wants to use. Despite the simplicity of this sign, those who come latter know that this area is reclaimed from the bottom to the top of the hill. They thus will not cultivate this plot.

5.1.1.2 Slashing and burning

Slashing and burning are the two major procedures of the swiddening. Thus, shifting cultivation is also known as slash-and-burn agriculture.

a. Slashing

An auspicious day for slashing the plot's vegetation plays an important role in avoiding the misfortune for all members of the family. The villagers set the auspicious day based on the fortune writing of the village magician. They believe that if they set a bad day, the head of the household will die of a sudden accident or one of his relatives will be put at risk. Those who do not know how to choose a good day will ask the help of a villager who knows how to do it or the village magician.

Based on the auspicious good day that has been set, farmers start to slash the cultivable land. In principle, the farmer who signs the ownership of the land has all rights to make the first cutting on this plot to inaugurate this work because this plot is considered to belong to him. Normally, the husband or the master of the house finds the cultivable land for his family and, therefore, is the first person who cuts trees on that plot. However, if the master of the house is a woman (in the case that her husband has died or she is single), she starts this work. Afterwards, all family members (except old persons and small children) take part in clearing the plot. Additionally, an exchange of labour and cooperation in clearing the land are common phenomena in the community. The helpers are normally cultivator's relatives, neighbours or other villagers.

b. Burning

Burning the plot is essential for the preparation of the land because it saves much time when it comes to cutting and clearing the fresh trees, and produces a large amount of fertilizer for the cultivated land and nutrients for the plants from the ashes. This is also a method utilized by the Trobrianders to give excellent

[1] Bronislaw Malinowski (1935). *Coral Gardens and Their Magic-A Study of the Methods of Tilling the Soil and of Agricultural Rites in the Trobriand Islands*. London: George Allen and Unwin Ltd. Ruskin House, England; American Book Company.

inputs to the land when the ashes are washed into the soil by the rain.[1] This is very important for the sloping land which is poor and rapidly eroded.[2]

The Yao farmers normally conduct this work from December to February because it is the dry season so that the trees burn more easily. Previously, farmers burnt the land in their traditional way which could burn extensive forested areas, but it protected crops from damage by grass (Figure 5.1). Recently, they have practised a new way of burning which contributes to decrease in forest deflagration, but makes grass grow more rapidly than before (Figure 5.2). It is found that the new burning method is more appropriate to new changing conditions because it can protect the forest from fire and some of the natural resources which is one of the important requirements for sustainable agriculture and food security.

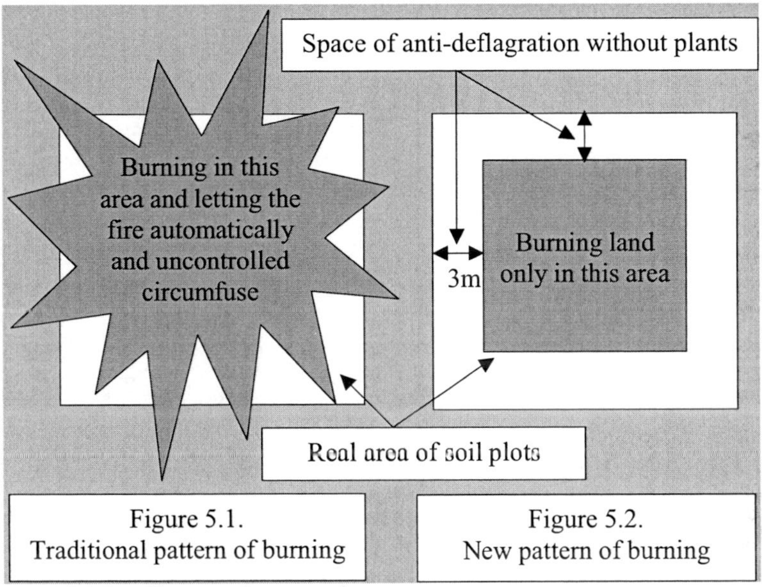

Figure 5.1. Traditional pattern of burning

Figure 5.2. New pattern of burning

5.1.1.3 Clearing the ground

In olden times, the burning without any control created large fires and killed all the roots of plants. Therefore, it was easy and time-saving to clear the ground. Small-scale farmers cleaned out their plots by taking the big trees aside to the corner or to the edge of the desired plot. Currently, by applying the new burning method, the farmers spend more time and labour to clear the land because various trees and scrubs are not consumed. This work is hard and time-consuming. Thus, like the case of the land slashing, all people are

[1] Bronislaw Malinowski (1935). *ibid*: 110.

[2] John Clammer (1993). "Fishermen, forest-eaters, peddlers, peasants, and pastoralists: Economic anthropology". In: Grant Evans (ed.), *Asia's Cultural Mosaic - An Anthropological Introduction*. Singapore: Prentice Hall: 159.

- Michael C. Howard (1996). *Contemporary Cultural Anthropology*. Fifth Edition. New York: HarperCollins College Publishers: 85.

involved in this work. They bank up all trees, sticks, and then burn them. Afterwards, they distribute the ashes on the plot with hoe and leave it for some weeks before cultivating. This provides excellent fertilizer for the plants.

Because the character of shifting cultivation is to burn and slash the sloping land, there are various conceptions and controversies about the damage done by ethnic minorities in Vietnam. The government, many international development organisations and agencies perceive the backwardness and the inefficiency of the swiddening. Additionally, it is seen as the main reason for deforestation and environmental erosion.[1] Previously, according to the researchers and some governmental agencies, the shifting cultivation was perceived as nomadic, harmful, wasteful and related closely to the self-sufficient economy; it is isolated from the rest of the world. Therefore, the aim of many policies (such as the policy on land tenure and allocation, the resettlement and new economic zones in Vietnam) is to reduce the shifting cultivation of ethnic minority people in the name of forest conservation. However, these policies lead to an uncontrolled emigration in large numbers, to deforestation and the resettlement of the Kinh people, the majority people, in the uplands.[2] Similarly, the misunderstanding and the misconception about shifting cultivation still exist in some other Asian countries.[3] It is evident that the farmers' traditional burning way is no longer appropriate for the changing environment and can create some forest fires. However, other procedures and steps of shifting cultivation reflect the high adaptation of the local farmers to the high sloping land and their environment.

5.1.2 Wet-land agriculture

The terrain of Sa Pa district is relatively high and sloping. Thus, the terraced field is a common kind of wet-rice cultivation in this region. Before the 1980s, terraced and swamped fields occupied a small proportion of the total Yao people's cultivated land.[4] Currently, they make up a large proportion of the

---

[1] Do Dinh Sam (1994). "Shifting Cultivation in Vietnam: Its Social, Economic and Environmental Values Relative to Alternative Land Use". London: International Institute for Environment and Development, HED *Forestry and Land Use Series* No. 3.

- Le Trong Cuc (1996). "Swidden agriculture in Vietnam". In: Rerkasem B. (ed.), *Montane Mainland Southeast Asia in Transition*. Chiang Mai (Thailand): *Chiang Mai University Consortium*: 104-119.

- A. Terry Rambo (1996). "The composite swiddening agroecosystems of the Tay ethnic minority of the northwestern mountains of Vietnam". In: Rerkasem B. (ed.), *Montane Mainland Southeast Asia in Transition*. Chiang Mai (Thailand): Chiang Mai University Consortium: 69-89.

[2] Neil L. Jamieson; Le Trong Cuc; and A. Terry Rambo (1998). "The Development Crisis in Vietnam's Mountains". Honolulu: East-West Center. *Special Report* No. 6: 20.

[3] Michael R. Dove (1983). *Theories of swidden agriculture, and the political economy of ignorance*. The Hague, The Netherlands: 84-95.

- Michael R. Dove (1984). "Government versus peasant beliefs concerning imperata and cupatorium: A structural analysis of knowledge, myth, and agricultural ecology in Indonesia". Honolulu: East-West Center, *Working Paper* No. 54.

- N. Myers (1993). "Tropical forest: The main deforestation fronts". *Environmental Conservation* 20: 9-16.

[4] Institute of Ethnology (1978). *Ethnic minorities in Vietnam (in the Northern provinces)*. Hanoi: Social Science Publishing House: 314.

completely cultivated land, much larger than the area of the burnt land in the Red Yao community in Sa Pa district.

The farmers have terraced fields in the relatively flat plots and nearby sources of water. The area of wet-rice fields is different from commune to commune (Table 5.2).

Table 5.2. Situation of wet-rice cultivation in the research areas in 2003

Research communes	Total (2003) (ha)	Compared with 2002 (ha)	Of which	
			New-rice area (%)	Local-rice area (%)
Tả Phìn	187.20	+ 56.09	93.6	6.4
Bản Khoang	120.66	+ 2.28	71.6	28.4
Nậm Cang	104.28	+ 43.61	88.7	11.3

Source: Department of Statistics of Sa Pa District People's Committee 2003.[1]

A fact is that areas of new rice fields are gradually increasing in number in all communes, whereas those of local rice are gradually decreasing. In addition, farmers still reclaim virgin land for cultivation. However, this area is not large.

5.1.3 Gardening

Compared with other Yao farming systems, gardening plays a minor role, making up about 5-12% of the farming systems. However, the crops in their home gardens are very diverse and differ from commune to commune. It is found that there are between 1-25 varieties in Tả Phìn communes, 1-29 varieties in Bản Khoang commune and 1-46 in Nậm Cang commune. This biodiversity is similar to those of many gardens in some other countries: 607 varieties in the Javanese gardens, more than 130 varieties in the gardens of Thailand and more than 60 varieties in the gardens of Africa.[2] It is found that their gardening and the biodiversity in the garden are essential to supply them with supplementary food and foodstuff. However, home gardens in Tả Phìn communes are less important than those of the two other research communes because the area of their gardens is very small and they are normally damaged by domestic animals.

5.1.4 Traditional classification of cultivated land

The Yao's knowledge of land classification is diverse and different from those of land surveyors (Table 5.3). Therefore, it is difficult for surveyors to assess current land use and to map a land-use system in this region without reference to farmers' viewpoint.

[1] Department of Statistics of Sa Pa District People's Committee (2003). "Table 02b/THN: Village synthesis - The basic household situation of farming in 2003". In: Sa Pa People's Committee (2003), *Report on survey of basic household situation of agro-forestry in 2003 in Sa Pa district*, number 121/ TK-ĐTH. Sa Pa 7/10/2003.

[2] Vandana Shiva (2001). "Globalization and Poverty". In: Veronika Bennholdt-Thomsen, Nicholas G. Faraclas and Claudia von Werlhof (eds.), *There is an Alternative: Subsistence and Worldwide Resistance to Corporate Globalization*. Victoria: Spinifex Press: 59.

Table 5.3. Yao's traditional classification of cultivated land

Criteria for land classification	Swidden milpa	Wet-rice field	Garden
Terrain	Upper milpa (*nậm hang đẩy*), low milpa (*ay đẩy*), inner milpa (*ưa nhừa đẩy*), outer milpa (*ưa khu đẩy*), high sloping milpa (*ưa chìa đẩy*), low sloping milpa (*đia đẩy*)	Fields at the back of village (*lạ ay lình*), fields at the head of village (*nậm hang lình*), earth fields (*đào tẩy lình*), fields with many rocks (*pì doòng lình*), fields nearby streams, terraced fields (*lình chàng hang*), relatively flat fields (*lình chàng ay*)	
Forest-based	Secondary milpa (*đẩy hu*), primary milpa (*kìm đẩy*).		
Varieties of crops	Maize milpa (*cà mẹ đẩy*), cassava milpa (*kinh đòi đẩy*), rice milpa (*bèo đẩy*), "*thảo quả*" milpa (*la hảo đẩy*), sweet potato milpa (*phẩn đòi đẩy*), peanut milpa (*píu sân đẩy*), arrowroot milpa (*quy hậu đẩy*), taro milpa (*hẩu đang đẩy*)	Glutinous rice fields (*bèo bụt lình*), ordinary rice fields (*bèo chí lình*), new-rice fields (*xang bèo nghim lình*), local rice fields (*lồ bèo nghim lình*)	Vegetable garden (*lay hun*), cassava garden (*kinh đòi hun*), arrowroot garden (*quy hậu hun*), *thảo quả* garden (*la hảo hun*), sugar-cane garden (*càm chĩa hun*), maize garden (*cà mẹ hun*)
Fertility of soil		Good fields (*lình chỉm*), bad fields (*lình chẽ*)	
Others			Mixed garden (*hun*)

5.2 Diversity of cultivated crops and their planting methods

5.2.1 Diversity of cultivated crops

The Yao cultivate different kinds of crops: food crops, vegetables, spices, fruit trees and other plants. Most of these are their own local varieties. Additionally, there are some new and hybrid crops, mostly staple food crops (Table 5.4).

Table 5.4 Diversity of food crops

Staple food crops = 43 varieties							
Rice = 32 varieties					Maize = 11 varieties		
Local = 29				New = 3	Local = 9		New = 2
Ordinary = 15		Glutinous = 14		Ordinary	Ordinary	Glutinous	Ordinary
Wet-rice	Dry-rice	Wet-rice	Dry-rice	Wet-rice			
40%	60%	64.3%	35.7%	3	7	2	2

Table 5.4 shows that the local farmers use rice and maize as their staple food crops. Compared to maize, rice is much more diverse. Taking into account the quantity of land used for rice growth and the number of rice cultivators, rice (Oryaza spp.) is considered the most important cereal in the world.[1] In the Red Yao communities, there are various kinds of rice (*bèo*). Based on the nature of rice, there are two kinds of rice: sticky rice (*bèo bụt*) and ordinary rice (*bèo chí*). Based on the origin of rice varieties, rice is also divided into two kinds: local rice (*lồ bèo nghim*) and new rice (*xang bèo nghim*). Based on the types of plots where the rice is grown, there is dry rice (*đẩy bèo chí*) and wet rice (*lình bèo chí*).

The Red Yao people plant local dry-rice varieties on the milpas. Contrarily, local wet-rice varieties and all hybrid rice varieties are grown in the swamped fields. Glutinous rice varieties are normally planted on the better land than the dry rice because they are very selective about the soil and are less productive. The dry rice grows on the higher sloping plots. This kind of rice is popular in many upland areas of Asian countries: in the Hmong communities in southern China, in northern Vietnam, Laos and Thailand; in the Yao communities in northern Vietnam, in China, Laos and Thailand; and in the Akha

[1] FAO (1997), cited in Joseph C. OOynu (2003). "Growing rice as a strategy to make income for the farmers around the swamped region of Kachonga, Toroto district". In: Vietnam - the Netherlands collaborative research programme (2003), *Proceedings of International Workshop on Environment and Sustainable Development*. Hanoi: Agricultural Publishing House: 105.

and Karen communities in Thailand.[1]

It is evident that the introduction of new varieties into the Yao communities and their application to production has diminished many local varieties. Although local rice varieties are more flavourful and delicious than the new varieties, they are less productive (26.3 cwt/ha compared with 40.4 cwt/ha) and more time-consuming. Therefore, to have enough rice to eat, local farmers mainly plant the new varieties. As a result, their local varieties have decreased from some 40 to 29 kinds of rice.

The preservation of local varieties differs from commune to commune and from household to household. This depends on the quantity of cultivable land (mostly) and their awareness of preserving their own flavoured varieties for their spiritual purposes and their eating demands. Comparing all research areas, the people in the two communes of Nậm Cang and Bản Khoang preserve more local rice varieties than the people in Tả Phìn commune because they have more cultivated land. Currently, the local people keep to their local sticky rice because there is not a new one. This variety is round, short, very glutinous and flavoured. In the New Year and in the traditional festivals, the Yao people regularly use the glutinous rice as an offering to their ancestors and other spirits. They want to give their ancestors their traditional food as a valuable offering to thank them for their supports. This is another reason for the maintenance of this kind of rice in their community. In addition, their traditional rice needs less manure and fertilizer than do the new ones. Most farmers are poor and cannot afford to buy enough fertilizer for all their new rice fields, if they sow all of their swamped land with the cross-bred rice. A similar situation also exists in the case of maize and taro.

It is found that the local farmers sow and plant the local rice mostly in their traditional way. However, they intensify fertilizers for their crops. Nevertheless, they limit the use of nitrate for the local rice fields because it can make the rice

[1] W. R. Gaddes (1976). *Migrants of the mountains: The Cultural Ecology of the Blue Miao (Hmong Njua) of Thailand*. Oxford: Clarendon Press.
- Robert Cooper (1984). *Resource Scarcity and the Hmong Response: Patterns of Settlement and Economy in Transition*. Singapore: Singapore University Press.
- Michael C. Howard (1996). *Contemporary Cultural Anthropology*. Fifth Edition. New York: HarperCollins College Publishers.
- Tran Huu Son (1996). *The Hmong's Culture*. Hanoi: National Culture Publishing House.
- Nguyen Van Minh (2000). "Agricultural adaptation of the H'mong in Vietnam (A case study of two mountain communes)". Hanoi: *Vietnam Social Sciences*, No. 6 (80): 75-95.
- Be Viet Dang, Nguyen Khac Tung, Nong Trung, and Nguyen Nam Tien (1971). *The Yao in Vietnam*. Hanoi: Social Science Publishing House.
- Pham Quang Hoan and Hung Dinh Quy (eds.) (1999). *Traditional culture among the Yao in Ha Giang province*. Hanoi: National Culture Publishing House.
- Jess G. Pourret (2002). *The Yao - The Mien and Mun Yao in China, Vietnam, Laos and Thailand*. London: Thames & Hudson.
- Peter Hinton (1967). *Tribesmen and Peasants in North Thailand: Proceedings of the First Symposium of the Tribal Research Centre*. Chiang Mai, Thailand.
- Paul W. Lewis (1984). *People of the Golden Triangle: Six Tribes of Thailand*. London: Thames and Hudson.

short and poor. It is evident that the local people have applied some modern technologies in cultivation, mostly in getting chemical fertilizers for their rice crops. However, based on the lessons learnt, they get to know the way of choosing and applying them to the next crop in order to achieve a better harvest.

Although the people have grown some new rice varieties for six years, they could not preserve or keep them for seeds. In fact, many households tried to keep these seeds by their traditional way. Unfortunately, most the seeds were mildewy. Therefore, the farmers had to buy the new-rice seeds from the local administrators when their season came. That is why these varieties are still *xang bèo nghim* ("new" rice) for them, although these kinds of rice have been introduced to them for a relatively long time. Moreover, many households still reserve some fields for their local rice varieties to keep their seeds in order to protect them themselves from hunger, when the local administrators are supplying them late in the new rice seeds.

Previously, in addition to rice and maize, other food crops, mostly the numerous taro varieties, played an important role in providing a considerable amount of food for the local farmers. Nowadays they are a supplemental food because of the abundant and good rice harvests of the six recent years.

The Yao people plant various kinds of vegetables and spices. All these plants are their own local varieties, except chayote (*quýt qua*). Compared to the past, they currently pay much more attention to an extension of the gardening and more investment in this work. Vegetables were previously planted on sloping land, intercropped with other crops, especially with the maize. Nowadays, vegetable gardens around and nearby the inhabitants' residences have become common. In these circumstances, farmers have more opportunity to care for crops in their garden than before. As a result, their gardens are increasingly verdant and lush. Their gardening meets farmers' demands for vegetables in summer. Additionally, many plants can be used as food for domestic animals and thus contribute to the development of local stock-breeding.

In previous times, the Yao farmers planted only a few fruit trees: lemon trees (*pìu suy*), plum and persimmon trees. Their fruit were only used for domestic purposes. Nowadays, however, many imported fruit trees exist in their communities. They are "*tam hoa*" plum trees, peach trees, pear trees, and new persimmon trees. Some of their fruit are used for both domestic and commercial purposes.

The Yao people practice of traditional disease prevention and treatment by using domestic herbal plants. Most of these plants naturally grow in the forest, along streams, in the paths, in the fields and in home gardens. In addition, the local farmers also grow some kinds of medicinal plants such as *thảo quả* (Amomum tsao-ko Crev. et Lem.), "conioselinum univitatim" (Ligusticum wallichii Franch.), *cây chân chim*, and *cây đỗ trọng* (Eucommia ulmoides Oliv.). Among these, the *thảo quả* and the "conioselinum univitatim" are used as cash crops. Many Yao households dispel hunger and poverty by selling *thảo quả*.

5.2.2 Seasonal calendars

Through their lives and production, the Yao have gradually fixed and settled seasonal calendars appropriate for crops. In addition, they now base agricultural practices on the government's calendar year as well. However, in some cases, this calendar is only suitable for the lowlands, rather for the warmer region than for their locality. Therefore, in the first two years when the local people applied imported crops to their cultivated land, their harvest was even poorer than the harvest of their local crops. As an example, the new rice of C70 is very suitable and favourable for the fields in the lowlands and in the delta with the warmer temperature, but not adaptable to a cold region as Sa Pa district. Therefore, in despite of their application of many modern techniques of sowing and planting to this variety, the local farmers still achieve a poor harvest. In some fields, its productiveness is even lower than those of their local variety which needs less fertilizers and labour. In another instance, if the local people apply the seasonal calendar of rice practiced in Tả Phìn commune to Bản Khoang commune, where is colder and drier than Tả Phìn, their paddies will be husky and then very poor. Therefore, in combination with the available experience in production and the new knowledge, the local farmers have gradually built for them themselves a seasonal calendar favourable to their environment. It reflects the typical characters of the locally and ethnically seasonal calendars in the ethnic communities in different regions.

Seasonal calendars are also different from crop to crop because of the crop diversity (Table 5.5 and Table 5.6).

* Notes of Table 5.5:

— Local rice (*lồ bèo nghim*)
— New rice (*xang bèo nghim*)
— Early maize (*chừ mẹ diêu*)
— Late maize (*mẹ chày*)
— Cassava (*bẻng đòi*)
— Sweet potato (*phẳn đòi*)
— Taro (*hậu*)
— Potato (*giẳng ỷ đòi*)

Table 5.5. Seasonal calendars of food crops

Work	Month											
	1	2	3	4	5	6	7	8	9	10	11	12
Slashing												
Burning												
Hoeing land												
Ploughing												
Harrowing												
Sowing seeds												
Planting rice seedlings												
Planting												
Fertilizing												
Irrigating												
Weeding												
Spraying pesticides												
Harvesting												

Table 5.6. Seasonal calendars of main vegetables and spices

Varieties	Month											
	1	**2**	**3**	**4**	**5**	**6**	**7**	**8**	**9**	**10**	**11**	**12**
Green bean (*tụm meng*)												
Lettuce (*lay chải*)												
Cabbage (*lay piêu*)												
Pumpkin (*phàn nhum*)												
Luffa (*lay dây*)												
Chayote (*quýt qua*)												
Tomato (*cù piêu*)												
Soya-bean												
Sesame (*sạ bẩy*)												
Green squash (*xộp*)												
Sweet potato buds (*đòi loẳng*)												
Green pea (*tập*)												
Yellow pea (*tập giẳng*)												
Colocynth (*pìu tạt*)												
Cassaba melon (*quà uôm*)												
Morning glory (*ông chày*)												
White cabbage (*lay chải pẹ*)												
"Rau tầu bay" (*lay may*)												
Kohlrabi												
Bamboo sprout (*hầu giẳng bẹ*)												
Onion (*kìu*)												
Perilla (*coỏng phâu*)												
Basil (*pờ la xít*)												
Ginger (*su*)												
Garlic (*phủn*)												
Capsicum (*phật chiu*)												
Saffron												

In a previous era, farmers harvested their rice crop in the beginning of September.[1] Now, their harvest comes sooner than before due to the cultivation of the new rice in addition to that of the local one. Additionally, other factors of their earlier harvests are the increasing warming of the earth and the intensification of the use of manure and fertilizers for the rice. Moreover, the harvesting time, especially for *thảo quả*, is shorter than before, about one and a half month which helps to protect their crops from theft or harm by animals (such as by buffaloes, pigs, mice, etc.).

Table 5.6 shows that the season of most vegetables lasts some months. In addition, some cultivated crops grow all year round. They are normally the spices. Particularly, some certain kinds of crops have two seasons a year. They are green beans and soybeans. Most green vegetables grow well in summer. They are mainly harvested in the end of summer. Therefore, the local farmers still have a shortage of different kinds of vegetables in winter. This shortage leads them to gather wild vegetables in the forest.

5.2.3 Different planting methods

The Yao's planting methods are various and diverse. They include monoculture, intercropping and mixed-cropping.

Monoculture is popular in the sowing and planting of rice, taro and some kinds of maize. The local farmers want to maintain the flavours of each rice variety; therefore, they grow them in separate fields. Sometimes, they intercrop one rice variety with another kind of rice, but only if these rice crops have similar biological characteristics and growing periods. In the case of taro, monoculture is the only planting method because this crop is very selective about the land; and it only grows well in its own plots without any other cultivated crops. Farmers who have a lot of cultivable land normally apply monoculture to their maize crops. They usually grow the ordinary maize and the glutinous maize in different soil plots because they are afraid that pollens of these maize varieties will cross, leading to a negative impact on their qualities.

A fact is that intercropping has long been a common planting technique among the Yao in Vietnam. Few soil plots have a monoculture.[2] Therefore, cultivable plots are places where the farmers not only produce food, but also where they maintain, protect and develop several varieties of indigenous plants. Green beans are popularly intercropped with maize. Traditionally, after farmers have sowed the land with maize seeds, they evenly distribute bean seeds over the surface of the maize plots. The bean plants themselves grow naturally. In addition, casaba melons, lettuces, pumpkins, and sweet potatoes are also intercropped with maize. This creates the milpa, with a combination of three crops of maize-casaba melons-green bean, of two crops of maize-lettuce, maize-pumpkin, and maize-sweet potatoes or the soil plots of a mixed-cropping

---

[1] Be Viet Dang, Nguyen Khac Tung, Nong Trung, and Nguyen Nam Tien (1971). *The Yao in Vietnam*. Hanoi: Social Science Publishing House: 76.

[2] Be Viet Dang, Nguyen Khac Tung, Nong Trung, and Nguyen Nam Tien (1971). *ibid*: 77.
- Institute of Ethnology (1978). *Ethnic minorities in Vietnam (in the Northern provinces)*. Hanoi: Social Science Publishing House: 316.

between all of them except sweet potatoes. The intercropping is also applied to some dry-rice fields. Some upland milpas include three different crops of dry-rice, sesame and *chỉ san* (which is similar to the sesame with black seeds and green seeds' nuclei). Additionally, many vegetables are normally intercropped with each other in the home gardens and in the sloping milpa.

In the case of the mixed-cropping, as mentioned above, seeds of five crops of maize, casaba melon, green bean, pumpkin and lettuce are sometimes mixed with each other and then sown in the same plots. The farmers mix all these seeds with the ashes and the phosphate or NPK. After that, they sow this mixture in the bottom of dug holes reserved for the maize. As soon as they sow such holes with the maize seeds, they cover it with earth. These seeds germinate simultaneously with the maize. Mixed-cropping is also very popular in the case of planting of different kinds of vegetables. The farmers normally mix some kinds of vegetable seeds with each other, and then they scatter these seeds on the surface of certain soil plots.

The Yao's care of the cultivated crops by increasing fertilizers has tended to develop over the past decade. However, in some certain steps of the growing process of some varieties, rice seedlings for instance, muck is indispensable for them. In addition, the local farmers gradually get some vegetable manure and chemical fertilizers for their milpas, their fields and gardens. On the one hand, the chemical fertilizers make some cultivated crops develop well with a high productivity. On the other hand, they contribute to erosion. For example, the new rice varieties grow very well in the fields where the local rice varieties grew. In contrast, local rice varieties do not grow well in the fields where the new rice varieties have been grown. One of the main reasons for this is that the local farmers normally added organic fertilizers to the local rice fields; therefore, the process of land erosion occurred slowly. Meanwhile, the new rice varieties require more water and more fertilizers than the local ones.

Nowadays, to protect cultivated crops from the damage caused by pests, the staffs of Sa Pa station of plant protection give farmers specific instructions for spraying pesticide for 8 ha of rice fields that are suffering from a disease of piriculariose, for 1 ha of atractylis fields and for some artichoke fields suffering from damage by termites. In 1999 the staffs of this station supplied the local people with 54 kg of powdered pesticides, 580 bottles of liquid pesticides, 50 packets of termite killers and 20 bottles of weed killers.[1]

In general, it is found that, by monoculture, the farmers can keep the special flavours of some cultivated crops. By intercropping and mixed-cropping, they can protect their soil plots from erosion and diversify their crops for their demands for food and foodstuffs all year along. In addition, fertilizers (both organic and chemical fertilizers) and different kinds of modern medication for plant protection have been gradually applied to agriculture in the Yao communities. These help them to increase the productivity of their crops and

---

[1] Department of Agriculture and Rural Development of Sa Pa district (2000). *Report on the work on direction for the agro-forestry development in 1999 - Trend, task, and plan of the year 2000*, No. 02/ BC-TK/1999: 8.

protect their crops from damages by harmful pests and insects. However, these modern chemical fertilizers contribute to more rapid soil erosion.

5.3Several usages of cultivated crops

The Yao people grow different types of plants and have different ways of using them. Agricultural products are used for the following purposes: seeds, food for daily meals (cooked rice and vegetable soups, etc.), desserts (cakes, stuffing of cakes, boiled food), drinks (rice alcohol), medicines, cash income, and as raw materials for house construction and for making articles for the home.

- As seeds: Good seeds play an important role in the growth of cultivated crops. After the farmers have carried all agricultural products to their homes, the female farmers are mostly responsible for selecting and keeping good grains, tubers and fruits for seeds. Their ways of selecting and keeping these seeds are based on their own experience. The criteria of selection for the seeds differ from crop to crop.

- For the purpose of food: Most agricultural products are used as food for the people (mainly) and domestic animals. Farmers have different ways of processing food. In previous times most Yao household lacked food from one to three months a year. Some households even had food shortages for 6 months a year. They therefore had to cook their food by mixing rice with taro, maize or cassava. Nowadays, most households have enough food for their families; thus, the cooked ordinary rice is very popular in their communities. In addition, they also make a series of rice dishes, such as cooked sticky rice, rice cakes and rice gruels. The stuffing of these cakes is made of green beans, sesames and *chỉ san*. Various kinds of soups are indispensable for the farmers' daily meals. Normally, they are vegetable and tofu soups.

The local farmers have three meals a day: in the morning, in the afternoon and in the evening. During harvesting season, they usually have lunch at the working site. The meal is cooked early in the morning or right at the work site. Daily meals include rice, vegetables and sauce.

- For the purpose of drinks: The Yao people live in the uplands and under cold conditions. Therefore, they traditionally drink alcohol to counter coldness and to meet their demands of drinking. Their alcohols are very diverse. They are different kinds of rice alcohols made from red glutinous rice (*bèo ừ củ*), rice for old men (*bèo ông*) and some other rice varieties (see: Appendix 2). In previous times, due to lack of food, many Yao farmers distilled cassava alcohol. Currently, they no longer distil this kind of alcohol because of the abundance of rice and because cassava alcohol causes the headache.

The alcohols have different tastes depending on the main raw materials used and the recipes for processing alcohol. For example, alcohol made of the rice with husks is more flavourful and delicious than one made of the unhusked rice. Alcohol made of red glutinous rice (*bèo ừ củ*) also has a different flavour compared to that made of "rice for old men" (*bèo ông*). In addition, even when alcohols are made from the same raw material but in different processings, they have different flavours. For example, there are two ways of processing red glutinous rice. The first is that the farmers mix this cooked rice with some traditional materials for about 4-5 days to ferment them. Afterwards, women will eat this rice and drink its undistilled essences. In this case, rice alcohol has a sweet taste. The last way is that the farmers distill this rice as usual, after they have fermented it by mixing it with some other materials. They only drink the distilled alcohol and do not eat the dregs. In this case, their alcohol has a fragrant and sharp taste.

- For medicinal purpose: All pharmaceutical plants (such as *thảo quả*, "conioselinum univitatim", *cây chân chim* and *cây đỗ trọng*) are used as medicine for disease prevention and treatment. In addition, with the view that "food, drink, and medicines share the same origin", the Vietnamese people have used food and drink in place of medicines to cure diseases from time immemorial.[1] Several western scholars also agree that food is not only a source of nutrition but also can be used as medicines and vice versa.[2] This is also a principle of Vietnam's traditional medicines. A dietary regime is considered the second most important of four modern treatment steps.[3] For Red Yao people, foods not only provide nutritious supplies necessary for human existence, but also prevent and cure some diseases. Some kinds of rice also can be used for the medicinal purpose. As an example, the "*bèo ông*" and the "*bèo ừ củ*" are used to treat the bellyache and asthenia. Particularly, the "*bèo ừ củ*" is normally used for improving the health of post-delivery women and for increasing their lactation.

Depending on the season, people select foods to meet their daily nutritional demand, protect their health, and suit each family economically. In summer, they have amaranth (*lay xeng*) or *lay lện* vegetable soup as febrifuges. In winter, cabbage, chilli and ginger are mainly used to maintain body temperature and prevent diseases caused by coldness. Vegetables and fruits having a red colour are preferred as they are thought to be good for the blood. Local people have different types of drinks depending on the season. In summer, in addition to the rice alcohol, Yao people prefer fresh green tea (*miền trà*), leaves of "*cây gai*" (*ghim nòm*), boiled water and well water. In winter, they prefer dry green tea and rice alcohol.

The Yao people divide food into two main categories: "hot" and "cold". Hot foods and drinks include chilli, ginger, garlic, pepper, lettuce, white radish, plums,

---

[1] Hanoi University of Medicines - Community Health Research Department, Vietnam Red Cross Society, Danish Red Cross Society (2001). *Goodwill Medicine Practice*. Hanoi: Medicine Publishing House.

[2] Cecil G. Helman (1990). *Culture, Health and Illness: An Introduction for Health Professionals*. Second Edition. Wight Publisher: 31, 37.

- Michael C. Howard (1996). *Contemporary Cultural Anthropology*. Fifth Edition. New York: HarperCollins College Publishers: 365.

[3] Hanoi University of Medicines - Community Health Research Department, Vietnam Red Cross Society, Danish Red Cross Society (2001). *ibid*: 5-6.

Four modern treatment steps are:
- First, adjustment of daily life style
- Second, adjustment of diet regime
- Medicines
- Last, surgical interference

Steps must be tried in the numerical order, then move to the next one if the former fails.

peach, *quang hậu* (a type of taro). Cold foods and drinks consist of green tea, amaranth (*lay xeng*), *lay lện*, sweet potato, banana, white cabbage. In principle, it is impossible for those who are using "cold" and "cool" medicines (*nẳm*) for "hot" disease (*chồm*) treatment to eat "hot" foods and drinks, and vice versa.

- Cash income: There has been a real change for the better in the Yao's life since one of their agricultural products, *thảo quả*, a plant that is maintained in semi-cultivated condition in the forest, has achieved a high monetary value. According to Tran Van On (2003), the output of this plant in the whole Sa Pa district reached 330 tons in 2002. Each household in the Yao communities had an average income of 8,350,000 VND/year from selling this plant. In comparison, each Hmong household earned 8,800,000 VND/year from this source. In both the communities of the Yao and the Hmong, many households earned up to 100 million VND/household/year by selling this plant.[1]

However, this income is unstable due to the *thảo quả*'s dependence on the weather and on the market. In rainy years, especially when it rains in the blossom season of this plant, the rain makes the *thảo quả* blossoms die and then the crop is very poor. In windy years, the wind makes the *thảo quả* blossom dry and then there is also a very poor harvest. Additionally, this crop cannot grow in very cold soil plots. Thus, farmers rarely grow it in plots located in the primary forest.

In addition, prices of this crop are also unstable. For example, before 1996 local farmers had to carry products of this crop to the Sa Pa market and then sold them to the Sa Pa General Store. At that time, their prices were very low. Since 1996, private traders have come into Yao communities to buy these products directly at much higher cost than before. However, the prices of this agricultural product still go up and down without a rule. For instance, prices of products of this crop suddenly rose in 2002. This made the traders pay a certain deposit to local farmers even when the farmers had not yet harvested their crop. In some cases, some traders coaxed the local farmers into selling their young crop to them. However, their prices were still high. At that time, prices of this crop were 140,000 VND/kg of the dry product and 80,000 VND/kg of the fresh product. As a result of this high value, many Yao households had enough money to buy televisions and motorbikes. Particularly, three households in Bản Khoang commune even bought cars by money from selling this product. In the five recent years, the price of the *thảo quả* has stopped going up; it even has gone down. For example, a kilogram of dry *thảo quả* costs 38,000 VND in 2002. In 2003, its price went up; then they were 60,000 VND per kilogram for the dry product and 14,000 VND per kilogram for the fresh product.

Apart from the *thảo quả*, the local farmers can earn money from selling some other agricultural products such as "conioselinum univitatim", peaches and plums. However, these incomes are unremarkable because these plants have limited outputs and are not very marketable.

- As raw materials for building houses and making house articles: In previous times, farmers rarely planted various kinds of bamboo because they

[1] Cited in Tran Van On (2005). "The medical plant resource and poverty reduction among ethnic communities in the northern mountainous area". Hanoi: *Anthropology Review*, No. 2: 36-37.

were available in the forest. In recent years, they have gradually increased the area of these plants by domesticating wild ones because of their scarcity and the farmers' increasing demands for consumption of these plants. This contributes to supplying them with some raw materials for building houses and making house articles, such as different kinds of baskets, chopsticks, scoops, spoons, and toothpicks.

5.4Different tools for production

The Yao normally use traditional production tools which they make themselves. These tools are relatively diverse. They include hoes (*poong*), ploughs (*lày*), harrows (*pà*), digging-sticks, sickles (*lìm*), hoes (*poong*), grass rakes (*nhiu*), bamboo screens (*chỉ bo bèo*), rice-plucking machines (*đèng chả*, *đèng niu*), bamboo tape fans, dossers, flat winnowing baskets (*seng*), panniers (*chỉ*), and wooden barrels. Each tool has its own function depending on its use. In addition to these tools, horses (mostly in previous times) and motorbikes (nowadays) are used to carry agricultural products from the fields to the dwelling house or storehouse.

Among these, there are different kinds of ploughs and harrows used for different soil types and plots. In the case of plough, there are two different kinds: the plough used for swamped fields (*lày lình*) and the plough used for high sloping milpas (*lày đẩy*). The *lày lình* is made of a "*cây dâu*" wood frame and a cast-iron ploughshare. Its shape is curved and one side shape is sharp. The *lày đẩy* has a similar form as the *lày lình*, but with both sides. As with ploughs, there are two different kinds of harrows: the harrow used for swamped fields (*lình pà*) and the harrow used for high sloping milpas (*đẩy pà*). Among these, the *lình pà* has single wooden teeth. The *đẩy pà* has double wooden teeth. Woods used for making the teeth of the *lình pà* are various. Meanwhile, to make the teeth of *đẩy pà*, the farmers select only hard woods of the "*cây xương cá*" (*xềng miềng đẻng*), of the "*cây gai*" (*đẻng ghim*), and of the "*cây đinh*" (*uồm chùn đẻng*).

Nowadays the Yao's available tools do not meet all of their demands of production because they are expanding their agriculture. Therefore, they buy some tools of the Kinh in the local market. These include hoes, mandrels, sickles, jute bags, plastic buckets, rice-plucking machines and threshing machines. However, many of these tools are worse than their traditional tools. As an example, hoes bought in the Sa Pa market are quickly worn out and broken; the farmers can use them only for one year because their blades are tempered for a short time so that they are not as sharp as the local ones. In comparison, the farmers can use their local hoes for a longer time, from two to three years. Therefore, the Yao usually fix these tools (making them sharper or fixing a shaft to a hoe and making it faster, etc.) before using them for their cultivation.

It is found that the Yao's traditional tools are still appropriate for their cultivation in the sloping land because the people know which tools are the best for which soil plots and how to make them for long-term use. However, some imported tools are essential and effective for the farmers to make up for their lack of metallic materials and to save time.

5.5Varied irrigation systems

Like many other minority uplanders in Vietnam, the Yao's agriculture is mainly rainfed. Water sources for their fields depend mainly on rainwater. Therefore, the local people only grow rice in the rainy season of a year.

To irrigate their fields, the Yao people traditionally construct a primary irrigation system based on their experience accumulated from one generation to another. According to their own regulations, representatives of every household who profit from water are responsible for digging ditches. They trench different fields to catch water from the head of the water source or from the ground water and to drain off water from their fields. To bring water into their fields, in some areas, they use bamboo trees as water pipes. Depending on each terrain of fields, this system is set tortuously around their villages.

The Yao people also make instruments of wood and other raw materials available in the wild to control the water level for their rice fields. They are used as governor valves to keep the water level in their fields not so high as to erode the land and not so low as to stunt their crops. In addition, this helps the fields located at the back of the watershed to have enough water during their season because water normally flows from the fields at the head of the water sources to the fields at the back of these sources.

Currently, besides their traditional irrigation system, they also have modern small-scale irrigation systems in some places where the fields are concentrated. These modern systems are built in Tả Chải, Can Ngài and Suối Thầu villages of Tả Phìn commune with 7.463 km in length; in Can Hồ A and Suối Thầu 1 villages of Bản Khoang commune with 2.36 km-long trench; in Nậm Cang and Nậm Than villages of Nậm Cang commune with 4.2 km in length.[1] A general guideline of the construction of some parts of the communal infrastructure, including the local irrigation system, is that "*state and people will do it together*". The government provides the people with a fund to buy raw materials and a labour free for the construction. The people carry these materials to places for construction. However, these systems only help them to lead water into the areas near their fields. In order to lead water right into their rice fields, their traditional instruments are indispensable. With this combination, complete irrigation systems for the concentrated fields have been much improved.

In many other fields, farmers use only their traditional irrigation systems because of the partitioned and complicated terrain. In addition, most farmers still use their own instruments to control the water level in their rice fields. These instruments are made of locally available raw materials, such as wood and different kinds of bamboo. Therefore, the traditional irrigation is still optimal and effective in these areas.

5.6Different beliefs and ritual ceremonies relating to cultivation

Like other farmers in Vietnam and in the Southeast Asia, the Red Yao people have a long-term hierolatry of many spirits. According to them, "everything is sacred" and spirits exist everywhere. The Yao adopted Taoism as

[1] Sa Pa District People's Committee (2005). *Report on the assessment of effects of irrigation systems funded by the Programme 135*, No. 75/BC-UB. Sa Pa: 7/6/2005.

a religion. It superseded their own earlier tribal religion which centred on three main deities: one in charge of natural waters, mountains, thunder, rain, etc; one in charge of living beings and another in charge of the dead.[1]

They classify the spirits into two different kinds: benign and maleficent spirits. The benign spirits regularly support and bless the people. However, it sometimes makes these spirits angry if the people worship them carelessly. In this case, these spirits will do the people harm. The maleficent spirits are considered to damage and harm the people, crops, and animals. The belief in the spirits exists not only in the Yao community in Vietnam, but also in other countries in Asia, such as China, Burma, Thailand, Laos, and Cambodia, etc. It is perceived to be one of the popular religions in Asia conforming closely to Edward Taylor's original model of animism (1871).[2]

The relationship between human and plants is demonstrated not only in the techniques of planting crops, but also in the ritual ceremonies regarding cultivation, the reciting of spells and incantation to wish a good harvest. This relationship was very clear in the previous time, when the local people lived mainly on the shifting cultivation. Until now, the people still maintain many taboos and ritual ceremonies relating to production to wish good harvests and good health.

5.6.1 Taboos and avoidances

The farmers observe taboos in some procedures of planting to avoid misfortune and poor harvests. They carefully fix an auspicious date and point of time for choosing the cultivable land, for slashing, sowing and caring for some crops, especially for paddy and maize. They usually base themselves on a shaman's magic manual to fix a good time.

In the case of slashing the land, good days are different depending on the age of the master of the house. However, they are based on a common set of principles for choosing a good day. These are: 1) a day that has no accident and bad news; 2) a good day corresponds to each age.[3] This order is influenced by the Chinese, as all the Yao's magic manuals are written in *Quan Hoả* (local Chinese) and transmitted from generation to generation in the family of the village magicians.

---

[1] Jess G. Pourret (2002). *The Yao - The Mien and Mun Yao in China, Vietnam, Laos and Thailand.* London: Thames & Hudson: 47.

[2] Cited in Nicholas Tapp (1993). "Karma and Cosmology - Anthropology and Religion". In: Grant Evans (1993), *Asia's Cultural Mosaic - An Anthropological Introduction.* Singapore: Prentice Hall: 301.

[3] Each person was born under the astrological sign of one of the 12 animals of the Chinese zodiac, which are associated with the Earth's 12 branches of ancient cosmology. These animals consist of mouse (*tí* in Vietnamese), buffalo (*sửu*), tiger (*dần*), cat (*mão*), dragon (*thìn*), snake (*tỵ*), horse (*ngọ*), goat (*mùi*), monkey (*thân*), chicken (fowl) (*dậu*), dog (*tuất*), and pig (*hợi*). This cycle lasts 12 years, the so-called "*giáp*" (12 year cycle). In addition, this person also was born under one of the ten signs of the Heaven's Stems. They are *giáp* (the first Heaven's Stem), *ất* (the second Heaven's Stem), *bính* (the third Heaven's Stem), *đinh* (the fourth Heaven's Stem), *mậu* (the fifth Heaven's Stem), *kỷ* (the sixth Heaven's Stem), *canh* (the seventh Heaven's Stem), *tân* (the eighth Heaven's Stem), *nhâm* (the ninth Heaven's Stem), and *quý* (the tenth Heaven's Stem). The real year of birth of a person is a combination of two signs of both the Heaven's Stems and the Earth's branches.

In the case of rice, farmers avoid sowing rice seed at the date of the mouse and the chicken because they are afraid that these animals will harm this crop. They also do not sow the land with rice seed at a thunder date because they are afraid that these seeds will not germinate or the paddy will be husky, and thus their harvest will be very poor. The local farmers do not go to their fields on 1st February (avoiding fowls) and on 2nd February (avoiding mice) because they believe that these animals will destroy their crops. To protect their crops from these animals' damage, they additionally close up their main doors and then they stick some glutinous cakes into the chink of the double door. This means that they stick the mouths of these animals to protect their crops from damage by these animals. Similarly, the farmers also do not work in their fields on 6th June because they are afraid that pigs will destroy their crops. They also avoid working on 7th July because they are afraid that paddy will be ashamed of their appearance; thus, the paddy will not continue to bear their gains.

Apart from the above taboos and dates of avoidance, local farmers also forecast good and bad days for many steps of growing rice (such as soaking rice seeds, sowing land with dry and wet rice seeds, transplanting wet-rice seedlings into terraced fields and harvesting them). To help rice seeds germinate equally and protect them from the damage by pests, the farmers select the following days for their soaking of rice seeds: *giáp tuất*, *ất hợi*, *nhâm ngọ*, *ất dậu*, *nhâm thìn*, and *ất mão*. To make rice seedlings healthy and grow well, the people fix the following good dates for sowing the fields with germinated rice seeds: *tân mùi*, *quý dậu*, *nhâm ngọ*, *canh dần*, *giáp ngọ*, *giáp thìn*, *ất tỵ*, *bính ngọ*, *đinh mùi*, *mậu thân*, *kỷ dậu*, *ất mão*, and *tân dậu*. Days for transplanting wet-rice seedlings into terraced fields and for sowing the milpas with dry-rice seeds are carefully selected and fixed. The good days for good growth of rice include *đinh sửu*, *bính tí*, *nhâm ngọ*, *quý mùi*, *canh dần*, and *tân mão*. Rice crops will be extremely productive when they grow in the days of *nhâm thìn* and *quý tỵ*. In addition, the Yao farmers will have a poor rice harvest when they fix the following days for transplanting wet-rice seedlings into the fields and sowing the milpas with dry-rice seeds: the days of *giáp tuất*, *ất hợi*, *tân mùi*, *nhâm thân* and *quý dậu* will make the rice fade and not develop well; the days of *mậu dần*, *kỷ mão*, *canh thìn* and *tân tỵ* will make leaves of rice reddish yellow, and it will be possible for the young rice to be eaten by mice. If rice seedlings are transplanted into the fields in the days of *canh tý*, *tân sửu* and *quý mão*, the rice will be damaged by pests. Rice will have no leaves if rice seedlings are transplanted into the fields in the days of *bính thìn*, *ất tỵ*, *đinh ngọ*, *đinh dậu*, *mậu thân*, *canh tuất*, *tân hợi*, *nhâm thìn*, *quý sửu*, *giáp dần*, *ất mão*, *đinh tỵ*, *mậu ngọ* and *kỷ mùi*. The Yao people also select and fix the best days for their rice harvest. The days of dragons and of snakes are considered good days for rice harvest because the farmers think that their rice ears will be as long as dragons and snakes.

Although they have selected and fixed good days for their above-mentioned work, according to the Yao farmers in Nậm Cang commune, their rice will decay and be consumed quickly if they do not select good days for storing the rice and maize in their storehouse after harvesting and for opening this storehouse for their first consumption of this produce.[1] Good days for storing these crops are *canh ngọ*, *kỷ mão*, *quý mão*, *tân tỵ*, *quý mùi*, *ất dậu*, *canh dần*, and *giáp tý*. If the farmers have not harvested their rice and maize crops yet, they pick some fresh rice ears and then store them in the storehouse on a lucky day to satisfy the rice spirits; then they can harvest in the following days. Based on the four seasons, the farmers choose good days for opening their storehouse for their first consumption of rice. Lucky days for this include days of *đinh mùi* and *ất sửu* (in spring); days of *giáp tí*, *giáp thìn* and *nhâm thìn* (in summer); days of *kỷ sửu*, *kỷ tí* and *đinh mùi* (in autumn); days of *tân mùi*, *giáp thân* and *nhâm hợi* (in winter). From that time, they no longer fix good days for their following consumption of rice.

In the case of maize, to wish a good maize harvest, the farmers comply with some certain taboos. They do not sow the soil with maize seed at the date of mouse and chicken because they are afraid that these animals will destroy the maize crop. They also do not the same work at a thunder date because they believe that maize seeds will not germinate or the maize corn will not be good. In addition, they avoid sowing maize seeds on the anniversary of an interment of a dead person in their family and seeing a post-delivery woman because they are afraid that their maize plants will be etiolated, unfruitful, or even die. However, in fact, some households still sow the land with maize at the date of anniversary of interment of a dead person in the family; but they must comply with some particular rules. If this anniversary falls in with a good day, the son and the daughter-in-law of the dead person should not sow the maize seeds. However, the daughter and the grandchild can do it.

Similar to rice, the local people also select good days for sowing soil plots with maize seed to wish a good harvest. Good days are selected and fixed based on much information written in the Yao magic manual that are encoded on different parts of a mouse considered a rice and maize killer. Each part of the mouse corresponds with certain days of some months. In January, May and September, there are the following good days: days of goat, monkey and chicken (which are located at the both ears of mouse), buffalo (located at its hind leg) and mouse (located at its tail). Lucky days of February, June and October coincide with days of pig, mouse (located at its two ears), buffalo (located on its back), horse (at its belly), dragon, snake (at its hind leg) and cat (at its tail). In the three months of March, July and November, there are three lucky days. They are days of dog, pig (at its ears) and mouse (on its back). Good days of April, August and December include days of tiger and cat (located at its ears).

The local people do not sow their land with maize seed on the bad days. According to them, there are different bad days depending on groups of months. In the three months of January, May and September, bad days coincide with days of snake (located at mouse's mouth), dragon (at its jaw) and goat (at its

[1] Previously, the Yao people in Tả Phìn commune built their storehouse in the milpas. Nowadays, they keep their agricultural products in the garret of their dwelling-house. Different from the Yao people in Tả Phìn commune, the Yao in Nậm Cang usually build their storehouse nearby their accommodation.

foreleg). Bad days of February, June and October include days of chicken (at its mouth), monkey (at its jaw) and goat (at its foreleg). In the three months of March, July and November, there are bad days of chicken (at its mouth), monkey (at its jaw) and goat (at its foreleg). Unlucky days of April, August and December comprise days of mouse (at its mouth), monkey (at its jaw) and dog (at its foreleg).

In general, some days have the same name but are located in different parts of the mouse. In principle, days located and encoded at the mouse's mouth and jaws are considered bad days for sowing maize seeds because the mouse will eat these seeds. Days located at mouse's foreleg are also considered bad days for this work because the mouse will damage the maize seed by using its foreleg to dig them up. Other days located at other parts of the mouse are considered good days for sowing maize seeds because the mouse cannot damage the maize crop by using its other parts (comprising its ears, its hind leg, its belly, its tail and its back). Therefore, the meaning of days is different depending on the mouse's parts where the days are located.

The Yao farmers always fix a good day for eating their new maize in the hope that their domestic animals will not suffer from diseases because of eating maize. They are the days of dog in March and of dragon in April (applied to the low areas where new maize crops grow), of horse in May, of snake in June, of mouse in July, and of pig in August. This proves that maize has been used as the main food for domestic animals for a long time.

- Other taboos and avoidances: The Yao conceive that a tiger and a bear will foretell a misery if someone happens to see them. The farmers in the two communes of Tả Phìn and Bản Khoang have the proverbs that are "*chiển la hu, sàn tải khu*" (meaning after seeing a tiger, the seer's generation and his two following generations will live in misery), and "*chiền la hùng, sàn niền chùng*" (meaning after seeing a bear, living in misery for three years). Similarly, the Yao people in Nậm Cang commune have their own proverbs which are "*triển lồng san niền sùng, triền hu y sí khu*" (meaning after seeing a dragon, living in poverty for three years; after seeing a tiger, living in misery all one's life).

In addition, local farmers have their own ways of dealing with their leftover food. They normally use the leftover cooked rice for livestock breeding. However, in some cases, they do not dare throw it into streams because they are afraid that the rice spirits will be angry with them for their waste of food. Therefore, these spirits will make their next harvest poor. They are also afraid that these spirits will make their rice kept in the storehouse damp or be damaged by pests and they thus will suffer hunger. To conceal their facts from the rice spirits and to avoid their punishment, they usually burn their leftover food to ashes. This also means that they protect their food crops from damages by birds and mice because they believe that these animals will eat and damage their crops if they have eaten their leftover food.

5.6.2 Forecasting the weather and the harvest based on some natural phenomena

The Yao people can forecast their general situation of a year based on some natural phenomena. As an example, they listen to the peal of the first thunder occurring in a year, the so-called new thunder (*xèng bọ ung* in Yao language), to forecast whether that year will be good or bad. In principle, the thunderclaps correspond with the timezones of a day. There are 24 hours a day. Each timezone includes two successive hours corresponding with one of the following times of animals: mouse, buffalo, tiger, cat, dragon, snake, horse, goat, monkey, chicken (or fowl), dog and pig. If the peal of thunder coincides with the timezones of mouse and dog, the farmers will have a very rich harvest but they will be unhealthy. If the peal of thunder coincides with the timezones of buffalo, tiger, cat, goat and monkey, they will have an extremely good year because they will be healthy and have very good harvests. If the peal of thunder coincides with the timezones of dragon, they will achieve only half the rice harvest and they will be ill. If the peal of thunder coincides with the timezones of snake, they will have an ideal year because they will achieve an extremely rich rice harvest, great success in breeding livestock and they will be very healthy. They will have a miserable year and their rice harvest will be extremely poor if the peal of thunder coincides with the timezones of horse. Contrarily, they will have a very rich rice harvest if the peal of thunder coincides with timezones of pig.

Similarly, based on the peal of the first thunder occurring in a year, the Yao can forecast whether the rains will be heavy or light in that year. Thus, they can forecast their rice harvest. In this case, the thunderclap is divided into two different kinds: claps of male thunder (*bọ ung câu*) and claps of female thunder (*bọ ung nhể*). Each kind of the thunderclaps corresponds with a different timezone. Among those, the "*bọ ung câu*" coincides with the timezones of mouse, tiger, dragon, horse, monkey and dog. The "*bọ ung nhể*" coincides with the rest of the timezones. Therefore, the people have a simple way of remembering the timezones of the both kinds of thunders because the timezone of "*bọ ung câu*" is always alternating with the time-zone of "*bọ ung nhể*". If the "*bọ ung câu*" coincides with the timezones of buffalo, tiger, horse and goat, it will rain in that year. If it coincides with the timezones of dragon, snake, monkey, chicken and pig, the people will have much water. If it coincides with the timezones of cat, they will meet many difficulties in their life. If it coincides with the timezones of mouse and dog, they will have a dry year. If the "*bọ ung nhể*" coincides with the timezones of mouse, buffalo and tiger, the farmers will have a successful year. If it coincides with the timezones of horse, goat, monkey and pig, they also have a good year but less successful than in the case of the foregoing. If it coincides with the timezones of cat and snake, they will have an average year (*pản kìa*). If it coincides with the timezones of dragon and dog, they will have a bad year. In the magic manuals of the Yao shamans, there is no information about a case in which the thunderclap coincides with the timezones of chicken.

The directions of the clap of the thunder also forecast different results of a year. If the clap of thunder comes from the east, the farmers will achieve 70% of the harvest; people and domestic animals will be healthy; and there will be a considerably dry month of June. If it comes from the south, it will give a signal that the people will achieve only 50% of the harvest; they will be unhealthy and meet some risks and accidents; and there will be an extremely dry month of August. If it comes from the west, people will achieve only 50% of the harvest; they will suffer from diseases; there will be a heavy rain in March and glazing hot month of August. If it comes from the north, the people will achieve very rich harvests, but they will usually have a quarrel and conflicts with someone else; it will rain heavily in May. If it comes from above, the people will obtain 10 rice plants by growing one rice plant; there will be many funerals in their villages; and there will be an extremely dry month of July.

In addition, the Yao people do not practise agriculture in some certain days of a year in order to avoid risks. For instance, the first day of March is considered a day of thunder by the Yao people. They do not work in their fields this day because they are afraid that they will be killed by thunder and by heavy rain. They also do not do this work in the days of tiger and cat (in this case, a cat is considered a panther) during January because they are afraid that these animals will kill them while they are doing farming. The people also do not work during the first day of summer because they are afraid that they will be unhealthy all year round.

Apart from the peal of thunder, the local people also maintain some taboos and avoidances relating to wind. In the day of wind (on 20th January), they do not do the following work: agricultural practices, whistling, sweeping the floor and blowing the firing because they are afraid that the wind will blow down their houses, trees and crops. Additionally, to avoid these risks caused by wind, one day before the day of wind, they stick some handfuls of *alang* grass along the paths towards their villages. In the right day of wind, they lay a stone on three leaves of this grass which are crossed and laid in front of their main doors to protect their houses from wind.

It is evident that some natural phenomena occurring first in a year are very important for the Yao farmers because they give signals of many things in that year, in terms of cultivation, health and life. This derives more or less from the dependence of the Yao's cultivation on the weather and rainwater.

5.6.3 Rituals and ceremonies in cultivation

Fearing both the punishment of the spirits and the threat of hunger, the Yao traditionally organize ritual ceremonies. The forms of worship differ from commune to commune. However, there are two main kinds of worships in the Yao communities: communal worship and household worship. These two types of worships exist not only in the Red Yao community, but also in other Yao sub-ethnic groups in Vietnam.[1]

5.6.3.1 Community worships (Xếp đẻng con)

This is the biggest and most important form of worship for the Red Yao people in the year. "Superior" shamans in the community are thus involved in this worship, which differs from commune to commune. However, in general, they observe some similar forms of worship.

In Tả Phìn commune, for instance, as soon as farmers plant out the rice seedlings (normally in May), they organize a communal worship in front of a cave sacred to their whole area to wish a good harvest, successful stock-breeding, good health and a peaceful year for all inhabitants. A special aspect of this ceremony is that participants are the Yao and the Hmong men. This differs from Tả Phìn commune, where all participants of Nậm Cang and Bản Khoang communes come only from the Red Yao ethnic group.[2] Before organizing this ceremony, all shamans and magicians discuss it with each other and choose a good date. They usually fix a date of dragon.

In their ceremonies, the offering and tribute are indispensable. Normally, they are the farmers' agricultural products in that year. Different from household worship, in communal worship all ceremonial tributes are shared equally by all households in the community. In the past, each household contributed rice and alcohol to their worship because they had no cash. Now, the cash displaces rice and is used to buy a pig and some chickens for their worship. Because they have four altars, they have to prepare four ceremonial tributes, one for each altar. The offering at the major altar in the joss-house is always much larger than those at the other altars. The worship at the main altar lasts two hours while the worship at the other altars lasts only one hour. Afterwards, all participants have a great feast.

During the seven days following the worship, local people forbade outsiders go to their villages for fear of a poor harvest. However, nowadays, while the people in Nậm Cang and Bản Khoang communes still observe this rule and exclusion, the people of Tả Phìn commune cannot maintain it because of the development of tourism in their community.

- In addition to the above-mentioned worship, the Yao people in Nậm Cang commune perform some other community ritual ceremonies.

+ Worship of the forest and village spirits (*síp tẩy chiêu miên*): Annually, at dates of 1st January, 3rd March, 6th June, and 2nd August, representatives of all households in the village have a meeting in the house of the head of the village. Each household contributes one chicken, a bottle of rice alcohol, an amount of rice and some joss-papers to this ceremony. Before the villagers organize their worship, the head of the village sticks a handful of branches of fresh trees in the

---

[1] Be Viet Dang, Nguyen Khac Tung, Nong Trung, and Nguyen Nam Tien (1971). *The Yao in Vietnam*. Hanoi: Social Science Publishing House: 262.
- Institute of Ethnology (1978). *Ethnic minorities in Vietnam (in the Northern provinces)*. Hanoi: Social Science Publishing House: 332.
- Pham Quang Hoan and Hung Dinh Quy (eds.) (1999). *Traditional culture among the Yao in Ha Giang province*. Hanoi: National Culture Publishing House: 260-270.

[2] Some Hmong households do not organize the same worship as those of the Yao because they are Protestants.

main door of his house to forbid strangers and non-participants to come into his house during the ritual ceremony. An altar reserved for the forest and village spirits is laid outside the house opposite the ancestral altar of the head of the village. During this ceremony, the head of the village calls upon the village spirit (*tẩy chiêu dùn phiêu*), the earth spirit (*tẩy chiêu miên*) and ancestral spirits of all households in the village to go back to the village and receive their offerings. This ceremony lasts about two and a half hours. A mandatory regulation for all participants is that they must participate in this worship from beginning to end. After eating, the participants have to go straight from the worship place to their own houses in order to keep their luck for them themselves and their families.

+ Ceremony of cleaning the village (*phùng vân khoi kìm*): The local people usually select days of monkey and of chicken in January to hold this ceremony to ask the spirits for rich harvests, good livestock-breeding and good health. One day before performing this ceremony, the people stick some notice boards along the paths to their villages to inform outsiders about their ceremony and forbid them to come into their villages for 3 days after their ceremony. This notice board also refers to the punishment applied to an offender who has to pay for the repetition of this worship. The villagers pay a certain amount of money to buy offerings, including a pig and ducks.

This ritual ceremony is held around a great tree at the back of their village.[1] Normally, there are three altars reserved for the three main spirits: the earth spirit (*xíp tẩy chiêu miền*), the spirit of pests (*xíp chàm miên*), and the spirit of diseases (*xíp vươn miên*). In this ceremony, the shamans use buffalos' horns (*ngùng choong*) to call God and the earth spirit and require their help to expel the spirits of pests and of diseases from their village as soon as these spirits have received their offerings. In this worship, the villagers also celebrate an anniversary of premature and derelict death (*tu thìn chìu*). Therefore, they reserve another altar for the people who died prematurely and in poverty. In previous times, they held this ceremony during one day and one night. They slaughtered a buffalo to prepare a feast for all participants. Nowadays, this ceremony only lasts about three hours; however, the villagers hold this ceremony in a larger scale every three years. In this case, apart from the above-mentioned altars, there is a big altar reserved for the forest spirit (*khoi kìm*).

It is found that the people in Nậm Cang commune maintain and conduct more community worships than do the people in the two communes of Tả Phìn and Bản Khoang do. However, they are not less underdeveloped than those of

---

[1] Currently, many workers who are building a road in this area want to fell this tree because this makes it easier for them to continue to build the road. However, their intention meets the fierce opposition of the villagers. This tree is very holy to the villagers because they hold their community ritual ceremony around it with the aim of cleansing their village from all bad things and then of receiving good things for their village.

The phrase of "(at) the head of the village" refers to the area close to the mountain because in earlier times, the villagers normally built their houses and resided close to the mountain. The phrase of "(at) the back of the village" refers to the area nearby the road where their village has been enlarged in the following period.

two other communes are. On the contrary, their community is socially and economically well-organized. Therefore, they have a good solidarity with each other and their living standard is much higher than those of the two other communes are. In reality, they expect support from the spirits in combination with their hard work.

5.6.3.2 Household worships

Each year, in addition to the community worships, the Yao people organize different small-scale acts of worship and ritual ceremonies in their families. Many of these ceremonies concern cultivation.

- Worship of paddy soul

The local farmers conduct many different kinds of paddy soul worship. They are the *Chẩu siêu miên*, the *Pưa sùn chây* and the *Chẩu bèo uồn*. The ways of worshiping differ.

+ *Chẩu siêu miên*

One day before the day of the beginning of autumn, the farmers take some joss-papers to their fields. Afterwards, they stick these papers on bamboo sticks which are laid in the middle of the fields so that these joss-papers are as high as the tops of the rice. By this way, only the rice spirit (*siêu miên* or *bèo uồn*) recognizes them and then she will support their rice fields. They do not stick these sticks with joss-papers higher than the top of the rice because they are afraid that all spirits will recognize them, and then they will take their rice. While they are sticking them into their field, they say an incantation that "*pủng siều thảo siều cung siều mẩu lẻng siều chìn, siều cung siều mẩu lẻng siều khiểu, pu dẩu sùn mìu miển tẩy tàu*" (meaning "rice spirit, please, come here to receive the money and then support our rice fields"). They hope that after the rice spirit has received their money and supported their rice fields, their rice will grow well.

+ *Pưa sùn chây* (conducted by the Yao people in Bản Khoang and Nậm Cang communes)

Normally, the farmers organize this ceremony as soon as they plant out the rice seedlings and fix a good date for their ceremony. The fixed date normally coincides with the day of dragon in April which is considered the time when the dragon brings water to the rice fields. It is essential for a family to ask for the help to the worship of a shaman who has a zodiacal sign in a positive relationship to that of the host of this family. Then, he fixes the date for holding this ceremony. In the past, it was conducted in the rice fields. The farmers made a bamboo altar and set it in their field, and then put the ceremonial tribute on it. The offering included a cock, an egg, a bottle of wine, and some joss-papers. This ceremony was performed in the evening when fewer people are around in order to protect the rice spirit (*xíp bèo uồn*) from hearing some comments of non-participants; then she will support their rice. While the shaman is praying and reciting the spells, he pours water into the field to wish that the field always has enough water leading to the abundance of ears and fat paddies.

Many Yao people still carry out this worship in their fields. However, some households organize the ceremony in their house yard. The ceremonial tribute includes a pig (if possible), 1-2 chickens, eight square glutinous rice cakes, 5 cups of rice alcohol, and some joss-papers. The way of praying is similar to that of praying in the field. However, they do not pour water into the field. Alternatively, they pray to the rice spirit and their ancestors to protect their crops from harm by pests leading to a successful harvest.

If farmers have had poor rice harvests for three consecutive years, they hold this ritual ceremony in a larger scale than other annual ceremonies. They believe that they have a bad harvest because the rice spirit is absent from their rice fields and, therefore, she cannot support them. In this case, they have to use a buffalo's horn to call her back. According to them, if they only say incantations, their sounds do not reach as far as the rice spirit can hear them. As a result, this spirit will not go back and support their fields.

This ceremony is one of the most important forms of worship of the Yao people each year because the people believe that it relates closely to the effectiveness of their rice crop. After finishing this worship, the shaman receives a pig leg (if they offer the spirits a pig) or half a chicken. This allotment is perceived as thanks of all family members to him for his help. Some young married people do not organize this worship in their own families. Alternatively, they take part in a ceremony performed in the house of their parents. Within the following 7 days, they avoid giving anything to outsiders and selling anything to them because they are afraid of a poor harvest.

+ *Chẩu bèo uồn*

Previously, the Yao farmers blamed the infertility of their rice on the spirits. When their rice did not grow well, they asked for the help of a shaman to divine and determine the spirit responsible. The offering includes a chicken, a bottle of rice alcohol, and some joss-papers. The shaman offered ancestral spirits and rice harming spirits these tributes. He burned the joss-papers and asked the ancestors to give some of these joss-papers to the harming spirits in order to evict them from the rice fields and to keep their fields from damage by these spirits. Currently, most households maintain this ritual ceremony only when pests heavily destroy their rice fields.

- Worship of pests for rice fields (*siêu chàm*)

The worship of pests for the rice and for other crops is very common in the Yao communities. In the period of May or June, when farmers recognize that insects damaging rice leaves, they pray to the spirit of these insects. However, before holding an official ceremony, a shaman always has a small ritual to find out the harming spirits. Afterwards, he conducts the ritual ceremony to give the offering to the spirits, and then require them to stop their harm. The offering includes one chicken, a bottle of rice alcohol, a certain amount of rice and some joss-papers. While the shaman is scattering rice over the field, he prays to the spirit and says incantations that each rice grain will change into a bird and then will kill all pestilent insects in this field as well as protect the field from all of these insects. As soon as he finishes praying, he sticks some branches of fresh trees at the head of this field and along the paths to this field in order to inform strangers that it is forbidden for them for seven days after the worship to come into this field. Currently, most households have ceased worshiping the pest spirits, and instead, use pesticide to crush the pests. Nevertheless, in some households of the shamans and of aged people, this ceremony is still carried out, in addition to the use of the pesticide.

- Festival of new rice (or harvest festival) (*nhân xèng hảng*)

After harvesting the rice, the farmers fix a good date, normally the dragon day, for the ceremony of the new rice in order to thank their ancestors and the rice spirit for blessing and supporting them with a good harvest. In some years, all villagers have the festival of the new rice at the same time because they fix the same good day. This ritual ceremony is regularly conducted at home with a shaman presiding. The ceremonial tribute consists of a pig with a weight of 10-20 kg (if possible) or 1-2 chickens, a bowl of fish, four empty bowls, four empty cups, four pairs of chopsticks, and some joss-papers. In addition, depending on the households, the offering is additionally complemented by different kinds of wild and cultivated vegetables, worms from bamboo shoots and young bees. Because it is a worship of the new rice, it is necessary for the farmers to offer their ancestors and the rice spirits a bowl of the newly harvested rice. In the past, they offered these spirits a bowl of the mixture of rice and taro. Currently, the new rice displaces the rice mixed with the taro. If they have not yet husked the new rice, they offer the spirits a bowl of the previously harvested cooked rice with a new rice ear put on the top of the bowl of the cooked rice. Alternatively, they boil three to four new rice ears; then they cook the previously harvested rice with the water which has been already used for boiling the new rice ears. Afterwards, they put these ears on the top of the cooked rice. After finishing the worship, these rice ears are tucked into the house girder or into a small gap of the kitchen. The shaman is invited to have a feast with the host's family.

The people maintain particular principles not only in the worship, but also in eating the ceremonial offering. As soon as they have finished this worship, they first feed their domestic animals (such as dogs, cats, pigs and chickens) with some of the food offerings to encourage them to take their responsibilities well. It is expected that dogs will keep the house successfully; cats will successfully protect rice and maize storehouses from mice; pigs and chickens will replace the people to catch diseases (if existent). After feeding these animals, the old people eat some of the food offerings earlier than the others do because they are old and especially respected by the others. In addition, the best thing that the people should do is that all of them eat the ceremonial rice in only one meal. If they cannot do it, they should finish this food in three times (not two times). While eating a meal, they avoid picking up food and putting it into their bowls. Alternatively, they put it into their mouths because they are afraid that the pismires will attack the cooked rice which is used for the farmers' lunch in the fields. As a result, they would have no lunch; then they would get hungry and could not work in the field. The Yao people in Nậm Cang commune additionally avoid scooping vegetable soups out of their pot into their own bowls because they are afraid that their rice will be quickly damp and damaged by parasites. During 7 days following the worship, the local people avoid giving outsiders anything because they fear a poor harvest in the next crop.

In general, it is evident that the Red Yao maintain various beliefs and ritual ceremonies relating to cultivation because their cultivation depends on the weather, particularly on the rainfall. They traditionally believe that the spirits cause all risks and misfortunes in their lives and their production. To overcome these risks, they worship the harming spirits. However, the worships and the ritual ceremonies differ from commune to commune. It is a tendency that people who live in tourist resorts cannot observe as many traditional rules and taboos as can those people in other communes.

5.7Division of labour and gender roles

5.7.1 In cultivation

The division of labour in cultivation among the Red Yao is relatively clear and similar to that of many other ethnic groups in Vietnam studied by Martin Linde-Rahr. This division is based on a combination of traditional norms and comparative advantages.[1] In Red Yao communities men are responsible for the heavy work that requires their good health and physical well-being: slashing, burning, clearing, ploughing and raking the land; digging a hole to sow maize seeds; spraying chemical pesticide; building storehouses; producing and repairing tools for production. Women bear the responsibility for clearing the ground, sowing seeds, transplanting rice seedlings into the fields, putting maize seeds into fixed holes dug by their husbands, weeding, clearing pests, harvesting, selecting and keeping varieties for seed. Their keeping of varieties for seed has many similarities to that of many other women in Vietnam and in other countries.[2] This work contributes to preserving agro biodiversity as one of the main sources for household food security.[3] It also reflects their profound knowledge of preservation of seeds and plants, especially of rice. Additionally, they are very knowledgeable about food processing.

Besides the major labour force of the family, additional labour is also involved in production. The old healthy people and the children are responsible for the easy work. They share the work of land clearing, weeding, and picking up of pests with the major labourers of the family.

Nowadays, the Yao's household economy is primarily market-oriented. Some farmers need more labour-force to plant out their rice seedlings and weed their *thảo quả* plots due to their agricultural expansion and lack of labour. The hired people include the Yao and the Hmong from the same commune, Tay and Kinh workers from other areas. The value of their working days is paid in cash or in food, mainly in rice. In this case, the cooperation is seasonal, purposeful and regular.

---

[1] Martin Linde-Rahr (2002). *Household economics of agriculture and forestry in rural Vietnam.* Göteborg University, Sweden: 1.

[2] Christine Helliwell (1993). "Women in Asia - Anthropology and the Study of Women". In: Grant Evans (ed.) (1993), *Asia's Cultural Mosaic - An Anthropological Introduction.* Singapore: Prentice Hall: 261.

[3] Vandana Shiva (2001). "Globalization and Poverty". In: Veronika Bennholdt-Thomsen, Nicholas G. Faraclas and Claudia von Werlhof (eds.), *There is an Alternative: Subsistence and Worldwide Resistance to Corporate Globalization.* Victoria: Spinifex Press: 59.

5.7.2 In the performance of ritual ceremonies

In this case, it is essential to refer to the role of shamans and village magicians because they are considered able to contact another world and negotiate with supernatural forces, including the spirits.[1] Jess G. Pourret also mentions their important role in worship in China, Vietnam, Laos and Thailand.[2]

An indispensable thing that a shaman has to do is to pass the ceremony of "*cấp sắc*"- a social and religious ceremony which determines a very important turning-point in the life of a man. This is also a popular rule and ceremony applied to all Yao men. After passing this ceremony, they are recognized as adults. This is especially important for the shamans. They accumulate a lot of experience not only in the ritual ceremony and in the magic act, but also through the "*cấp sắc*", they can receive the support, the blessing and the supply of "the force of the other world," of various spirits to help them to complete their worships successfully.

The shaman plays a significant role in ritual ceremonies in the Yao communities. Like the head of the village and the village elders, the shaman's voice and sayings are very prestigious and influence some of the villagers' behaviour.

5.8 Social control of land, water resources and crop diversity

5.8.1 Land allocation and land tenure

During the colonial period, most farmland in Vietnam was owned either by French plantation owners or by large Vietnamese landlords: 52% of the land was owned by only 3% of the indigenous population and more than 60% of farmers across the country were landless in the mid-1940s.[3] The French colonists established their monopoly of natural resource management and of the uplands. They were considered the paramount land proprietors. If the grassroots population wanted to exploit soils for cultivation, they had to beg the land proprietors and give these proprietors aid. The various forms of aid were their heavy burden. The proprietors possessed some forest lands that were rich in precious trees, some rivers that were abundant with fish, and beehives. The proprietors even possessed some forests and land demesne in the name of the whole commune, and then gave them to the new inhabitants in order to make these people dependent on them as "dependent peasants".[4]

After the Geneva Accord of 1954, and particularly from 1960 to 1980, the government made many land reforms. Land began to be collectivized in the late 1950s, as Communist ideology gained in strength. As a result, according to Quy-Toan Do and Lakshmi Iyer (2003), 86% of all peasant households and 68% of total farmland, were brought into cooperatives by 1960, and 90% of all

---

[1] Tran Hong Hanh (2000). "The prevention and cure of disease among the Dao Quan Chet (in some hamlets in Da Bac district, Hoa Binh province, Vietnam)". Hanoi: *Vietnam Social Sciences*, No. 6: 52-74.

[2] Jess G. Pourret (2002). *The Yao - The Mien and Mun Yao in China, Vietnam, Laos and Thailand.* London: Thames & Hudson: 63.

[3] Quy-Toan Do and Lakshmi Iyer (2003). "Land Rights and Economic Development: Evidence from Vietnam". *World Bank working paper* 3/2003): 4.

[4] Institute of Ethnology (1978). *Ethnic minorities in Vietnam (in the Northern provinces)*. Hanoi: Social Science Publishing House: 48.

peasant households in the north of Vietnam in the mid-1960s. In this period, while individual rural households were privately allocated 5% of farmland, they derived 60 to 70% of their earnings from this small plot.[1] In general, this was the difficult period of the agriculture in Vietnam because agricultural output declined significantly. The agricultural co-operatives held back and restricted forces of the peasants in production because they were only interested in the working point; and, therefore, they ignored the quality of production. However, in this period, according to Thomas Sikor and Dao Minh Truong (2001), in some areas of the Northern Mountains, the cooperative movement contributed to the intensive farming. The arrangement of cooperatives for working promoted the cooperation in managing water sources and reclaiming wet fields as well as in changing the management of the wet fields in reality.[2]

The economic crisis in the early 1980s led to a major policy reform by the mid-1980s. In the period of 1981-1995, there were many economic reforms, mainly concerning agro-forestry. In 1986, Vietnam struck out in a new direction towards a market economy. Since the late 1980s, this direction has intensified the fact that the household was determined as the basic economic unit. In the case of an agricultural country, this is a very important factor for its development. Agriculture has been decollectivised. According to some researchers, the innovation progress of Vietnam has been a breakthrough made by land reforms, especially manifested themselves by the Land Law in 1988 (the so-called Resolution 10) and Land Law in 1993.[3] In general, Resolution 10 granted land rights to individual households, while the 1993 Land Law made these rights pledgeable and tradable.

Since 1988, the shift away from cooperatives to decollectivisation has resulted in a marked increase in agricultural production, mostly in rice.[4] The new agricultural policy launched in 1988 made the household the key unit of agricultural production. By Resolution 10, the government allocated the wet fields to the farmers from the fields of the former cooperative for their long-term use. According to Esta Ungar (1994), this resolution called for dismantling the collective system of agriculture which had been the cornerstone of economic policy for the previous thirty years. Through this, the property relations between the agricultural household and the state were changed, giving farmers control over allotted agricultural and forestland for varying periods. It further opened the way for peasants and urban households to receive some forms of title to

---

[1] Quy-Toan Do and Lakshmi Iyer (2003). *ibid*: 4.

[2] Thomas Sikor and Dao Minh Truong (2001). "Agricultural policy and land use changes in Black Thai villages of Northern Vietnam (1952-1997)". Hanoi: *Anthropology Review*, No. 6: 44.

[3] Esta Ungar (1994). Gender, Land and Household in Vietnam. *Asian Studies Review*, Vol. 17, No. 3: 61-72.
- Deanna Donovan, A. Terry Rambo, Jefferson Fox, Le Trong Cuc and Tran Duc Vien (1997). *Development Trends in Vietnam's Northern Mountain Region*. Honolulu: East-West Center, and Hanoi: National Political Publishing House.

[4] Esta Ungar (1994). Gender, Land and Household in Vietnam. *Asian Studies Review*, Vol. 17, No. 3: 61.

land-use rights and to habitation sites.[1] In the Sa Pa district, Red Yao people were allocated new wet-rice fields from the wet-rice fields of the agricultural cooperatives based on a principle of allocation that each household received an amount of good and bad land which were located distant from and nearby their residences. Therefore, their allocated new land was normally dispersed and quite small-scale. In comparison, their milpas were available and inherited from their parents and the ancestors. In this period, the Yao individual households had rights to use allocated lands and cultivate in these plots. However, they were not allowed to exchange or mortgage them.

In 1993, a new Land Law was issued to make up for the transaction of land in order to promote the farmers to invest and put their efforts for further economic efficiency. According to this law, the government allocates land to organizations, households and individuals for their long-term use. In principle, land is given to households or individuals as users for annual cropping for 20 years and for perennial cropping for 50 years without a fee. The users have rights to exchange, transfer, rent, inherit and mortgage their allocated land. In addition, they are allowed to receive the Land Use Certificates (LUCs). However, there are some limitations of agricultural land use for individual households as users as follows: 1) Agricultural land area for planting annual crops allocated to users in provinces in the Mekong Delta is less than 3 ha; and allocated to users in provinces and cities in the central regions is less than 2 ha. 2) Agricultural land area for planting perennial crops allocated to users in the delta is less than 10 ha; and allocated to users in the midland and in the highland is less than 30 ha. 3) The committees of the local governments or the local administration manage bare land, denuded hills, wasteland and coastal land depending on the land-fund of the respective region and the production capacity. 4) The village committees manage public land in the villages. However, this area must be less than 5-percent farmland of that village.[2]

As a result, the LUCs given to the individual households gradually increase in number. Data obtained from different sources show that there is a difference between the urban and rural households in the granting at LUCs. By the end of 1994, about 24% of households on average in a province had been issued LUCs. In 1997, 44% of land users received LUCs, but the LUCs given to urban households only reached 3%. At the end of 2000, LUCs in the rural areas made up 90% of the land users while the figure was only 16% in urban areas.[3] In the Red Yao communities in Sa Pa district, the 1993 Land Law had no remarkably strong impact on the land allocation to the local farmers because they still use and manage their land which is allocated by Resolution 10. A remarkable difference is that, by this law, they legally receive the LUCs for their long-term uses based on the quantity of their current land. About more than 70% of the Yao individual households received LUCs in 1997. This figure gradually

[1] Esta Ungar (1994). *ibid*: 67.

[2] *Land Law* 1993. Hanoi: National Political Publishing House.

[3] Quy-Toan Do and Lakshmi Iyer (2003). "Land Rights and Economic Development: Evidence from Vietnam". *World Bank working paper* 3/2003): 8.

increases in their communities. In Yao society, most heads of households are men. Therefore, they normally undersign to receive the LUCs for their households. As apposed to the case of some ethnic minorities in the Central Highland of Vietnam whose extensive lands were sold to some Kinh immigrants in the mid- and the end-1990s, the Yao farmers mainly keep their allocated land for their cultivation because of the importance of the land for their food production. A similar situation exists in many Hmong households. As evidence, some Red Yao people have rented some milpas and sloping soils of the Hmong yearly to cultivate because they have had a shortage of milpas. The payment for their rent is from 200,000 VND to 500,000 VND/year depending on the quantity of their rented land. However, they cannot persuade the Hmong people to transfer this amount of land to them for their further use. Despite of unremarkable impacts on the Yao households, the 1993 Land Law creates and ensures a more secure feeling of the farmers to continue to invest more capital, labour and intellectuals in production.

In reality, in addition to the land management by the individual households, at the community level, the community still plays a particular role in using and managing the land, mostly the forestland. According to the data obtained from the Bureau of Forest Management, up to June 2001, villages, kinships and social organizations are managing 2,348,295 ha of forest and forestland of the whole country. This area belongs to 1,203 communes or 146 districts of 24 provinces and cities directly under the central government. According to Tuan (2002: 9-10), in the Northeast and Northwest of Vietnam, this kind of forest includes 1,529,961 ha. Forests managed by the communities mostly comprise the poor secondary forests and the forests which are reforested from the farmers' previous milpas. However, according to Phuong (2002: 91), in some areas, some communities are managing medium forests (80-120m^3) and rich forests (over 120m^3).[1] In the Red Yao communities, forests managed by their communities normally include sacred and holy forests and secondary forests which are reforested from their previous milpas. In addition, there is a system of customary law referring to different regulations of the community in order to protect these forests for their ritual purpose and for livelihoods. However, the 1993 Land Law did not legalize the land-use right of these communities. Therefore, a new Land Law issued in 2003 is an additional step towards this end.

Compared with previous Land Laws, the most remarkable point of the 2003 Land Law is to refer to the land-use rights of communities and kinships to the land, particularly the agricultural and forestland (belonging to the agricultural land, in the new classification of land by the government).[2] Article 9 of this law

---

[1] Cited in Vuong Xuan Tinh (2004). "The role of community in the use of forest land among the Northern minority people (tradition, changes and implementation of the 2003 Land Law)". Hanoi: *Anthropology Review*, No. 4: 23-34.

[2] Land Law 2003, Article 13 and 71. In: *Land Law* 2003. Hanoi: The eleventh National Assembly of the Socialist Republic Vietnam, Session 4, 21/10/2003-21/11/2003; Law number 13/2003/QH11.

points out that the community includes the Vietnamese people who live in the same hamlet, in the same lowland village, in the same communal subdivisions, in the same highland village, and in similar residences sharing the same habits and customs or belonging to the same lineage. The government allocates land to all these people or legally recognizes their land-use rights.[1] The community as the legal land user also receives LUC which is kept by the legal representative of that community. The redistribution of forestland and forest sources in the local communities has not ensured the eradication of poverty, but it has indeed created opportunities for the people to improve their situation.

In the Yao communities, their customary laws still play an important role in the natural resource management, particularly in land and water use. In the past decade, many increasingly conflicts relating to land and water for cultivation have occurred in Yao communities because of their rapid population growth and shortage of these productive materials. To solve these conflicts, their customary laws have played an important role. However, it is found that if the farmers have an increasing shortage of productive materials, it is very hard to prevent them from conflicts concerning them. In this case, their customary law cannot solve these problems completely. Alternatively, the government's law has more advantages.

Apart from some above advantages of the Yao's customary laws, in some cases, their laws are quite complex where the land laws of the central government have been implemented at the local level. In some areas of Red Yao communities, there is a history of land disputes, particularly in the period of implementing "Resolution 10" and the 1993 Land Law. A reason for this is that many households asked for their ancestral land back. According to their traditional regulations, a farmer who first reclaimed virgin land has rights to use this land forever and nobody offends against this rule. However, this rule is opposite to the government's laws which regularly refer to the land reallocation to the people.

5.8.2 Management of water resources

Management of water resources is also indispensable because this is the second important productive source for the Red Yao. In combination with governmental campaigns for sedentarization and fixed cultivation, the government has supplied the households who fixed their residences with some constructions to help them with their living and production. These constructions include seven running water systems and three irrigation systems.[2] Additionally, the central government also issues different regulations for watershed protection in relation with its laws and documents of forest protection and development.

Apart from the government's laws, Yao customary laws still play an essential role in protecting their holy forest and water sources, particularly the watershed. Based on this law, the people are not allowed to make a mess, to graze cattle and to build their houses nearby the watershed. In previous times,

---

[1] Land Law 2003, Article 9, in: *Land Law* 2003. ibid: 6.

[2] Sa Pa District People's Committee (2005). *Report on results of effectuation of the Programme 135 in the period of 1999-2005 in Sa Pa district*: 4.

their customary law punished an offender. In some cases, depending on the seriousness of his offence, he had to pay a fine, such as paying for a community ceremony. However, nowadays, only a few young people do not observe their laws despite criticism from their co-villagers. This is a problem in some Yao villages when few young people have chances to go out of their communities to earn money from non-farming activities. However, all Yao still observe their rule of protection of the holy forest where they normally organize their community worships. In this case, this means that they can protect their watershed through protection of their holy forests.

In addition, Yao farmers also fix a set of community rules to protect and improve their traditional irrigation system for their long-term use. Based on these rules, those who profited from water sources take turns maintaining their irrigation system periodically by picking up leaves out of their drainage ditches and gutters and dredging their beds. In principle, they do this work whenever the water in their ditches is running slowly or is filled up with leaves. So far, they have strictly observed these rules. This contributes to strengthening the solidarity of the Yao communities and to their awareness of the importance of natural resource management for their cultivation.

5.8.3 Management of crop diversity

Compared with the land and water, control of crop management by the central government is less of a focus. However, this has some impacts on the increase of high agricultural productivity. In this case, the government has not obliged local farmers to plant the new varieties introduced by some programmes of agricultural extension at the local level. Alternatively, staffs of the local departments of agricultural extension mainly encourage the farmers to apply new varieties, mostly rice and maize, in their cultivation practices.

Particularly, in the case of planting opium poppies, the government required local farmers to give up this crop because of its disadvantage as a drug. Prior to 1994, many Yao and Hmong households grew opium poppies on their high sloping land. However, since 1994, they have stopped growing these plants for two reasons. Firstly, they have recognized its disadvantages as introduced by the local administrators. Secondly, they have completely performed the Decision 24-CP dated on 22/1/1979 and the Instruction 99-CT dated on 8/4/1991 of the government.[1] In addition, all local administrators and villagers helped the opium addicts undergo detoxification. As a result, from 1993 to 1994, 24 opium addicts in Nậm Cang commune (including 19 Hmong farmers and 5 Yao farmers) underwent detoxification. Since that time, all poppy fields have been replaced by fields with food crops (such as maize, potatoes, etc.) and of other plants. In

[1] Cabinet Council (1979). "Propaganda for the upland people against free planting of opium poppies and smoking of drugs. Decision No. 24-CP dated 22/1/1979". In: Parliament Council of Ethnic Groups. Session X (2000), *The policy and law of ethnic groups of the Vietnam Communist Party and the government*. Hanoi: National Culture Publishing House: 500-502.

- Chairman of the Council of Ministers (1991). "Propaganda for the people against planting of opium poppies". In: Parliament Council of Ethnic Groups. Session X (2000), *The policy and law of ethnic groups of the Vietnam Communist Party and the government*. Hanoi: National Culture Publishing House: 761-762.

this case, the obligation of the central government played a dominant role in halting planting of this crop in the mountain areas.

In addition to the diversity of cultivated crops introduced by the local administrators, the Yao people have their own ways of preserving and managing their different crops. This manifests itself in their experience and knowledge of cultivation. Among those, women farmers play a dominant role in managing their traditional crops.

5.9Summary

Cultivation plays a key role in producing food for Yao households. As local farmers are the mountain people, they mainly and traditionally choose shifting cultivation and wet-rice terraced farming as their adaptation to the high sloping and infertile land. In addition, they have gradually paid attention to combining these types of cultivation with the development of gardening and forestry. However, their horticulture is traditionally minor to other types of cultivation. In addition, their cultivation differs from commune to commune.

The Yao's systems of land classification and their selection of cultivated crops appropriate for and compatible with the land and the weather help them to recognize the land's potentials. Based on that, they work out a plan of evaluating the soil for their production. In addition to their local varieties, they increasingly plant some new varieties with higher productivity. This leads to diminished amounts of some local varieties, mainly rice. Although these local varieties have a lower productivity than the new ones, they need less water and fertilizer and adapt well to the high sloping land. In addition, they provide more delicious and flavourful meals for the people.

Under the pressures of population growth, increasing shortage of land and environmental degradation, some of the Yao's traditional ways of cultivation are no longer appropriate for the changing environment. Therefore, it is necessary to apply the strength of modern agricultural technology to their cultivation in combination with advantages of their traditional cultivation systems.

Knowledge and experience of cultivation are different from gender to gender, from profession to profession and from commune to commune. This manifests itself in the labour division in the Yao households and communities. Their division is based on the traditional norms and on the existence of comparative advantages. Normally, men are mainly responsible for the heavy works or for making decisions in their families. Women mainly take responsibility for domestic work, for planting and taking care of the crops, and particularly for selection of crops for seeds. It is found that women play a dominant role in producing and processing food for their households because they spend much more time for their cultivation and they are knowledgeable about keeping crops for seed. In their small-scale societies, male shamans play an indispensable role in performing ritual ceremonies and acts of worship which are key cultural and religious aspects of their communities.

Nowadays, the Yao's cultivation meets not only their domestic demands but also commercial requirements. Some of their valuable agricultural products, particularly *thảo quả* that is normally planted in the forest, have become main sources of cash income for their households. Therefore, their living standard is improving.

The Yao communities manage natural resources as their main productive source following both customary laws and the central government's laws. The government's laws are gradually dominant; however, in some cases, customary laws still play important role, particularly in protecting holy forest and watershed lands.

Chapter 6
LOCAL KNOWLEDGE OF ANIMAL HUSBANDRY OF THE RED YAO PEOPLE

6.1 Importance of animal husbandry in the Red Yao communities

As mentioned in the second and the third chapters of this study, animal husbandry accounted for about 21% of the total agricultural productivity per year in the period of 2000-2005 on average. This activity is essential to the economic development of the Red Yao communities. Although animal husbandry is less extensive than food cultivation, it supports many foodstuffs for the local people. In addition, some people also benefit from selling some of their animal products to small traders in Sa Pa town.

In the ethnic communities, the animal husbandry plays a supplementary role in the development of cultivation, supplying cultivation with a source of muck and dung. Therefore, it contributes to improving land fertility and increasing crop productivity. In this way, the people have more opportunities to achieve good harvests. In this case, successful harvests meet the demands for food of both the people and their domestic animal. Therefore, the animal husbandry and the cultivation in the Yao communities are closely related. This seems to support an assertion by Shiva (2001). According to Shiva, awareness that the people feed and nourish themselves by nourishing other beings is the basis of the sustainability.[1] Similarly, in farming societies, the raising of animals is considered an adjunct to peasant farming. This situation gradually became common in these societies.[2]

Like cultivation, the development of animal husbandry differs from commune to commune (Figure 6.1). In the three research communes, Bản Khoang commune ranks first in the development of animal husbandry; the second rank belongs to Nậm Cang commune, then to Tả Phìn commune. Bản Khoang commune is one of the remote areas of Sa Pa district. The people here reside in more dispersed places than those in other communes so that their domestic animals are rarely affected by epidemic diseases. Moreover, in case they fall sick, they are kept in check isolated from all healthy domestic animals. The diseased and ill animals are moved to the burnt land or kept them in a fixed house, a traditional method of disease prevention of the local people in this commune. A similar situation is the case with the people in Nậm Cang commune. Although the people in this commune live closely together in the valley, many of them raise and keep their domestic animals distant from their own dwellings. Therefore, they remarkably protect their animals from diseases.

---

[1] Vandana Shiva (1998). *Globalisation, Gandhi and Swadeshi: What is Economic Freedom? Whose Economic Freedom?*. New Dehli: RFSTE.
- Vandana Shiva (2001). "Globalization and Poverty". In: Veronika Bennholdt-Thomsen, Nicholas G. Faraclas and Claudia von Werlhof (eds.), *There is an Alternative: Subsistence and Worldwide Resistance to Corporate Globalization*. Victoria: Spinifex Press: 57-66.

[2] John Clammer (1993). "Fishermen, Forest-eaters, Peddlers, Peasants, and Pastoralists: Economic Anthropology". In: Grant Evans (1993), *Asia's Cultural Mosaic - An anthropological Introduction*. Singapore: Prentice Hall: 165.

Figure 6.1. Result of animal husbandry in the research communes in 2003
(Unit: head of animals)

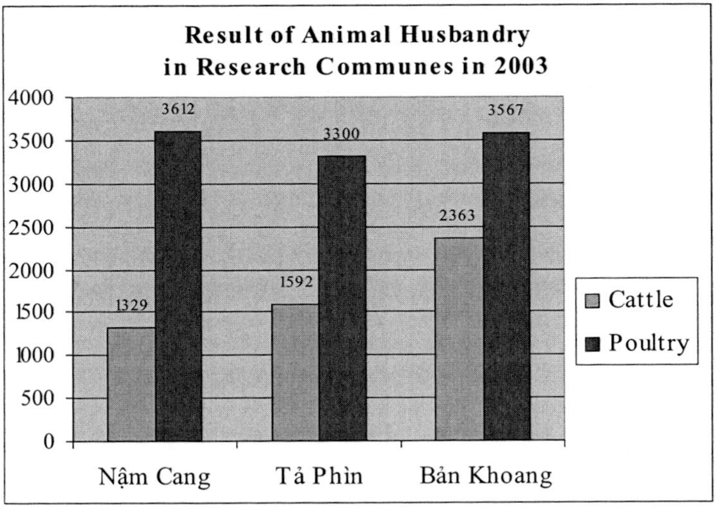

Source: 1) Sa Pa District People's Committee. 2003, *Statistical Yearbook*;
2) Data collected by the author in research communes.

Livestock breeding of the Red Yao people is more expansive than that of the Hmong and of other ethnic minorities in the same commune. For instance, the domestic animals raised by the Yao are regularly more numerous than those raised by the Hmong, except the hybrid cow. This is also acknowledged in many different yearly census and reports by the Department of Agriculture and Rural Development of Sa Pa district.

6.2Various domestic animals and aquatic products

The Yao ethnic group raise both cattle and poultry. Their cattle include water buffalo, cow, pig, goat, horse, dog and cat. Their poultry includes chickens, ducks and white-winged ducks. The raising of cattle is much more dominant than that of poultry. This situation exists not only in the Red Yao communities but also in many other ethnic groups of Vietnam.[1] Moreover, the development of their animals is different from one commune to another (Figure 6.2 and Figure 6.3). In addition, the farmers also practise fish-farming and raise other animals.

[1] Bui Quang Toan, Cao Duc Phat, and Vu Thi Ngoc Tran (1993). "The real situation and development orientation of farm household economy in mountainous regions". In: Institute of Agricultural Programming and Planning (1993), *Agriculture in the hilly and mountainous regions - Current situation and prospects*. Hanoi: Agricultural Publishing House: 48-58.
- Tran Binh (2001). *Customs of economic activities of some ethnic groups in the northwest Vietnam*. Hanoi: National Culture Publishing House.

Figure 6.2. Breeding of main cattle in the research communes in 2003
(Unit: head of cattle)

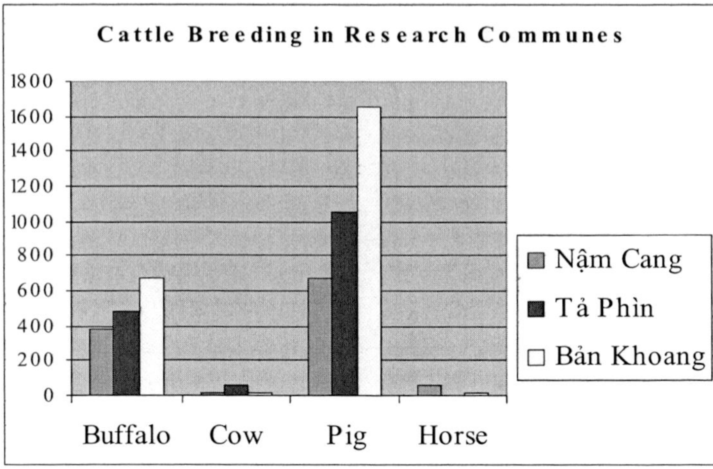

Source: Data collected by the author in research areas in 2003

Figure 6.3. Poultry breeding in the research communes in 2003
(Unit: head of poultry)

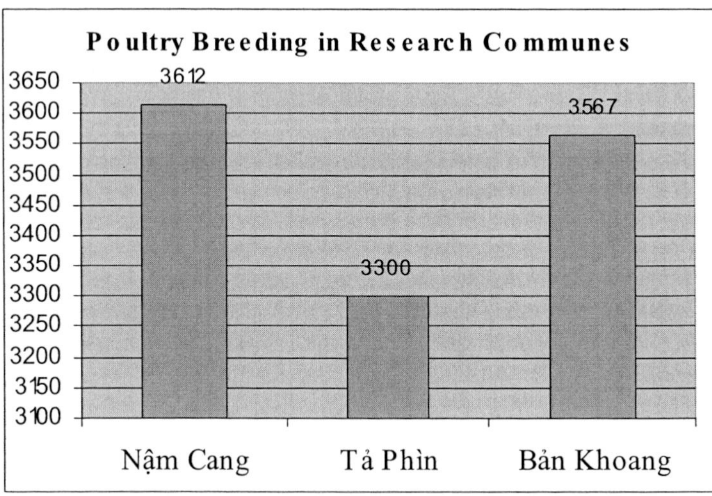

Source: Data collected by the author in research areas in 2003

6.2.1 Cattle

6.2.1.1 Water buffaloes

For the farmers, the water buffalo plays an important and indispensable role in their agriculture, particularly in preparing and in tilling the land as well as in transportation. The Kinh people who have long history of wet-rice cultivation consider this animal as a "master of the fortune." It has a great position in agriculture both in Vietnam and in many other countries in the world, especially in Southeast Asia.[1] Like other farmers who have traditionally long-standing wet-rice cultivation, the Yao people raise buffaloes to pull a plough, a harrow and timber.

Previously, the poor had no buffaloes for cultivation. Therefore, they had to hire or borrow a buffalo to practise their cultivation. Currently, many households raise this kind of animal. As an example, a farmer in group 2 of Sả Séng village (Tả Phìn commune) had 14 buffaloes and buffalo calves in 2000. In 2003, he had only nine buffaloes because three buffalo calves had died of an epidemic, and two others were sold because he needed money to buy fertilizers for his crops and furniture.

Normally, in the season of cultivation, the local farmers in Tả Phìn commune keep their buffaloes in a house or stanchion them by a tree near their dwelling to protect their crops from damage by these animals. After the harvest, the buffaloes practice free-range grazing in the forest, on the hills and the grassy areas near the fields. In comparison, the people in the two communes of Bản Khoang and Nậm Cang keep their buffaloes in the shelters in the high grazing plot isolated about 2-3 km from the dwelling land. Therefore, they can protect these animals from diseases. This way is similar to those of the Yao people in Hoa Binh province and to the Hmong in Son La province. However, these two ethnic groups keep their buffaloes in the valleys which are about 1-2 km or more distant from the farmers' dwelling land.[2] To prevent the buffaloes from losing the way home, the Yao farmers regularly tie a signed bamboo bell to their necks.

Food for the buffaloes is different according to the period. Five years ago, when the people did not have enough to eat, the food for their buffaloes was only grass. Nowadays, in addition to grass, when the buffaloes are ill or when it is too cold, the farmers cook a rice soup for them.

The buffaloes do not only satisfy the farmers' demands for the pulling force in their cultivation, but they also have become a valuable commodity. When farmers have more than three buffaloes, they normally sell some of their buffaloes with the price of 5.5 million to 6 million VND/ buffalo. They consider these animals as very valuable assets, testifying partly to the wealth of their families.

---

1 John Dixon, Aidan Gulliver, and David Gibbon (2001). *Farming Systems and Poverty: Improving Farmers' Livelihoods in a Changing World*. Principal Editor: Malcolm Hall, FAO, Rome, Italy. Also available at: www.fao.org/DOCREP/003/Y1860E/y1860e00.htm.

2 Hoang Xuan Ty (1998). "Buffaloes' valley of the Yao and the Hmong (in Hoa Binh and Son La provinces)". In: Center for Ecological and Forest Studies (1998), *Indigenous knowledge of agriculture and natural resource management among the people in the uplands*. Hanoi: Agricultural Publishing House: 167-168.

6.2.1.2 Pigs

The pig is a traditional domestic animal in many Asian countries. However, many central Asian peoples, from Chinese Turkestan right across to Persia do not raise pigs because they are Muslims.[1] In the case of Red Yao communities in Vietnam, similar to many other Southeast Asian countries, pig breeding is extremely typical of their households. Every household breeds pigs, minimally from two to three pigs and maximally more than ten pigs. In the past, the pattern of free-range in the burnt land and near the farmers' dwelling-land was very common. Currently, the half-domestic and half-free-range pattern has become gradually common in the Yao community. In addition to local pigs, the Red Yao people also raise imported pigs (or hybrid ones).

a. Local pigs

In the past, the people raised pigs free-range in the burnt land to protect them from a disease. Nowadays, when the crops are in season, they impound the pigs in a structure near the dwelling house to protect their crops from damage by these animals. During fallow periods, the pigs free-range find food for them themselves. However, at that time, this is very harmful for some vegetables because they are growing and tend to be in key stages of development. Therefore, the free ranging of domestic animals can damage or eat the vegetables in the home garden. In the house located in a relatively high sloping place, pigs are normally kept in their shelters to protect them from injury or death by falling into the depth. Generally, they breed naturally. The local people sometimes keep a good pig for a breed or castrate it.

Compared with other domestic animals, pigs are carefully cared for. They are fed twice a day. The main food for these animals includes maize, cassava and some wild plants. Since 2000, rice has also been one of their foods because the farmers have achieved some good harvests by combining the hybrid rice planting with the increased use of fertilizers. Wild plants used for a pig food include *xì cầu thông*, *lay chần*, *tu mìa phiên*, *hùng tỉa dàm*, *tùng mìa bung*, *gục xàng nòm*, and *ngùng giỏ nòm*, etc. Additionally, some cultivated vegetables in the home garden are also used as supplemental food for them. The people cut these vegetables into small pieces and then mix them with the offal rice and maize. Afterwards, the food for pigs is ready.

In the recent years, the local pigs of the Red Yao have become a favourite food supplied to many restaurants and hotels in Sa Pa town. A roasted suckling pig is a favourite meal. Thus, some households pay much attention to the breeding of their local pigs to supply suckling pigs for the local market in the town. In addition, this market helps the Yao people to maintain and develop their indigenous variety of pigs.

b. Imported and hybrid pigs

In the past, the inhabitants raised only local pigs. However, starting in 1997, the district and communal agricultural extension departments have chosen

---

[1] John Clammer (1993). "Fishermen, Forest-eaters, Peddlers, Peasants, and Pastoralists: Economic Anthropology". In: Grant Evans (1993), *Asia's Cultural Mosaic - An anthropological Introduction*. Singapore: Prentice Hall: 165-166.

some households for experimental breeding of hybrid pigs. In the first half of 1997, the new pigs were introduced to Tả Phìn commune. At that time, each experimental unit received three breeding pigs and some money to build a house for them. Another programme of breeding of hybrid pigs was conducted in the same commune through March 2003. Like the first time, some households were chosen for this experiment. The communal department of agricultural expansion provided each household chosen with some 2 million VND to build a house for the experimental pigs and 300,000 VND to buy two breeding pigs weighting about 10 kg per pig. The farmers themselves supplied the food for these pigs. According to an agreement between the department of communal agricultural extension and the experimental households, the households had to pay for their breeding pigs if they survived.

However, until now, this department has received no payment from the farmers due to their failure in the new pig breeding. Most breeding pigs died. In the first experiment in 1997, among 15 experiment households, only one farmer succeeded in raising this new race of pig. However, he did not have to pay for his breeding pigs adopted by the local agricultural officer to encourage him in developing his flock of new pigs.

In principle, the feeding and breeding system of the hybrid pigs in the Yao community is realized similarly to the cases in the lowland and in the delta. This means that the people keep the pigs in their sties and feed them three times a day. However, in fact, they defer to the guidelines of the local agricultural officers during about the first month or the first two months as soon as they have received the new breeding pigs. Afterwards, most experimental households apply their traditional ways of raising animals to the breeding of hybrid pigs because they do not have enough money to buy food for them any more. Thus, although the growth of the new pig is more rapid than of the local ones, this growth is still much slower than it should be according to the previous plan of the experiment. These new pigs grow well, but it is very difficult for breeders to sell them to the regional market. That is why the people normally consume the new pigs during traditional and New Year festivals, in the ritual ceremonies and use them as the meals to feast the people who help them to build or repair their own houses.

6.2.1.3 Ox/cows, horses and goats

The Yao also raise cows, horses and goats. Cows have been bred in the Yao community since 1995, when the communal agricultural officers supplied some households in the two villages of Tả Chải and Suối Thầu (Tả Phìn commune) with some new breeding cows in order to introduce the cross-bred cow to the villagers. The way of breeding cows is similar to that of raising buffaloes. The cow is regularly free-ranging grazing on grass and only kept in its house at night or tied to a tree nearby the dwelling house. Currently, many households want to breed this race because of their commercial demand. Raising a cow is much more financially beneficial than raising a buffalo.

In the past, the horse was an important means of transport for the local people. Therefore, many households raised a horse and used its force to transport timber, goods, and items (such as rice, salt, and others) from the market to their homes. Nowadays, thanks to better roads, the people can ride on their motorbikes to the hall of the People's Communal Committee and even to many villages in some places. As a result, horses have gradually decreased in number. Nowadays, only a few households raise these animals. The mode of breeding horses is based on the natural environment. The horse is free-range in the forest or on the hill, grazing the grass. This animal rarely dies of epidemic diseases. In winter, in the high and remote areas, the weather makes it catch cold; thus, it is kept in its shelter to protect it from wind and cold.

Like the horse, the goat is also a familiar domestic animal of local inhabitants. They are the local race, and the system of breeding is similar to that of horses.

6.2.1.4 Dogs and cats

These are the farmers' pets. As discussed above in the part of the history of the Yao ethnic group, a dog is considered a spiritual and holy animal and most households raise them. The people raise them to keep their house and to catch some small wild animals, such as wild mice, birds, and weasels, etc. They are a local race that is clever and relatively healthy due to their adaptation to the environment, and they are good hunters. Thanks to their special characteristics, many Kinh people and other ethnic groups want to raise the Yao's dogs. This motivates the Yao people to raise them to keep their good breed. Farmers normally sell the puppies to buyers and keep the mothers to preserve the good breeding characteristics and continue to propagate them.

Most farmers raise cats to catch mice. They are pets and friends of the children. It is easy for local people to raise them. They live in the same house with the people. They eat the people's leftovers. They nuzzle in the farmers' blanket or nestle themselves in the ashes close by the cooking fire. These cats protect the farmers' agricultural products which are kept and stored in the smoking-shelf and in the storehouse from damage by mice.

The surplus food of the Yao people is also the main food for dogs and cats.[1] However, when these animals are ill, pregnant, or post-delivery, they are treated carefully. Then a rice soup, sometimes with the pig fat, is prepared for them. Thus, according to the Yao people, the breeding of these pets is easiest.

6.2.2 Poultry

Chickens and ducks have been raised for a long time. In addition, some new animals have been introduced into the Yao community as an experiment. These flocks of the poultry tend to be expanded to meet the demands of the local people and of the tourist market.

6.2.2.1 Chickens

Chickens are familiar animals of the Red Yao. Most households raise these animals in different number. They mostly breed the local race. Their own chickens

---

[1] This is also one of food sources for the dogs raised by the Bushmen in the Dobe area in Australia. Some of their surplus food probably went to the dogs, who ate what they left over (Richard Lee (1969). "Kung Bushman Subsistence: An Input-Output Analysis". In: A. Vayda (ed.), *Environment and Cultural Behaviour*. Garden City. New York: Natural History Press: 73).

have a small shape, but they are firm, sweet and flavourful. Thus, in the recent years, they are a favourite meal in many hotels and restaurants in Sa Pa town.

The Yao breeder raises chickens free-range in the burnt land to protect them from epidemic diseases and feeds them by salvaging rice and maize which have been leftover in the fields. However, due to increasing theft, many households breed their chickens near their dwellings.

In addition to local chickens, some households have experimentally raised the race of *Tam hoàng* chicken (or the hybrid chicken) since 1997. Many of them are unsuccessful in breeding this new race because they have no experience in raising it and in protecting it from a disease. On the contrary, some experimenting households succeeded in this work because they communicated with the Kinh people and learn a new method of breeding hybrid chicken from them. They even interbreed their local chickens with *Tam hoàng* to generate a new type of chicken. However, they prefer their local race to the others because they easily raise these ones thanks to their available experience, and it is harder for these chickens to become diseased due to their adaptation to the environment. Additionally, it is rare that these chickens break their own eggs while incubating because their weight is lighter and their meat is much more flavourful than that of the *Tam hoàng* chickens. Therefore, the farmers easily sell their local eggs to the restaurants and hotels in the town. However, in conversations and interviews with some other farmers who succeed in raising *Tam hoàng*, they said that they had only a few difficulties in breeding *Tam hoàng* and that this kind of chicken grows more rapidly than the local chickens A current challenge for them is that it is difficult to sell the new chickens due to the lack of a market for them.

They raise *Tam hoàng* to meet their eating demands or to sell them to other Yao villagers and to the Hmong people in the same commune. In addition, they also invest more money and labour in breeding the local chicken, and then sell them to the restaurants and hotels in Sa Pa town. Normally, they do not sell the eggs that the chickens produce because they want to increase their flock of chickens by encouraging hens to incubate their own eggs. Eggs bought in the market are not used for breeding purpose, but as a meal because, according to the local people, they are not so good and it is easy for them to be unsound and diseased if derived from ill hens.

Chicken breeding is mainly based on traditional methods of animal husbandry. Their food consists of ground maize and cassava. Additionally, some food plants for pigs are also food for chickens. In the past, the mode of chicken breeding was free-range in the burnt land to protect them from epidemic diseases and to use the available food in nature and from the harvest. Nowadays, many households raise them in a house near to their dwelling house to protect them from a theft and to breed them easily. In addition, the market demand is also a motivation for the farmers to pay more attention to animal raising, particularly to the breeding of their local race.

6.2.2.2 *Ducks*

Like the chicken, local ducks have been a free-range breed for generation. They find their food in the river, in the stream nearby the dwellings or in the fields as soon as farmers have harvested their crops. Thus, they do not have as much weight as the others raised in the lowlands. However, they are very firm and flavourful. In addition to the free-range breeding, many households with a good harvest feed the ducks with the same food as that of the chickens. Therefore, like other domestic animals, their ducks grow much more rapidly and gain more weight than in the past. Many households build a house for them to protect them from cold and theft.

6.2.2.3 *White-winged ducks*

The Yao people traditionally have no white-winged duck. In the recent years, the staffs of the department of communal agricultural extension have supplied farmers with 15 white-winged ducks per household as an experiment. They intend to develop this race in the whole Yao community if their experiment succeeds. Unfortunately, most experimental flocks of white-winged ducks died. In Tả Phìn commune, the farmers achieved a bad result in breeding this race; most of the ducks died. Two households succeeded in raising them and then intended to develop flocks of white-winged ducks due to their more remarkable benefits over the breeding of the local ducks. In contrast to Tả Phìn commune, the farmers in Bản Khoang commune relatively succeed in raising this race. In spite of some dead white-winged ducks, most birds are very healthy and grow rapidly. According to the local people, the reason for their success is that the weather in Bản Khoang commune is probably more favourable for this race than in Tả Phìn commune, and the terrain here is relatively high and set aside so that it is hard for epidemic diseases to infect this area.

Many farmers who succeed in the experimental phase want to develop this race because of the high benefit of raising it. However, their great challenge is lack of experience and capital. They need more information about how to raise this variety and the capital for it.

6.2.3 Fish-farming

The fish-farming of the Red Yao has been considered an additional income. This activity has only met their domestic demands. This is also a common phenomenon in other northern regions of Vietnam.[1]

The Yao people raise both local fish and new ones that they buy in the market from the Kinh. The farmers in Tả Phìn commune normally buy the fish from the same ethnic group in Bản Khoang commune. Many households have a long-term tradition of raising fishes in the wet-rice fields. Therefore, the season of raising fish goes together with the wet-rice crops and the fish are normally small. Over the past 10 years, some households in different villages have raised them in small ponds they have dug with an area of 25 m^2 to 150 m^2 near the

[1] Bui Quang Toan, Cao Duc Phat, and Vu Thi Ngoc Tran (1993). "The real situation and development orientation of farm household economy in mountainous regions". In: Institute of Agricultural Programming and Planning (1993), *Agriculture in the hilly and mountainous regions - Current situation and prospects*. Hanoi: Agricultural Publishing House: 53.

dwelling-house or in the area of the garden. Particularly, some households in Nậm Cang commune have several small fish and shellfish ponds with an area of 3-200 m^2. Their fishes include crucian carps, carps and cirrhina molitorella.

Usually, when the fish are as big as two fingers, they are gradually harvested. Nowadays, by raising fish in the ponds and feeding them with ground offal rice, they are bigger than before, even with a weight of 0.3-0.4 kg. The local farmers regularly keep the biggest fishes for breeding purposes.

6.2.4 Other animals

Because inhabitants live near the forest and have a long tradition of exploiting natural resources, they domesticate and breed some wild animals they catch themselves. These animals include various kinds of birds, which are kept for ornamental purposes. In recent years, they are solely for tourists due to increasing tourist demand.

The Yao farmers domesticate wild honeybees and keep them in the hive in their home garden or adjoining their dwelling house. In the past, the wild honeybees grew in the forest. The people collected their honey when they went to the forest and found them. Now, they spend much more time in cultivating and in their other interests. Therefore, they domesticate and keep the wild bees in their dwelling-land and in the garden. This makes it easier to collect the honey. Their way of domesticating the wild bee is traditional. They keep the queen-bee in a fixed hive. Afterwards, workers will fly to the new hive to see their queen. Every day, the workers go out of their hive to suck the nectar out of various flowers and then go back to their hive. They increasingly grow in number in their new hive. The honey that the farmers own depends on their flock of honeybees and the florescence of the flowers. Normally, the honey is collected to meet the domestic demand of the farmers' households. Currently, many farmers also sell the honey to tourists and visitors.

In short, compared to the past, the domestic animals, especially pigs and chickens, grow more rapidly due to the abundance of food. For example, in the past, farmers had to spend one year to breed a local pig of 8 kg in weight to a weight of 40 kg. Now, they achieve the same result in eight months. Similarly, a breeder spent four months to raise a newborn chick to reach a weight of 1 kg. Now, the breeding time is shortened to just three months. In the case of buffaloes and horses, their growing time has not remarkably changed because their main food is the grass. In the past, in the period of October-February, they were hungry due to lack of grass and fodder. Currently, in this period, many people feed them with maize and rice soup.

6.3Various modes of breeding

Their mode of animal breeding is half-domestic and half-free-range. Before 1990, the mode of the free-range was most significant and dominant. In that period, they kept their animals, except the ducks, in the burnt land and they fed these animals every two or three days. In reality, in the past, their chickens mainly grew up wild and lived off the farmyard refuse. The farmers practised their cultivation there in combination with the feeding of the animals. However, their animals still grew up more rapidly than now because they found food for themselves in the forest and around the fields. This situation is similar to the case of breeding some domestic animals practised by some Indian farmers.[1]

Particularly, in the case of the ducks, the Yao farmers always breed these animals in their dwelling-land because their ducks easily search for their food along the stream and in the ponds. In addition, in this way, the people can protect their ducks from getting lost on the way back home. Particularly, after harvesting, they breed their ducks in the rice-terraced fields. In this period, the ducks grow rapidly up by eating the remaining rice in these fields. Therefore, this is also the season that the ducks lay their eggs. Moreover, in this season, the farmers normally build a small coop in the fields for their ducks to keep their eggs. Up to now, they still maintain this way of breeding the ducks. In comparison, the farmers have tended to keep and to breed their other animals near their dwelling-land resulting from a movement of the new raising method by the local administrators since 1990. A short time after this change, many farmers had to return to their traditional modes of breeding because many of their animals died of diseases and grew slowly because the new breeding methods. However, up to now, the two half-domestic and half-free-range modes are always combined with each other in the Red Yao communities to achieve a better result and to protect their animals from epidemic diseases.

In the case of some cattle raised on grass, the people in every village reserve some grazing areas (*ngùng seng* in Yao language) for them. In principle, these areas depend on the total area of each village and there are at least two different grass plots. In the total research areas, the people in Nậm Cang commune reserve the largest grass plots for their cattle. The grass plots for the cattle in Bản Khoang commune rank second in the area and last are the grass plots for the cattle of the people in Tả Phìn commune. Normally, some households share grass plots of about 0.5-1 ha in area. For the larger areas, for example, an area of 2-3 ha is shared by about 30-40 households for their animals. In the case of buffalo breeding, the farmers themselves take turns caring for their animals and for the grass plots. In the case of goats, they only select grass plots with small rock caves for these animals because the goats can seek shelter from the wind and the rain in the caves.

When the grass is eroded, the Yao people move their animal herds to another grass plot, because their herds cannot find food in one location all year around. However, their way of moving the animal herds is different from those of other pastoralists in the world. Because the Yao people are not pastoralists but farmers, they do not move their homes from one grazing area to another, but only move their animal herds according to the season. This situation differs from that of many pastoralists in the world, like the Qashgai of Iran and the Evenks of Siberia, who practice transhumance which is a pastoral way of life in which people move with their herds from one grazing area to another according to the seasons.[2]

[1] Maria Mies (1986). *Indian women in subsistence and agricultural labour*. Women, Work and Development 12. Geneva: International Labour Office: 77-78.

[2] David Hicks and Margaret Anderson Gwynne (1996). *Cultural Anthropology*. Second edition. New York: HarperCollins College Publishers: 135.

In many cases, farmers keep some of their cattle, mainly the buffaloes, the horses and the goats in the area of their grass plots. However, in this case, they have to fence these plots with small trees, bamboo trees or with stone. In addition, the people never fence the grass plots for their goats with the stone, but with other materials, as the goats can easily go over stone fences.

Apart from their traditional protection of domestic animals from diseases as mentioned about, since May 2003, the new method of animal raising and protection has been introduced into some villages. Pigs and chickens are injected with particular medicines made by the village veterinarians to prevent them from some common diseases. As a result, they die of diseases more rarely than before. However, the local people irregularly maintain these injections for some animals because of the lack of money to buy medicines. Therefore, in some cases, they only give their animals medicine when these animals catch a disease. As a result, the injection is not very effective.

6.4Different utilizations of domestic animal products

As mentioned above, in the past, the Red Yao people used all domestic animals for their domestic purposes. This utilization of the Yao people is similar to those of other ethnic minorities in Vietnam.[1] The Yao people used the buffaloes and the horses for transport and pulling forces in cultivation. Similarly, this function of these animals manifests itself in the ploughing of the fields and in the threshing of grain by the farmers in the Middle East, China, Africa, South America, India and some parts of Europe. Particularly, they use wooden or metal plows and threshers pulled by horses, donkeys, or water buffaloes.[2]

The other animals, except dogs, provide different kinds of meat for the yearly traditional ritual ceremonies, and nutritious meals for unhealthy persons. Traditionally, the Yao people do not eat horses and dogs, although they are aware that these animals are edible and used as a source of food by other ethnic groups. These avoidances derive from their beliefs and values which they choose to exploit the resources. In other words, their dietary habits are often closely associated with religious beliefs. Apart from transportation purpose, buffaloes are used by the Red Yao farmers as a source of meat for the communal and large feasts.

However, the people have not used buffalo for ritual offerings. This situation originated from a legend handed down from one generation to another. Up to now, many village shamans and many other villagers remember a legend that a buffalo was used as a sacrifice for the funeral of an old woman. A very short time afterwards, one of her grandsons died. The villagers believed that this

[1] Institute of Ethnology (1978). *Ethnic minorities in Vietnam (in the Northern provinces).* Hanoi: Social Science Publishing House.
- Pham Quang Hoan and Hung Dinh Quy (eds.) (1999). *Traditional culture among the Yao in Ha Giang province.* Hanoi: National Culture Publishing House.
- Tran Binh (2001). *Customs of economic activities of some ethnic groups in the Northwest of Vietnam).* Hanoi: National Culture Publishing House.
- Vuong Xuan Tinh (2001). "Food security of the R'mam". Hanoi: *Ethnology Review*, No. 5: 1.

[2] David Hicks and Margaret Anderson Gwynne (1996). *Cultural Anthropology.* Second edition. New York: HarperCollins College Publishers: 137.

woman had previously received the sacrificed buffalo, but was old too to care for the animal. Therefore, she asked her grandson to do this work. Since then, the Yao people have no longer sacrificed a buffalo to a dead person.

Apart from these holy reasons, in the case of horses, the farmers do not eat this animal because they are afraid of catching a disease from eating it. In their villages, they raise horses only for transportation, and keep it until it dies. In this case, they believe that this horse gets a disease. Thus, it dies of this disease, so that the people do not dare eat this dead horse.

Originating from the association with religious beliefs, food taboos also exist in other groups of people in the world. As an example, most Rastafarians are vegetarians, although they may eat small fish. However, they do not eat pork and beef because these kinds of meat are considered pollutants.[1] Similarly, most Hindus in South Asia do not eat beef because the cow has an important place in their religion. According to Heston (1971: 192), the cow is "worshiped as a symbol of warmth and moisture, as earth mother, and as a producer of milk and indirectly clarified butter, so essential in sacrificed."[2]

In the Red Yao communities in Vietnam, the local people do not eat dogs because, as mentioned in the second chapter of this study, this animal is considered the progenitor of the Yao ethnic group and worshiped. The dog is a sacred animal as a totemic emblem in the Yao communities.[3] Few young Red Yao people also have as same action and behaviour as those of the Walbiri, although they do not consider that they will be stupid not to eat dog meat as their totem, but will regret a very delicious dish. However, if they want to eat a dog dish, they have to have it outside their villages. On the contrary, they are afraid that their ancestral spirit will punish them. In this case, they will probably no longer receive support from their ancestors, or will catch a serious disease.

Some animals are also used for other purposes. It is important that the ducks and the chickens support the people not only as a source of meat but also by providing eggs for the farmers' food and for breeders. Apart from this, domestic animals also supply the farmers with different kinds of dung for cultivation. The Yao people normally fertilize their fields, mainly fields of their staple food crops, with dung from their animals. This also exists in many other farming communities based on non-mechanized agriculture.[4] In the case of fish-farming, products of this Yao's activity only meet the farmers' demand because of their low quantity and

---

[1] Michael C. Howard (1996). *Contemporary Cultural Anthropology*. Fifth edition. New York: HarperCollins College Publishers: 310.

[2] Heston (1971); Cited in Michael C. Howard (1996). *ibid*: 310.

[3] This food taboo of the Red Yao is similar to the case of Australian Aborigines. The Aborigines refrain from eating their totems or harming them (Michael C. Howard. 1996). However, there is a difference in eating taboos among these groups of people depending on the area. According to Meggitt (1962: 208), the Arapda of central Australia strictly avoid eating their conception totems whereas the nearby Warramunga will eat their conception totems if someone else kills these totems. Similar to the Warramunga, the neighbouring Walbiri do not place restrictions on eating their conception totems because of their assertion that "men would be stupid not to eat such foods when available." (Meggitt 1962, cited in Michael C. Howard (1996). *ibid*: 312).

[4] David Hicks and Margaret Anderson Gwynne (1996). *Cultural Anthropology*. Second edition. New York: HarperCollins College Publishers: 137-138.

their small scale. The small-scale fish-farming of the Yao people is similar to those of some other uplanders in the north of Vietnam.[1]

During the past 10 years, with tourism as one of the main sectors of the regional economy, the farmers' animal husbandry has expanded to meet both their domestic demands and their requirements for additional cash income. The tourists' enjoyment of some local agricultural products, including local domestic animals, creates a great opportunity for the farmers and encourages them to expand their animal husbandry and preserve their local flavourful and valuable varieties.

The Yao sell their domestic animals (such as pigs, chickens, ducks, dogs, etc.) to their neighbours and to the Kinh people. Regularly, they sell them after their traditional New Year, in summer (or in the tourist season) and at Christmas. The money earned is used to buy different new seeds, fertilizers, gasoline, salt, clothes, cloth and other essential items. However, in this case, they still give their priority to the purchase of some important materials for their cultivation. In this way, their cultivation had gradually developed. In general, the animal husbandry of the Red Yao farmers is still a self-sufficient economic activity, but it also has become one of the primarily market-oriented economic activities in some farm households in this region.

6.5Various beliefs and ritual ceremonies regarding animal husbandry

6.5.1 Selection of days for building sties and coops

As discussed in previous chapters, the Yao people are Taoists. They believe in the existence of supernatural forces and different kinds of spirits. They also perceive that everything has its own soul, and their animals are no exception. The Yao notion of the "*vẩn*" (soul) seems to derive from the popular religion of the Chinese people. Their notion of soul is similar to the "*hun*" of the Chinese people and to the "*khwan*" of the Thai people in Vietnam and Thailand. Therefore, similar to some cultivated crops, in the case of animal husbandry, there is a spirit who manages and supports the souls of domestic animals. In addition, in some important steps of the livestock breeding, they will receive much support from the animal spirits and achieve an auspicious result if they select a right day for these steps and vice versa. The following tables show different results of Yao's selections of good days for building pigsties and chicken coops (Table 6.1 and Table 6.2).

[1] Bui Quang Toan, Cao Duc Phat, and Vu Thi Ngoc Tran (1993). "The real situation and development orientation of farm household economy in mountainous regions". In: Institute of Agricultural Programming and Planning (1993), *Agriculture in the hilly and mountainous regions - Current situation and prospects*. Hanoi: Agricultural Publishing House: 53.

- Tran Binh (2001). *Customs of economic activities of some ethnic groups in the Northwest of Vietnam*. Hanoi: National Culture Publishing House.

Table 6.1. Selection of a good day for building a pigsty

Month	Good day	Note
January	Days of dragon and dog	
February	Day of dragon	
March	Day of cat	
April	Day of monkey	
May	Day of chicken	
June	Day of snake	
July	No good day	
August	Day of pig	Not selected because it coincides with the pig
September	Day of cat	
October	Day of tiger	
November	Day of tiger	
December	Day of tiger	

Table 6.2. Selection of a good day for building a chicken coop

Month	Good day	Direction of coop	Result
January	Days of monkey and goat	In the western direction	80 pairs of chickens
February	Days of monkey and horse	In the eastern direction	80 pairs of chickens
March & May	Days of cat and chicken[1]	In the western direction	80 pairs of chickens
April	Day of goat	In the southern direction	80 pairs of chickens
June	Day of goat	In the western direction	80 pairs of chickens
July,Sept.,Nov.	Monkey, goat and chicken days	In the western direction	190 pairs of chickens
Aug.,Oct.,Dec.	Days of cat, goat and monkey	In the western direction	120 pairs of chickens

Based on these tables, it is clear to distinguish good days in months and dates, with the case of pigs and chickens. However, in some cases, good days overlap with each other. In addition, when these good days and dates coincide with the name of each animal corresponding with the table, the farmers will not fix these dates for building houses for these animals. Particularly, table 5.2 shows that farmers also focus on different directions for the coop because this relates to the result of their chicken breeding.

[1] Like the case of the pig, the farmers do not select the day of chicken to do very work relating to chickens, such as building chicken coops, buying and selling them because this coincides with the chicken.

When we look at the Chinese religion, it is important to refer to one of the main structures of this religion, which is a system of geomancy or so-called *feng-shui* practised by the Chinese and some Chinese minorities. This is a system of divination for the location of homes and graves, residences of the living and those of the dead. It is based on a complicated system of correspondences between time and space, the seasons and years, animal categories, colours and directions. Durkheim and Mauss (1970) examined this system as an example of "primitive classification."[1] It is reasonable to link the system of geomancy by the Red Yao people in Vietnam with the *feng-shui* system by the Chinese and Chinese minority people for two reasons.

Firstly, the Red Yao people originate from China, which is referred to in their system of myths. Secondly, the shaman's fortune-writings are written in Chinese and the Yao shaman prays and recites incantations in local Chinese as well. Thus, it seems that the Red Yao's system of geomancy originates from the Chinese *feng-shui* system. In addition, it is impossible to separate the Yao's beliefs in the system of geomancy from their beliefs in supernatural forces.

6.5.2 Selection of days for keeping the breeding animals in their new houses

Related to the above beliefs, the Yao people are careful to keep their animals in the new houses. For example, the pig is a valuable and typical animal in the Yao communities. Thus, it is important to select and fix the right days for many main steps in raising this animal, including days to keep it in its new sty. When the farmer selects good days for this work, their pigs will survive and be fat. If not, they will be thin or even die (Table 6.3).

Table 6.3. Selected days relating to results of the pig breeding

<table>
<tr><th>Month</th><th>Survival</th><th>Death</th><th>Fat</th><th>Thin</th></tr>
<tr><td>January</td><td>Day of cat</td><td>Day of chicken</td><td rowspan="3">Days of monkey, mouse and dragon</td><td rowspan="3">Days of snake, chicken and buffalo</td></tr>
<tr><td>February</td><td>Day of horse</td><td>Day of mouse</td></tr>
<tr><td>March</td><td>Day of monkey</td><td>Day of tiger</td></tr>
<tr><td>April</td><td>Day of dog</td><td>Day of snake</td><td rowspan="3">Days of pig, cat and goat</td><td rowspan="3">Days of tiger, horse and dog</td></tr>
<tr><td>May</td><td>Day of horse</td><td>Day of mouse</td></tr>
<tr><td>June</td><td>Day of goat</td><td>Day of buffalo</td></tr>
<tr><td>July</td><td>Day of chicken</td><td>Day of cat</td><td rowspan="3">Days of tiger, horse and dog</td><td rowspan="3">Days of pig, cat and goat</td></tr>
<tr><td>August</td><td>Day of mouse</td><td>Day of horse</td></tr>
<tr><td>September</td><td>Day of snake</td><td>Day of pig</td></tr>
<tr><td>October</td><td>Day of snake</td><td>Day of pig</td><td rowspan="3">Days of snake, chicken and buffalo</td><td rowspan="3">Days of monkey, mouse and dragon</td></tr>
<tr><td>November</td><td>Day of mouse</td><td>Day of horse</td></tr>
<tr><td>December</td><td>Day of snake</td><td>Day of pig</td></tr>
</table>

[1] Nicholas Tapp (1993). "Karma and Cosmology - Anthropology and Religion". In: Grant Evans (1993), *Asia's Cultural Mosaic - An Anthropological Introduction*. Singapore: Prentice Hall: 295.

It is found that that this system is diverse and complicated. It is very hard for a shaman to remember all these rules. Therefore, he has to fix good days by looking at his magic manual.

6.5.3 Definition of days for buying breeding animals

Like the crops, a good breeder plays an important role in developing the Yao's animal husbandry. It is easier for a good breeder to be against a disease and to be grown up. Normally, the local farmers keep some healthy and good animals for breeding. However, in some cases, for example, when their animals die of diseases, they buy the breeding animals from their neighbours or from other people in another commune. In this case, a good day for buying these animals is indispensable because it relates to the result of their breeding. The local farmers normally apply this rule to buying cattle because these animals are normally costly. The following table shows this rule of the Red Yao people (Table 6.4).

Table 6.4. Bad days for buying cattle (buffalo, horse, pig and goat) for the breeding purpose

Month	Bad day	Result
Jan., May and Sept.	Days of dragon, snake and horse	They would be thin or die
Feb., June and Oct.	Days of goat, monkey and chicken	
March, July and Nov.	Days of dog, pig and mouse	
April, August and Dec.	Days of buffalo, tiger and cat	

6.5.4 Selection of an auspicious day for piercing the buffalo's nose

It is obvious that buffaloes are very important for the farmers. Therefore, farmers take care of them carefully. In addition to the regime of care and taboos relating to these animals, good days are also selected for piercing buffaloes' nose and for stinging their nose. The good days are days of *mậu thìn*, *kỷ tỵ*, *tân dậu*, *giáp tuất*, *ất hợi*, *tân tỵ*, *ất dậu*, *mậu tí* and *kỷ mão*. In this way, they can easily control their buffaloes as they do the farming. On the contrary, they would have many difficulties in controlling these animals if other days were selected.

6.5.5 Animals as one of the criteria for forecasting the result of a year

Apart from these above taboos, some animals are used as one of the criteria in forecasting the result of a new year. Based on shamans' magic manuals and farmers' experiences, the sounds and chirps of some animals will foretell the people bad or good things during the whole year. At midnight on 30 December in the lunar calendar, all family members keep silent and listen to which animal cries first. If they hear the sound of a cat or a chicken at first, they believe that a certain person in their family will be seriously sick or their crops will be poor. The sound of a mouse foretells an agriculturally strenuous year. The sound of a pig signals a successful harvest and stock-breeding, but the ill-health of man. The sound of a horse implies a good year because the horse will carry home the agricultural produce, meaning a good harvest. The sound of a buffalo shows good crops and a funeral in the family. The cry of a dog is considered the best sound, and therefore its sound is a wish of the Red Yao because it foretells a very successful harvest, wealth and good health for the family. In contrast, the people are scared at hearing the sound of an owl because they are afraid that all bad things will come to them, such as hunger, sadness, and disease. Usually, they hear the sound of domestic animals first, because they are kept near their dwelling-house. The wild animals normally cry in the early morning and it is rare for the people to hear them. Thus, if the people hear the sound of the wild animals, they believe problems foretold by the wild animals.

In general, as with cultivation, the animal husbandry of the Red Yao people still contains many aspects of Taoism and geomancy. That is why the local people usually combine their breeding techniques with the taboos in the livestock raising for the best achievement in this domain.

6.6Division of labour and gender roles in animal husbandry

In agriculture, including animal husbandry, it is important to highlight the role of farmers in the Third World in producing food and in feeding the world.[1] The sexual division of labour is clear in the case of animal husbandry in the Red Yao communities.

The Yao men are mainly responsible for selecting good days for building the animal houses, selecting animals for breeding and building houses for animals. In addition, the grazing of cattle (such as buffalo, cow, horse and goat) and the practice of fishing-farm are also their work. A common phenomenon in the community is that many boys cluster into groups nearby their animals grazing in the grass-plots, in the forest, on the hill and in the fields without cultivated crops or they ride on their buffaloes and horses. Through my survey, some households hire their nephew to care for their grazing buffaloes. On a monthly basis, he lives in the house of the owners of buffaloes and has a meal there. Based on an agreement between the owner of buffaloes and his parents, after a fixed period, he will receive a buffalo calf as a payment for his work.

In comparison with the labour division of men, women play a significant role in feeding people and various animals. In this way, they nourish themselves and other people. The Yao women are mainly responsible for the feeding of pigs, chickens, ducks and other poultries. In addition, they also spend time gathering the wild vegetable food for their domestic animals. This is also one of the domestic works practiced by many women in other ethnic minorities in Vietnam and in some other countries.[2] It can be said that this is a natural age-old

---

[1] Vandana Shiva (2001). "Globalization and Poverty". In: Veronika Bennholdt-Thomsen, Nicholas G. Faraclas and Claudia von Werlhof (eds.), *There is an Alternative: Subsistence and Worldwide Resistance to Corporate Globalization.* Victoria: Spinifex Press: 60.

[2] Do Thuy Binh (1995). "The mountainous environment and the mountain women". In: Institute of Strategic Forecast (1995), *Gender, environment and development in Vietnam.* Hanoi: National Politics Publishing House: 129.

- Maria Mies (1986). "Indian women in subsistence and agricultural labour". *Women, Work and Development 12.* Geneva: International Labour Office: 76-77.

- Christine Helliwell (1993). "Women in Asia - Anthropology and the Study of Women". In: Grant Evans (ed.) (1993), *Asia's Cultural Mosaic - An Anthropological Introduction.* Singapore: Prentice Hall: 260-286.

sexual division of labour among both the Yao people and other ethnic groups in Vietnam. However, in the current period, the division of the same work between men and women is being found in many households. This change is clearly seen among young families or in the families of the communal administrators.

Apart from the role of farmers in livestock breeding, in recent years, the communal and village veterinary surgeons primarily play a particular role in protecting domestic animals from certain diseases. Normally, every village has a veterinary surgeon. Most are men because they are more fluent in Vietnamese than women are. The village veterinarians take part in three short training courses a year in the town to get different kinds of information relating to agriculture. These courses include one course of animal husbandry, one course of cultivation and one course of veterinary work. In general, they are normally involved in comprehensive training programmes of agricultural development. After finishing their training courses, they go home and then cooperate with the local administrators to impart news and information that they got from the courses to other villagers. The participation and contribution of these communal and village veterinary surgeons mainly results from a series of various governmental policies and development programmes implemented in the mountainous region in general and in the Red Yao communities in particular. Particularly, there were two programmes of hunger eradication and poverty reduction for the period of 1998-2000.[1] In addition to other effects, these programmes play a significant role in improving the capacity of the local cadres, including of local veterinary surgeons.

6.7Summary

In comparison with cultivation, animal husbandry by the Red Yao is less extended and effective. This is a small-scale, mainly natural and supplementary economic activity. However, it is an indispensable economic activity in Yao communities and it gradually increases the number of domestic animals.

The local people have accumulated a lot of knowledge and experience in choosing the breeding animals, managing their grazing plots, selecting and processing different kinds of food for their domestic animals as well as protecting and curing their animals from certain diseases. Many of these kinds of knowledge are still valuable today.

Despite their efforts, in some cases, farmers meet some difficulties in developing their animal husbandry because they lack information and experience in breeding some new and hybrid animals. In addition, in recent years, they have faced some animal diseases because they move their domestic animals to their

[1] WB (2001). *Project appraisal document on a proposed credit in the amount of SDR 87.9 million (US$110 million equivalent) to the Socialist Republic of Vietnam for a northern mountains poverty reduction project*. Rural Development and Natural Resources Sector Unit, East Asia and Pacific Region, Report No: 21233-VN: 4.

- Decision 135/1998/QĐ-TTG dated 31/7/1998 by the Prime Minister, "An approval of the socio-economic development programme for especially difficult mountainous and remote communes". In: Parliament Council of Ethnic Groups. Session X (2000), *The policy and law of ethnic groups of the Vietnam Communist Party and the government*. Hanoi: National Culture Publishing House: 667-677.

residences and then breed them there. Their traditional ways of breeding animals on their milpas are more effective than the new ways introduced by the local administrators and caused partly by reaction to fear of theft.

Knowledge and experience of breeding animals differs from commune to commune and between genders. In general, the people in the two communes of Nậm Cang and Bản Khoang are more knowledgeable about raising horses and goats than the people in Tả Phìn commune because there are more grass and grazing plots in these two communes. However, the farmers in Tả Phìn commune have more knowledge and experience in raising the new animals, mainly hybrid pigs and chickens as well as cows, than the people in Nậm Cang and Bản Khoang communes because these new races are first introduced into Tả Phìn commune. In terms of gender, the knowledge and the labour division is also different between men and women. Men are mainly responsible for grazing the cattle (such as buffaloes, cows and goats), selecting good days for building their animal houses, buying the breeding animals and building their houses. In comparison, women mainly take responsibility for planting and gathering the vegetable plants for their domestic animals, processing food for these animals and feeding them. However, in recent years, there is a labour exchange between men and women, mainly in the families of young people and of local cadres.

The cultivation and the animal husbandry of the Red Yao people are closely related. They are two main economic activities of the ethnic minorities in Vietnam, including the Red Yao. The cultivation products supply food for both the people and the animals. The livestock breeding supplies crops with valuable cattle manure. In addition, the money that the local people earn from selling the domestic animals is mainly used to buy the seeds and tools for production as well as the fertilizers to expand and develop the cultivation. Therefore, the development of cultivation goes together with the expansion of animal husbandry and vice verse. By this way, the local people can gradually increase the output of food and foodstuff which contribute to improving their situation of food security.

Chapter 7
LOCAL KNOWLEDGE OF FORAGE ECONOMY OF THE RED YAO

7.1Hunting

For thousands of years, human beings lived mainly on hunting and gathering. Their food sources depended on nature's offerings.[1] Many peoples in the world have maintained the economy of nature-based food collection, especially forest-based food, until now. Hundreds of millions of people still depend on the forest, with differences from region to region and from one ethnic group to another given the various available ecological conditions, levels of agricultural development and the regional consumer markets.

In Vietnam, approximately 24 million people live in or around forests and depend directly on forests for their livelihood. Most are part of a subsistence economy. It is also a common supplementary economic activity in the Vietnam mountainous areas. Before 1968, the year of the implementation of settlement in the mountain regions of Vietnam, many ethnic groups had to live mostly on the forest because of their traditional nomadic life.[2] Previously, the forest was considered an endless food source for the people; and this was, therefore, a reason for the tenacious maintenance of the forage economy.[3] Here, forest products meet their demands for an important food source and provide materials for basic household items and housing construction. The forest provides a source of income for the local people through their harvesting and selling of bamboo, firewood, different kinds of herbal plants, of fruits, fodder and wild animals.[4] In general, it can be said that the available natural food and other forest products are considered supplementary sources for food security of the upland people.

Although the Red Yao have made great strides in agriculture in recent years which contribute to the eradication of hunger and alleviation of poverty for local inhabitants, the forage economy continues to play an indispensable role in their lives. It supplied local people with an important food source, especially during seasonal periods of hunger, in the case of a poor harvest and during the wars.

There are two basic types of the forage economy: hunting and gathering. These are the most common activities of peoples who live near the forest in many

---

[1] M. O. Cosven (1974). *Outline of history of the primitive culture*. Hanoi: Literature – History – Geography Publishing House.

[2] Be Viet Dang, Nguyen Khac Tung, Nong Trung, and Nguyen Nam Tien (1971). *The Yao in Vietnam*. Hanoi: Social Science Publishing House.

- Institute of Ethnology (1978). *Ethnic minorities in Vietnam (in the Northern provinces)*. Hanoi: Social Science Publishing House.

- Be Viet Dang (1985). "Some issues of the socio-economic development in the Northern mountainous provinces". *Ethnographic Review*, No 1: 16-17.

[3] Institute of Ethnology (1978). Ethnic *minorities in Vietnam (in the Northern provinces)*. Hanoi: Social Science Publishing House: 44.

[4] Epprecht M. and Heinimann A. (eds.) (2004). *Socioeconomic Atlas of Vietnam. A Depiction of the 1999 Population and Housing Census*. Swiss National Centre of Competence in Research (NCCR) North-South, University of Berne. Berne: 42.

countries in the world.[1] Hunting and gathering are the two main activities of the forage economy as practiced by the Red Yao in Sa Pa district.

7.1.1 Functions of hunting

Hunting contributes to supplying supplementary food for the mountain people. Foodstuff from wild animals partly supports the inhabitants as a source of protein and improves their nutrition.[2] In the case of the Red Yao people, this is also their favourite food.

It is found that hunting is also a measure that protects the farmers' harvest and their domestic animals from destruction caused by some wild animals. Mice like to eat the new ripening rice. They are one of the most dangerous animals for the rice fields of the Red Yao people. Squirrels and bears are called the maize eaters. During the maize harvest, these wild animals destroy most maize plots. Thanks to their good understanding of the ways of these animals, the local people often set a trap on their agricultural plots. Afterwards, these animals will fall into the trap when they attempt to eat the crops. According to the stories of some Yao village elders, their pigs and buffaloes were often killed or caught by tigers. Some households lost most of their herds of pigs, with even some 10 pigs killed in one night, because tigers had caught them. Furthermore, foxes catch fowl and ducks. That is why the Yao's animal husbandry in the past was extremely precarious and inefficient. According to the local people, in some years, they could harvest just half of their actual yield because of the wild animals. However, in the last twenty years, the scarcity of these wild animals and the increasing density of houses and populations have decreased this loss.

Hunting is additionally one of the amusements of the Yao people and it reinforces the cooperation and solidarity of the people in their communities. All hunters share every duty and every achievement of their hunting, especially in collective hunting. They stand together and coordinate every action to achieve a successful hunt. The hunting feasts and the share of hunting products bring further joy and intimacy to all the hunters.

7.1.2 Forms of hunting

There are two different forms of the hunting: communal and individual. Communal hunting is normally conducted to hunt the large wild animals. The self-awareness and the sense of community manifest themselves clearly in this form of hunting. Many hunters, mostly the male villagers, are involved in the communal hunt. In the past, there were many dense forests in this region with many large animals living there. The participants of such hunting were open

---

[1] G. P. Murdoch (1967). *Ethnographic Atlas*, Pittsburgh: University of Pittsburgh Press.
- Richard B. Lee and Irven DeVore (eds.) (1968). *Man the Hunter*. Chicago: Aldine.
- Thayer Scudder (1971). "Gathering among African woodland savannah cultivators - A case study: The Gwembe Tonga". *Zambian Papers*, No. 5. Zambia: University of Zambia.
- Kathleen D. Morrison and Laura L. Junker (2002). *Forager-Traders in South and Southeast Asia: Long-Term Histories*. Cambridge: Cambridge University Express.

[2] Tim Ingold, David Riches, and Jame Woodburn (eds.) (1988). *Hunters and Gatherers 2: Property, power and ideology*. Oxford: Berg.
- Richard B. Lee and R. Daly (eds.) (1999). *The Cambridge Encyclopedia of Hunters and Gatherers*. Cambridge: Cambridge University Press.

hunters. Therefore, some hunts involved most of female villagers in it. Nowadays, the forest has been largely destroyed and thus few wild animals can survive there. A hunting group currently consists of three of five hunters. However, the hunting scales differ from community to community in Sa Pa district. Communal hunting is more common in Bản Khoang and Nậm Cang communes, where the forest has remained relatively dense, than in Tả Phìn commune. As soon as the hunters discover the track of a certain wild animal in the forest or in crop plots, they lay some traps on stretches of the narrow and sloping path where this animal passes, and then it falls into one of the traps. The hunters share some work with each other: pursuing the animal, directing the hunting dogs, catching the animal, etc. These hunts sometimes last a few days because the hunters have to track the wild animal, waylay it, then surround and catch it. Because the hunt is also at night and is of long duration, the female villagers are not able to take part in such the hunt.

Individual hunting is increasingly common at present, as the large wild animals have become gradually rare because of the decrease of forest areas. This is mainly observation hunting. The hunted and trapped animals are usually small. They are different kinds of birds, mice, wild fowl, bamboo rats, monkeys, musk-rats, and even small wild boars, etc. The hunts are usually carried out in the early morning or the late afternoon. Some kinds of hunting, mostly hunting for small wild boars and monkeys, last all day. The hunters are male villagers. However, in some cases, female villagers and children also hunt or trap some small animals while they work in the upland plots.

7.1.3 Diversity of hunting artefacts and tools

The hunting artifacts and tools of the Red Yao people are diverse and abundant, in terms of both sorts and sizes. They are the hunting harquebus, various traps and snares, cross-bows, spears, different kinds of fishing nets, torches, flashlights and the hunting dogs.

Red Yao people use various traps and snares to catch animals. Local people use different kinds of traps depending on each wild animal. To catch those birds and mice which go to the upland fields and eat the *thảo quả* plant, rice and maize there, the people lay traps with *hỉa chang* and *chảng bọ ton*. *Nọ hang*, a kind of string-snare, is used to snare those birds which usually perch on the branch of a tree with ripening fruits. The birds are normally slightly wounded when they fall into the snare.

To protect birds from severe injuries while they are caught in the snare and then to tame them and keep them for ornamental purposes, the Yao people use *nọ lồng*, meaning a cage. They divide this cage into two parts. They confine a prey bird in the close part of this cage. The door of the rest part is opened to wait for the snaring bird. Here, there are some foods available for this bird. When the snaring bird flies past this cage, it will hear a voice of the prey bird, then creep into this snare and finally be caught in it.

A kind of bamboo triangle trap, the so-called *hau chang*, also belongs to the small traps to snare birds and mice. As soon as the animals fall into these traps, they will die of their broken necks caused by a sudden and strong spring of the trap.

As to the size of the trap, there are two kinds of traps. They are the big trap (*chang hô* or *tẩm chang*) which is used to trap the big wild animals (normally the chamois, wild boars and bears) and the small trap (*chảng bọ ton*) which is used to trap the small animals (mostly mice, wild fowl and various birds). A documentary picture of some traps of the Red Yao shows the difference in size of such the traps. To hunt and trap the big animals, the hunters must use bigger and more solid hunting artefacts and tools than those used to catch the small wild animals, and vice versa. These big traps do not kill the larger animals, due to their large size and strength. Normally, when a big animal falls into the trap it will drag the trap up to a certain point of its path. To catch it, the hunters follow its tracks marked on the ground or in the trees and plants along the path.

The Red Yao's ways of setting the traps are also diverse. They can hang a snare or a trap on a tree branch, or put it on the ground and then disguise it with leaves, or bury it in a dug hole and then cover it with the branches and leaves of a tree. For example, the hunters can catch a bear by shooting or trapping it. To trap it, they plunge several sharp neohouzeaua sticks into the upland slope. Afterwards, they create a loud noise in the opposite direction of the trapped area. The bear hears that noise, then runs into the direction of the trapped area and falls into the trap. Another way of trapping the bear is that the hunters put some buffalo bones on a wooden plank laid about 1 meter above the ground. At the same time, they plunge many sharp knives into the ground and lay them under the plank. The hungry bear will climb up this plank to take the bones and then will be killed or heavily injured by falling on these knives. In general, the local people set the different traps and snares depending on each wild animal.

Choosing the location of traps plays an important role in the hunting because it makes the springing of animal traps possible, easy and efficient. The hunters fix the appropriate trapping places based on their own experience. The ideal places are normally bends in the path or narrow stretches of the path where the animals probably pass or where they must go through because of the uniqueness of this path. The hunters sometimes understand and have a thorough grasp of the animals' movements. As a result of this understanding, they can fix the right place to lay a trap. In this case, the trapping place will be fixed in the exact position where the animals will walk as they go through the stretch of this path. Consequently, it is obvious that the animals will be caught in the trap.

Setting a trap to catch an entire animal is only successful for the small wild animals. For the bigger animals, traps only wound them slightly and restrict their movements and speed. Normally, the hunter goes on an inspection tour of the trap 3 or 4 days after he laid it. If he sees that the trap is lost, he will follow the tracks of the animal marked by its hurt legs. The new marks, such as a broken tree or some branches of a tree, etc., signal to hunter that the trapped animal is a short distance from him.

In addition to the variety of the traps and ways of setting them, the Red Yao people have also accumulated much experience in the making of hunting harquebus. Until now, all their hunting harquebuses are artifacts. The traditional hunting gun differs from the modern one in ammunition. Their traditional shot is made of silex. The gun powder has been introduced into the Red Yao community only in recent years. The local people buy it in the Sa Pa market. This weapon is only used to hunt and shoot large wild animals. In many cases, although the big animal falls into the trap, it is still so healthy and powerful that the hunters cannot catch it. Thus, the hunters shoot it dead or injure it seriously before carrying it to their village.

Hunting dogs often participate in the large-scale hunting because they are good at scenting. They can smell the tracks of the trapped animal and then follow their scent. The hunters rush after these dogs based on their noise to catch the trapped animal.

7.1.4 Diversified knowledge of the habits and the rules of some wild animals

Local inhabitants know thoroughly the movements and feeding patterns of wild animals. For example, the squirrel, the monkey and the bear are fond of eating maize. Therefore, they usually go to the maize plots when the maize harvest is coming. Knowing this, the Yao people often lay traps in the maize field during August and September every year to catch these animals. The mice however enjoy rice. Thus, when the rice is ripening, mice destroy many rice fields. To protect the rice from this destruction, the local people set many mice-traps at the corners and edges of the rice fields.

The season of flowering and fruit attracts many animals which enjoy honey, such as the bear. Bears often frequent the beehives to eat honey because they like it very much. Thanks to the thorough understanding of this animal's habit, hunters often lay a trap on the ground surrounding the stump of a tree which has a beehive, when they find the footprint of a bear there. In this case, it is easy for the bear to be caught in the trap. For the Red Yao community this is also the season of honey collection in the forest and the hunting season for birds.

The hunting season for herbivorous animals, such as the muntjac and the chamois, is normally during May to the end of July every year because this is the season of tender grass. In this period, these animals usually go to the secondary forests near the residential areas of the villagers to search for food so it is possible to trap them then.

The Yao people have great experience in seeking and snaring different kinds of birds (*nọ*) because of their thorough knowledge of the birds' life. For instance, to catch or shoot the *nọ dìn chịa* - a black bird equal in size to the human fist, the hunters usually search for them along the stream because they are fond of worms which normally living in the bush along the stream. The Yao also set snares in cassava fields to catch the *nọ poòng sạ* - a bird as large as the human big toe with red and black feathers, a very fine blazing red beak and having a gregarious life- because they enjoy the cassava. Some other birds are only found in the jungle, such as the *nọ chiềm chìn*, *tầm nọ* (meaning the big birds), *nọ quề*, *nọ noong*, *nọ khọng*, and the pigeon (*nọ gồ*). The *tầm nọ* is about

1.5 kg in weight, with white feathers and has a gregarious life. These birds often perch the branches of the trees in the jungle. The hunters find these birds' shelters at about 9 pm or 10 pm by shining the light of a torch or flashlight on the trees and their branches. The *nọ quề* is extremely fond of earthworms and several kinds of wild fruits. It is approximately 0.4 kg or 0.5 kg in weight, has ash-coloured feathers and lives in couples. It is normally caught in the snare in the season of flowering and fruit. The *nọ noong* is about 1.5 kg to 2 kg in weight, with yellow-white feathers. It lives only in the forest. Therefore, the hunter must go there to catch it. An increasingly rare bird is the *nọ khọng*. Its beak is about 20 cm long and as big as the buffalo's horn. It is approximately 3 kg or 4 kg in weight and only lives in the forest. In addition, some other birds live both in the forest and in the residential areas of the inhabitants. They are the nightingale (*nọ mẩy*), *nọ tre* (a kind of bird which is nearly as big as the domestic chicken), the Chinese laughing-thrush (*nọ giằng*), the sparrow (*nọ chi líp ton*, meaning the small bird), the *nọ pờ pẻo* (a bird is as big as a bowl with yellow feathers), and the *nọ nhíp* (having a similar shape as the *nọ pờ pẻo*'s).

The local people maintain their hunting activities in other seasons of the year as well, but this is not highly effective because it is more difficult for the hunter to find and catch the wild animals. At that time, hunters must go to the remote primary forest to set their traps and it takes them a long time to catch these animals.

The rules of gregarious or single life of some wild animals are thoroughly understood by many local inhabitants, mostly by the male villagers. The size of the hunting group differs from one hunt to another based partly on the Yao's knowledge of these animals' rules. The gregarious animals consist of the deer, the chamois, the muntjac, the wolf, the monkey, various kinds of mice and birds. Meanwhile, the bear searches for feed alone.

In general, their thorough knowledge of the ways and habits of some wild animals helps the local hunters to save time and labour for successful hunting. The local people have accumulated this knowledge for a long time. Their hunting activity derives partly from the protection of their crops from destruction by wild animals. Additionally, this activity meets the demand for food and entertainment of the local inhabitants, especially when they have leisure time.

7.1.5 Diversity of the share of hunted animals and their usage

7.1.5.1 Variety of the share of hunted animals

In olden times, when communal hunting was very common, the hunted animal was shared with the hunter who shot first straight into that animal and with the shaman who organized and presided over the ritual ceremony of the forest spirit. The rest of animal was given in equal parts to all hunting participants. Nowadays, this rule remains in the Yao community. However, hunting products are gradually limited because of the increasing scarcity of the wild animals, especially the big ones. This leads to decreasing hunting profits for local hunters.

Meanwhile, in individual or family hunting, the hunted animal belongs obviously only to the hunter or to his family. In many cases, the successful hunter also invites some of his relatives and neighbours to come to his home and then feasts them with his hunting booty. The relationship between the hunter and visitors, therefore, is increasingly consolidated in such a feast.

7.1.5.2 Variety of the usage of hunted animals

When the hunt is successful, the animal caught is used for many different purposes for a ritual offering, foodstuff, goods, medicine, ornament, and other purposes.

- As the ritual offering:

It can be said that this is the Yao's first use of the hunted animal, especially of the big animals. As soon as the individual hunting is over, the hunter carries the animal into his house. In a communal hunt, when the hunters finish their hunting, they carry the animal caught into the house of the person who first shot straight into the animal. The whole animal or some body parts are used for one of the indispensable offerings to the ritual ceremony. By this offering and the shaman's witchcraft, the forest and ancestor spirits will receive it as a gift, thanking them for their support for the successful hunting.

- As a foodstuff:

Normally, if the hunted animal is large a part of its meat is prepared for a feast that is organized in the house of the hunter who shot it first. The rest is shared equally with all participants. However, the shaman and the hunter who shot first straight into that animal will receive a bigger part of its meat than the other hunting participants. If the animal is small, it is cooked for the feast in the house of the hunter who shot it first or who trapped it. All participants and the shaman enjoy that feast after the worship is over.

- As goods:

In previous times, the Red Yao people used the entire hunting product for their domestic purposes, which improved their nutrition. However, in the past ten years, especially as tourism has developed rapidly and remarkably in Sa Pa district, the hunting products are more or less used as goods for tourism. The ornamental bird is one of the favourite items of tourists when they visit villages of the ethnic minority people. This fosters the interest of the local people in taming and domesticating different kinds of wild birds, and then in keeping them for ornament and sale.

Additionally, some pharmaceutical parts of certain wild animals are valuable. Previously, in addition to the supply of the foodstuff for the family, some wild animals were exchanged for the daily necessary items, such as salt, productive tools, etc. Nowadays, they are used for the commodity market. For example, bear legs and the bladder, gall, the ulcer of the porcupine and the bones of the chamois are extremely valuable in the market. However, it is currently more difficult for the hunters to catch these animals because they are increasingly rare. This makes the price of these animals more expensive and more valuable in the regional market and in the whole country. Many Kinh traders go to the villages of the minority people to find and buy them.

- As medicine:

The Yao people have an age-old tradition of community health care using their own herbal medicine. Their traditional medicine includes various materials, including the wild animals. For example, the bear legs and its fall are soaked in rice alcohol and then used as a drink to prevent and cure pain. The ulcer of the porcupine is able to treat stomach aches. The bones of the chamois can be cooked to make glue to cure arthritis. The inhabitants' experience in using these medicines has accumulated from generation to generation.

- As ornaments:

As soon as the local hunters catch a big wild animal, they normally keep certain parts of it (such as the head of the chamois and the bear, the tiger claws, etc.) for ornaments, and decoration of the house. The people hang them up at the wood wall or at a certain column of the house or somewhere inside the house where it is easy for the visitor to see them. These hunting products represent the hunter's talent and his pride, especially when he receives praise from his visitors.

Another common ornamental animal is the bird. It is easy for the local people to tame it. The Yao often tame some kinds of beautiful birds with fine singing voices (such as the nightingale and the Chinese laughing-thrush), and keep them for ornament and sale.

- Other purposes:

The value of some animals is not only to supply the Yao family with foodstuffs and decorative articles, but also for use in making some articles for daily use. For instance, the chamois hide can be used to make a drumhead.

7.1.6 Various beliefs and ritual ceremonies related to hunting

7.1.6.1 Ritual ceremonies regarding the hunt

In olden times, originating from the belief that everything has its own soul, the Yao people believed that all wild animals are controlled by the forest spirit. Therefore, they always organized a ceremony to worship the forest spirit to say thanks to him for his support of their successful hunting as soon as they had caught a certain wild animal, especially in case of a big beast.

In case of communal and large-scale hunting, the ceremony is frequently organized in the house of the hunter who was the first to shoot straight into the animal. This hunter has deserved the main credit for the successful hunt and is thus is worthy of such an honour. This also means that his fellow-hunters recognize his hunting talent. Another reason for the Yao's maintenance of this worship is that if they organize this ceremony in the house of one of the other hunters, the host of that house will not be able to develop his animal husbandry or shoot straight into an animal, but will shoot a fellow hunter in the coming hunt.

In the case of the individual hunting, it is obvious for the hunter to organize the worship of the forest spirit in his own house. However, in this case, he will invite some of his relatives and neighbours to enjoy the feast at his home and share the hunting achievement with them.

The local people arrange various forms of worship. These ceremonies are different, depending on each hunted wild animal. However, they are based on their traditional principle that if they catch a big wild beast, they must organize a large-scale ritual ceremony and vice versa. According to the inhabitants, wild beasts include the bear, tiger, panther, chamois and wild boar. Small animals include the monkey, deer, muntjac, stag, several kinds of wild birds and mice. The large-scale ceremony normally lasts about two or three hours, while the small-scale worship lasts around one hour. In every ritual, it is indispensable to have a rite of smearing the blood of the animal on the head of the hunting gun with which the hunter shot first straight into that animal. This rite informs the forest spirit about the hunting achievement and asks this spirit for continuous support of this gun in the next hunt.

In addition to the hunted animals, the additional ritual offering, the so-called gift, consists of a bottle of rice alcohol, one silver coin (if this is the small-scale worship) or two silver coins (for large-scale worship) covered by a bundle of raw rice and some traditional votive papers. In this ritual, the shaman worships the forest and ancestor spirits and offers the gift to them to inform them about the successful hunt and to express the hunters' gratitude towards these spirits for their support. Additionally, he also prays to these spirits for continuous good luck in future hunting. The Red Yao people strictly maintain their ceremonies and worships after they have finished their hunting because they are afraid of misfortune in the next hunt, such as a hunt or when the hunters shoot straight into each other while they are hunting animals.

The shaman plays an important role in these ceremonies. He is both the organizer of the ritual and the connector between the hunters and the forest and ancestor spirits, reporting the hunters' newest achievement to these spirits. He is also the representative of all the hunters to thank these spirits and request luck in the next hunt. That is why he always receives a small gift for his worthy efforts as soon as the worship is complete. He normally gets about 1 kg of the hunted animal's meat if that animal is big or a certain part of that animal if it is small.

7.1.6.2 Taboos and avoidances concerning hunting

Local hunters strictly maintain and comply with some particular taboos regarding hunting, in addition to the celebration of the ritual ceremony. They maintain that this makes their hunting successful and helps them avoid some misfortunes and risks in their productive work and life.

As one of the first taboos, the worship must be organized in the house of the hunter who shot first straight into the animal because the hunters are afraid of a misfortune in the coming hunt. The rite of smearing the blood of the animal on the head of the gun represents this taboo. The size of the worship is also one of the beliefs of the local people in the hunting.

In addition, the local people also maintain some other taboos to protect their domestic animals and the breeding from damage by wild animals. For instance, as soon as they catch a wolf, panther or tiger, they do not organize the ritual ceremony inside the house of the hunter as usual, but outside his house because these animals are considered to harm and giving misfortune to human beings. Another reason is that they are wild eaters of the Red Yao's domestic animals, so that they are not treated as the local people's animals. That is why they are not taken into the house. When the people organize the ritual with the offering of such animals, they put this offering on a small table in the courtyard in front of the main door. The way of worshipping and praying is similar to other ceremonies. When the worship is over, the people carry this offering into the kitchen by the back door to prepare and cook it for the feast. When they finish cooking, they bring the meat into the sitting room and enjoy it.

Although a day with thunder is considered a bad day for cultivation, it is a very good day for hunting. It derives from a Red Yao myth which has been well memorized by the local hunters. The myth is that one day a snake hid in a hollow tree. There was suddenly thunder and the snake stuck out its tongue. At that exact moment, a hunter reached the place and shot it dead. It suddenly stopped thundering as soon as the snake died. Thenceforth, the people believe that the god of thunder intended to kill that snake. However, the hunter did it for him.

The Yao also uphold some taboos concerning the hunting of pregnant wild animals. Although it is impossible for us to find out the local inhabitant's written regulation of these taboos, this regulation has been maintained and orally transmitted from generation to generation. The hunters never catch or kill the pregnant animals. It is also their moral and belief. The hunter whose the wife is pregnant observes this rule strictly because he and his wife are afraid that their foetus or their infant will meet a misfortune or die if he shoots such an animal dead and eats it.

7.2Gathering

7.2.1 Functions of gathering

Gathering of food and materials is a relatively common activity of the uplanders. In previous eras, especially in the nomadic stage when the agriculture was not expanded, the gathering of the available natural products played an important role in supplying the people with the daily food. This was similar to the dependence on the nature of most of the foragers in Australia, the BaMbuti, the Cree and similar groups of northern Canada, and of the Punan and other isolated tribes of Southeast Asia. According to Michael C. Howard (1996), the importance of hunting and gathering for these societies varies, but gathering generally provides the bulk of what is eaten.[1] The available food source is very important for the local people in surviving after a poor harvest, misfortune, war or natural disaster. It has the function of alleviating hunger for the local people. Sometimes, this is the household income and the savings of the local inhabitants.[2]

In societies where agriculture is relatively expanded, gathering is an additional economic activity that supplements the available food supply for the local people when they suffer hunger or lack of cultivated food.[3] The Yao people, mainly women, traditionally go to the forest to gather wild plants for their households. However, they practised this activity more frequently in the

---

[1] Michael C. Howard (1996), *Contemporary Cultural Anthropology*. Fifth edition. New York: HarperCollins College Publishers: 81.

[2] R. Neil Byron and J. E. Michael Arnold (1999). "What futures for the people of the tropical forests?". *World Development* 27 (5): 792.

[3] W. D. Sunderlin, A. Angelsen, and S. Wunder (2003), "State of the World's Forests". In: FAO (2003), *Forests and poverty alleviation*. Rome: Italy. 61-73.

past than now because their current food crops are more abundant, especially in Nậm Cang commune. In addition, processing the wild animals and plants meets their fondness for some special local dishes. Some natural products are fed to domestic animals and thus contribute to developing the husbandry of the local people. Gathering also provides them with various herbal medicines.

7.2.2 Diversified knowledge of the gathering products and the gathering season

The Yao gather many forest products, including several kinds of animals and plants, and other products exclusive of the timber. In a study by Neumann and Hirsch (2000), they also found that all of the poorest people in the world collect non-timber forest products.[1]

7.2.2.1 Wild animals

Gathered wild animals consist normally of different kinds of bees and aquatic products in nature (such as fish and shrimp in rivers and streams, crabs and different kinds of shellfish in springs and rock crevices). The frequency of and results from gathering differ from season to season.

The bee (*muổi*) and the bee's products, mostly its honey, are the favourites of the Yao people. There are different kinds of bees. Honeybees include "*ong khoái*" (*bèng muổi*), "*muổi mung*" and *muổi nhười*.

To collect the honey, the local people must have good knowledge of the life of bees and different bees' ways of producing honey. People have accumulated much experience in this domain. For example, to collect the honey of the *bèng muổi*, local people usually search for the beehive in the rock caves during the season of bloom and fruit lasting from February to May each year. The collectors normally include two villagers. One stands under the bee nest and is responsible for keeping a piece of the nylon cloth which has been already opened out and waiting for the fall of the honey. Another collector uses a stick to poke at a beehive to make his honey flow down to the available nylon cloth kept by his fellow-collector. In comparison, hollow trees are nests of the honeybee *muổi mung*. To collect the honey of these bees, the people break up a certain part of that tree with a hammer and then put their hands into that hole to extract the honey from the bee-nest. In the case of the *muổi nhười*, a very poisonous kind of wasps which builds its nests on the branches of trees in the home gardens and in the forest, the local people usually collect young wasps during about August and September every year. At this time, there are many young wasps of *muổi nhười*. They are the favourites of the Yao people. When the people find the nest of these bees, they fire the rice straw under their nest or on the ground around the tree with the bee nest. The smoke of the straw drives the bees, except the young bees, out of their nest. Afterwards, the collector takes the young bees out of their nest.

To avoid bee stings while gathering the honey, the Yao have their own means of protection. Normally, they collect the bee honey carefully and try hard

---

[1] Roderick P. Neumann and Eric Hirsch (2000), *Commercialisation of Non-Timber Forest Products: Review and Analysis of Research*. Bogor, Indonesia: Center for International Forestry Research, Rome: FAO.

not to break up the beehive. According to them, bees only make a rush at someone and then sting him when their nest is broken or touched powerfully. In some cases, for example, when the beehive is big or the bees are large and poisonous, the collectors wrap their head and arms in a cloth or take a raincoat on to protect themselves from the bee stings.

Fresh water fish from streams is a favourite dish in the Yao community. The local people often catch these fishes at leisure. However, the most frequent and effective gathering of fish coincides with the period of March-July every year. It is not ideal for the local inhabitants to catch the stream fish in winter because the very cold temperature in this region makes the fish rare. As a result of this coldness and the scarcity of fish, it is hard for the fisher to catch them. In previous times, the inhabitants caught more fish than at present. At that time, they could catch about 5 kg to 6 kg of fish or more. Currently, the amount of fish available in nature is gradually decreasing due to population growth and the increasing fishing. Thus, the people only catch from 0.5 kg to 2 kg of fish in each fishing time. Sometimes, they even go home with empty handed.

Different kinds of shrimp, crab and shellfish are also caught while the people search for and catch fishes. However, these aquatic products are normally less plentiful than the fish. In addition, these products provide some feed for the ducks. The flock of ducks search for this feed along the springs near the Yao villages.

7.2.2.2 Edible wild vegetation

The flora of the Hoang Lien Son Mountain is very abundant and diverse. Nowadays, there are 167 vegetation families in this region, comprising about 70% of the Vietnam's total flora families.[1] Among them, there is the edible vegetation used as food, foodstuff and herbal plants.

- Edible wild plants used as food and foodstuff consist of different kinds of wild vegetables and tubers, various kinds of the mushroom family (such as the mushroom and the cat's ear), several kinds of wild blooms and fruits.[2] The Yao people usually gather the wild plants to supplement the green vegetables and foodstuff for their daily meals. They are the "*rau dớn*" (*lay chuốt*) (collected all year round); "*rau tầm bóp*" (*lả peo lay*) (February - August); *man xặt*, "*rau móc*" (*tùng chan mia*), *lay gùng bẳng* (July - September); *chẩn moảng lay* (March - April); *ghỉm tuy* (all year round); *mà tẩy loòng tuy* (from September to October); the top of rattan (*đàng phim*) (all year round); *là cỏ phim* (all year round); *mìa chạn* (March - October); pennywort (*tửu chan mia*) (from February to July); *lay chiền* (all year round); "*rau tàu bay*" (March - May), etc.

---

[1] Ha Van Tue (1997). "Flora and Vegetation Structure of Hoang Lien Mountains: Some Initial Results of the Research". In: Sobey, R. T (ed.) (1997), *Biodiversity Value of Hoang Lien Mountains and Strategies for Conservation*, Proceedings of Seminar and Workshop, 7-9th December 1997, Sa Pa district, Lao Cai province, Vietnam; SEE Forest Research Programme, London (ISBN 1873070 13 6): 10.

[2] Institute of Ethnology (1978). *Ethnic minorities in Vietnam (in the Northern provinces)*. Hanoi: Social Science Publishing House.

- Be Viet Dang (1985). "Some issues of the socio-economic development in the Northern mountainous provinces". *Ethnographic Review*, No 1: 16-17.

Wild vegetables and grasses for feed for animal husbandry are also plentiful and diverse. There are both green vegetables for the people and vegetables just for domestic animals. They consist of *xì cầu meng* (April - June), *ngùng nhỏ tuy* (April - June), *nặn* (all year round), *xì cầu thông* (all year round, but mostly in the period of October to January), *mà đổ tuy* (February - April), *hầu hắp đang* (all year round), *hùng tỉa dàm* (all year round), *pưa sùng tuy* (February - April), the trunk of green banana trees (*nậm chiu*) (from October this year to February next year), *mìa loòng* (March - August), *sà cầu mèng tuy* (February- August), excluding wild vegetables for the people. They are the feed mostly for pigs and for some kinds of poultry. Meanwhile, grass is the indispensable feed for some kinds of cattle, such as the buffalo, cow, goat and horse. This feed is gathered all the year round in nature. However, in spring and summer, there are many tender grasses. In addition to the maize, all these plants are the main feed for domestic animals because it is not hard for the local farmers to search for them in the wild.

The Yao people are extremely fond of bamboo sprouts and their products. The bamboo-sprout season is normally short, lasting about one or two months a year. The local people have their own ways of choosing the right period for bamboosprout collection, depending on each kind of bamboo. Wild bamboo sprouts include small bamboo sprout (*hầu đìa bẹ*) collected during February to March; large bamboo sprout (*hầu im bẹ*) (February - March), "*xặt*" bamboo sprout (*hầu xô bẹ*) (only in September), neohouzeaua bamboo sprout (*hầu pỉa bẹ*) (only in November) and thorny bamboo sprout (*hầu ghim bẹ*) (only in March).

Various kinds of the mushrooms are found and gathered by the local inhabitants. Because of these varieties, their seasons are different. They include the agaric (*chầu cúc*) gathered from January to July every year; the cat's ear (*chầu sút*) (all year round, but mostly in the time period from March to May); *chầu đập ngoỏng* - a white mushroom growing on the decayed wood and gathered from July to September when it is about 4 cm high; *chầu pịa* - the black cat's ear growing on the decayed wood in the home garden and in the forest, gathered all year round; *ngủng gái chầu* - a white mushroom growing on the ground and gathered from April to July; *chầu công* - also a white mushroom growing on the ground and gathered in the same time like the *ngủng gái chầu*; and *chiêu cốp* (January - March).

Some kinds of blossoms and fruits can be eaten by the people and used as feed for domestic animals. These are the flowers of wild banana trees (*chìu toọng meng*), which are gathered all year round. Additionally, the local people collect some kinds of wild fruits for their children, such as the fruits of the wild bullage (*pìu heng*) (April and May); fruits of the wild mulberry (*xà phoong piu*) (March - May); the wild persimmon (*pỉu cháy*) (September and October), the green wild banana (*chìu meng*) (all year round), the red wild banana (*chìu sí*) (two seasons a year, from January to March and from July to September) and *pìu pẻng piu* - wild fruits has a size as big as the human finger which grow in raceme and have a green skin when they ripen. These fruits are also used as feed for pigs.

Wild tubers also have contributed remarkably to overcoming periods of hunger of the uplanders when they lived as nomads and took part in the co-operatives as well as during the Vietnam-China war in 1979. The Red Yao people had a serious food scarcity resulting from their participation in the agricultural cooperatives during the years of 1969 to 1974. At that time, it was very common for them to lack food for three to five months a year. Particularly, some households had no cultivated food to eat from 6 to 8 months a year. The hunger season normally lasted from March to August every year.

In addition, the China-Vietnam war in 1979 had negative impacts on the food security of the Red Yao. This situation differed from region to region. In Sa Pa district, the people in Tả Phìn commune were influenced by this war more than were the people in Bản Khoang and Nậm Cang communes. When they had to move from their villages to another place within about two weeks, they were ravenously hungry that whole year because both Chinese and Vietnamese soldiers ate most of their stored food.

To supplement their food in this period, the local people had to go to the forest to find and gather several wild tubers exclusive of other forest products. They are the wild yam (*đòi chu*), the brown tuber (*kiềm giàng*), *mà tầy*, *seo mi tỉ*, "*củ móng ngựa*" - a kind of wild tuber in the shape of the horse-shoe, etc. In the Yao's folk poetry, the inhabitants still maintain the following song: "*ừ chay chỉ san lố nhần khí; kiềm giàng, đòi chu nủn nhần làng*." This song means that corns of the *chay chỉ* (*cây mỳ*) are reserved for village elders because it is easy to eat these; brown tubers and wild yams are reserved for young villagers because it is hard to eat them. In general, at a certain historical stage, these wild tubers helped the uplanders to limit serious periods of hunger.

- Some kinds of wild edible plants used as medicine are herbal plants. Normally, these grow along the sides of rivers and streams, by the roadside, in home gardens and in the forest. In the Hoang Lien Mountains, there are 53 kinds of herbal plants used for the community health care in recent years.[1] In the Yao communities, herbal plants are also growing around the residential areas. They are used for the treatment of common diseases such as influenza, bellyache, headache, body pains, etc. To gather some rare and valuable herbal plants, the people, mostly the herbalists, have to go into the deep forest and jungle. In this case, these plants are normally used for the difficult deliveries and to treat serious diseases such as stomachaches and fractures.

7.2.2.3 Other gathering products

The local people also gather some other forest products to meet their daily and production demands. These include materials for building accommodations for both people and domestic animals (such as woods, different kinds of bamboos, neohouzeauas and alang grass), fuels (such as firewood and leaves of trees), materials

---

[1] Dinh Van My (1997). "Biodiversity of Medicinal Plants in the Hoang Lien Mountains". In: R. T. Sobey (ed.) (1997), *Biodiversity Value of Hoang Lien Mountains and Strategies for Conservation*, Proceedings of Seminar and Workshop, 7-9th December 1997, Sa Pa district, Lao Cai province, Vietnam; SEE Forest Research Programme, London (ISBN 1873070 13 6): 42.

for making productive tools and hunting artefacts (such as woods, bamboos, ivory bamboos and silexes) and materials for producing family handicrafts.

- Materials for house construction for both people and domestic animals: The Yao's traditional house is made of wood. Therefore, wood is an indispensable material for construction purposes.

Normally, the local people live in their house for a long time. This house costs much labour of the local people and wood for their house in the first time of building this house. Thirty years later, or even more, they start to repair that house or build a new one. Alternatively, when the children grow up and then get married, their parents allow them to live in another house nearby their parents' house.

Before they build the new house, they must prepare the wood for this house construction. The quantity of wood for a house can be plentiful or little depending on the size of the house planned. Local people spend much time in this preparation, from about 5 years to even 10 years. Previously, they freely exploited the timber. Nowadays, they must give their application of the timber exploitation to the leader of the local administration before they cut down timber in the forest to build their house. They cut down trees only when they receive the local administrators' permission to the timber cutting. They normally receive this permission a short time after they give their application to the local administrative cadre. However, in some cases, there is some illegal logging, without permission. Timber is also the essential material for building huts in the burnt plots, for storehouses and animal shelters.

Many kinds of bamboo and neohouzeauas are gathered to make screens and walls for the huts in the upland fields and to be used as main materials for building houses for young and poor families. However, these trees are not plentiful in the Yao community, so that they are normally used as additional materials to build houses for people and domestic animals. In addition, they are main raw materials for weaving screens and fences of the home garden to fix the boundaries of gardening areas and to protect the farmers' gardens from destruction by some domestic animals.

Before pieces of sheeting made of mixed cement were introduced to the Red Yao people, the alang grass was the major raw material for roofing their houses. These grasses are very abundant and diverse in this region. They grow rapidly and abundantly in the upland fallow-fields. Many Yao households still use them to roof the houses for their domestic animals and some very poor households continue to roof their homes with these grasses.

- Materials for fuels: firewood is the most common fuel in the mountainous areas, especially where there is much forest.[1] The Red Yao inhabitants in Sa Pa district use firewood gathered in the forest as their major fuel. Although they use the electricity connected to their house from small-scale

---

[1] Be Viet Dang, Nguyen Khac Tung, Nong Trung, and Nguyen Nam Tien (1971). *The Yao in Vietnam*. Hanoi: Social Science Publishing House.

- Epprecht M. and Heinimann A. (eds.) (2004). *Socioeconomic Atlas of Vietnam. A Depiction of the 1999 Population and Housing Census*. Swiss National Centre of Competence in Research (NCCR) North-South, University of Berne. Berne.

hydropower, this energy only meets their demands for some of their electric lamps and for a television. To meet their other demands (such as for cooking, for making their house warm in winter and for drying *thảo quả* fruits), firewood is extremely important.

Firewood reserves and distances from the residential areas to the forests differ from one commune to another. For example, it is easier for the Red Yao in Nậm Cang commune to collect firewood than for the Yao in Tả Phìn commune because the forest in Nậm Cang region surrounds their residential area. Sometimes, the people can collect firewood behind their house or get it in the forest plots about 300m - 400m from their house by foot. It is not very hard for the people in Bản Khoang commune to collect this fuel because the forest in this region remains relatively plentiful and is not very far from the local farmers' residential area. The Red Yao people normally gather firewood and then carry it to their home as soon as they finish their work in the upland fields.

Firewood consumption also differs from commune to commune and from household to household. To meet the demand for fuel for daily cooking, each household collects about two ivory bamboo dossers of firewood per day, equivalent to approximately 60 kg of firewood/day. However, the people gather firewood in certain months of a year, mainly in the dry season. Moreover, there is a quantitative difference in the firewood gather in different communes.

Many households in Tả Phìn commune have to burn less of this fuel than their really demand because of the two following reasons. First, the firewood is increasingly rare. Second, the people lack labour for this collection because they are busy following the tourist to sell products of their handicrafts. In comparison, the people in Bản Khoang and Nậm Cang communes consume as much firewood as the actually need. They consume this fuel not only for their daily demands (such as for cooking and making their house warm in winter), but also for the desiccation of a great amount of *thảo quả* fruits.

As mentioned in the previous chapter, the planting and selling of these fruits in the communes of Bản Khoang and Nậm Cang are more dynamic than in Tả Phìn commune. This means that the requirement of firewood of the people in these two communes is much higher than in Tả Phìn commune. The drying of *thảo quả* requires a lot of firewood. A ton of fresh *thảo quả* fruits consumes $5m^3$ of firewood. Therefore, the available dry firewood cannot meet this requirement.

The local people cut some trees down or cut off branches of some trees to get fresh firewood, despite the local administrators' prohibition of felling trees for firewood. They prepare enough firewood for the *thảo quả* desiccation in the year before they dry these fruits. They keep firewood in the huts or heap it up in the forest area where they will make a drying-room. During that time, the fresh firewood becomes gradually dry and ready for the desiccation process.

In Yao communities, the output of *thảo quả* fruits differs from household to household depending upon the forestland area where the people grow these plants and upon its fertility. The forestland in Nậm Cang commune is normally much more fertile, plentiful and suitable for the growth of the *thảo quả* plant than in the rest communes. The area of these plants in Tả Phìn commune is the smallest in comparison with the other research locations. In this commune, the households have at least about 50 kg of dry *thảo quả* fruits and at most approximately 1.5 tons of these dried fruits. In comparison, the minimum output of dry *thảo quả* fruits of the household in Nậm Cang commune is 500 kg and the maximum is about 3 tons of these dried fruits. If we multiply these outputs with the firewood requirement for the desiccation, we will recognize the very great consumption of this fuel in the Yao community. This contributes to violation of the prohibition of cutting down trees for firewood.

Leaves of wild trees are also used for fuel and are commonly used to start a fire and to cover up the fresh *thảo quả* fruits. In addition, they are considered the "signal" for the completion of the drying process. The Yao people usually finish this process when these leaves are dry and ash-grey. They mainly collect different wild leaves in the drying stage of *thảo quả* fruits which normally coincides with September and October every year in the lunar calendar.

The local inhabitants have a tradition of burning incense at every ritual and ceremony. The raw material for their incense is the skin of a tree called "*mẹ hung*". The people gather this skin only on the seventh day of the lunar month every year because they believe that if they take them on another day, their ancestors and other spirits will disagree with them. They gather enough skins of "*mẹ hung*" for the whole year. They start to burn this dry skin as the incense on the fourth day of the lunar month.

- Raw materials for making productive tools and hunting artefacts: Wood and different kinds of bamboo are also used to make some productive tools (such as the rake, some parts of the plough, the handle of the hoe and the knife, the float of the fishing net, etc.). The fishing trap and basket, the frame of the traditional fishing net and the birdcage are made of ivory bamboos, rattan (mostly) and normal bamboos. The large bamboo can be used to lead underground and spring water to the pool of the Yao households and to the rice fields.

Some available raw materials can be used to make some parts of the hunting tools and weapons. In addition to the above use of the wood, it is used to make the hunting gunstock. Until now, all hunting guns are artefacts made by the local hunters themselves. The wood gun is unique in this area. In the past, silex was collected to make bullets. However, now local people do not search for silex because it is so scared in the area. Instead of searching for these bullets in nature, they buy them in the Sa Pa market and then use them in their traditional way.

- Raw materials for producing household articles: The Yao have an age-old tradition of making some household articles from raw materials in the forest. They make different kinds of baskets and other articles from rattan, normal bamboo, large bamboo and ivory bamboo. These materials are also used to make chopsticks and toothpicks. Some other household articles (such as scoops, spoons, tables, desks, different types of wardrobes, cupboards and cabinets, and bathtubs) are also made of the wood.

7.2.3 Gathering instruments

7.2.3.1 Instruments and tools for the collection of some wild animals

The Yao people have various instruments to collect wild animals. They use different tools and instruments depending on each species. For example, to gather bees, they use the most following common tools, sticks to poke at the beehive. Their hands are used to collect bee honey and young bees. Pieces of fabric and nylon cloth are used to catch the honey. Many different kinds of bottles and pots are used for containing the honey.

Instruments for fishing and collecting other aquatic products are both very abundant and diverse. They include both traditional and modern instruments of the Yao people. In principle, the modern fishing instruments have the same shape as their traditional instruments. The differences exist in their materials and sizes. Fishing instruments include the casting-net (*mủng*), the fishing-net (*làn vâng*), the racket (*chao chọ bẻo*), the fishing coop (*cẳng lùng*) and the containing instrument (*đinh*).

Some fishing instruments (such as the *cẳng lùng*, the *đinh* and the frame of the *chao chọ bẻo*) are made from rattan, ivory bamboo and normal bamboo which are available in the forest. These instruments are still the artefacts of the local people.

The design of the casting-net is that one end of the net is tied up and the other end is attached by an iron chain which helps the net to sink rapidly as soon as it has been cast. This tool can catch fishes quickly and correctly.

The local people currently use two different fishing nets to catch fish. The first kind of fishing net is the traditional one, with a frame made of irony bamboo and its net made by weaving cotton strings together. The local inhabitants make this net themselves. The second fishing net is the new one which has been introduced in the Red Yao community for about 20 years. Its net is made of plastic strings which are bought in the regional market. The local people use the fishing net in a way which is different from using the casting net. It is possible for the people to catch fish quickly when they use the casting net. Contrarily, they have to spend a longer time to catch the fish when they use the fishing net. It can be said that the fishing net can be used as a "trap". When fish touch the net, they will be caught in it.

Another instrument used for a fine catch of fish and other aquatic products is the tool of electric wires. With this instrument, the local people can catch a great amount of aquatic products, mostly fishes in a short time. However, in some cases, they can have some small-scale accidents while they use it, due to carelessness. Although it is not deadly, it can injure somebody. Therefore, only young people use this instrument to catch of aquatic products.

Although most of these instruments are for catching fish, some can be used to catch other aquatic products as well. For example, in addition to catching fish, the *chao chọ bẻo* can be used to catch shrimps and crabs. The *cẳng lùng* is laid in the spring. The fishes and the shrimps will fall into it.

7.2.3.2 Instruments and tools for gathering wild vegetation

The most elementary and available tool for gathering different kinds of wild vegetables and mushrooms is the local farmers' hand, mostly the female hand. It is relatively easy for the local people to collect these plants by hand because the useful parts of plants are mainly their branches and tender tops.

Some productive tools are additionally and effectively used to gather particular forest products. For instance, to take several tubers out of the earth, the local people use the spade, the hoe, the stick and the knife. Another example is that in some cases, it is hard for them to gather some kinds of tough wild vegetables by hand so they have to cut these plants with a knife or sickle.

One of the most multifunctional tools of the Red Yao people is the dosser. Local farmers use this large basket that can be carried on their backs for various purposes. However, its main functions are those of container and to transport tools. Farmers often use it to carry different kinds of seeds to the lowland and upland fields. They also use it to carry the firewood and other forest products as well as to bring their agricultural products home. This tool is additionally used to store food.

Some productive tools are used for the gathering of the available forest products, mostly wild vegetation. Most of them are the Red Yao's artefacts made of the available raw materials in the forest. They are really multifunctional and handy.

7.2.4 Variety of purposes and usages of products from gathering

The products from gathering in the wild are used for several purposes. They can be processed into food and foodstuffs for people and domestic animals. They are also raw materials for building houses, making productive tools and household articles. Some wild plants also serve as fuels. Additionally, they are used as goods and herbal medicine.

- As food and foodstuff for people and domestic animals: this is the major purpose for the local farmers.

For example, the bee and its products (honey and wax) can be used in various processes. In the season of the bee collection, the young bees are cooked with oil and salt as the local inhabitants' daily meal. This is one of the Yao's favourite dishes. The bees' honey is normally used as a drink in the Yao community.

Most of the wild vegetation meets the Yao families' demands for green vegetables and foodstuffs. They supply a great amount of vegetables for their domestic animals.

- As the raw materials for building houses and cattle-sheds, for making productive tools and household articles and for the fuel: As mentioned, some products of gathering can meet such daily requirements of the Yao. They supply local people with raw materials to produce many tools and instruments for their production and daily life. This is a common phenomenon in subsistence societies.

- As goods: The gathering of forest products by local farmers traditionally met most of their daily demands. However, in the recent years, the Yao have begun to use some products of gathering for commercial purposes.

For example, if the people collect a lot of honey, they will sell some depending on the amount available. The Red Yao do not use the beeswax for their own household use. However, they still collect it and then sell it to the Hmong people. The Hmong people dye their cloths and put a good shine on their clothes by using this wax.

The stream fishes are a great favourite of both local people and tourists. The local people sell these fishes to the regional restaurants. In summer, the stream fishes are figured in many restaurants in this region.

Many wild pharmaceutical plants are well-known and provide valuable goods. A few Yao people, mostly the herbalists, collect them. They then process these plants for their domestic demand and for sale according to medical prescriptions. In addition, many Yao women collect and sell them in the Sa Pa market or sell them according to fresh medical prescriptions to the Kinh who live in Sa Pa town. The purchasers boil these medicines and use their steam for a sauna, and use their decoction for baths to treat tiredness and influenza.

- For the medicinal purposes:

There are abundant and various ways of using and processing the wild animals and vegetation as medicine. Besides their use as food, bees and their honey are also effective medications that cure many diseases, especially the stomach ache and diseases of the digestive tract. Bees can be cooked along with often food or soaked in rice alcohol, and then used for treatment of diseases and health care in general.

Normally, the most common parts of herbal plants, especially small plants, used for treatments are the stems or trunks, branches and leaves. Additionally, local people also use their fruits, pips, roots or tubers, skins of medicinal plants and of their fruits, etc. for the treatment. In general, the Yao people do not use just a single part of the herbal plants to treat diseases, but use a combination of many different parts of the plants to make a medical prescription, depending on each disease. The prescriptions are, therefore, various in their species. They are used to treat common diseases as well as for over-all strengthening and prevention of malnutrition.

These medicinal herbs are normally used in the form of herbal teas and decoctions. Additionally, they are cooked as vegetable broths or used as salad, as many are green vegetables appropriate for daily meals. For example, soups of the *"rau tầm bóp"* (*lả peo lay*) and the pennywort can cure some diseases caused by high temperatures and fever. The raw wild banana can cure the diarrhoea.

7.2.5 Variety of domestication of some products from gathering

The Yao's knowledge of taming some wild animals and the domestication of some wild vegetation is vast and valuable. However, nowadays, most villagers cannot remember all the stories of the domestication of these animals and plants because of their oral transmission. It is just possible for us to search for some of these stories in the fortune writings of some well-known shamans in Yao villages.

The Yao's legend of the appearance of rice and its domestication can be found in their fortune writings. Among the local rice varieties of the Red Yao people, the *Bèo chìm kìm* (wild ordinary rice) derives directly from its uncultivated origins, as its name implies. The Yao people in Nậm Cang commune also have a legend of their domestication of rice from a wild variety brought by a mouse. Until now, this legend has been kept in the fortune writing of the shamans. According to this legend, the lineage of *Phàn* resided first in a certain area in China. At that time, the head of this lineage was the leader of the Yao people. All the people had nothing to eat. Therefore, they had to collect different kinds of wild tubers, fruits and vegetables to eat. One day, a mouse came into their community, brining with it an ear of an unknown grain plant. The Yao people picked this ear up off the ground; then, they sowed land with its grains. A short period after this sowing, the young plants sprouted from these grains. Thenceforth, this plant has become the staple food of the local people. This is how rice appeared in the Yao community. Later, a dragon brought water to the people. As a result, their rice developed well. Therefore, the dragon is considered a symbol of water. From that point on, the people only plant their rice after the day of "*thanh minh*", which was a day the dragon brought water to them and which falls on March fifth, the so-called grave visiting festival.

Thanks to the sacred appearance of rice, the local farmers believe that a certain spirit manages each part of the rice. Thus, to manage all the rice, there are various spirits. They are the spirits of rice ears and grains, of the rice stem, and of rice roots.

In addition, according to this legend, much rice in the Yao fields died during a drought that lasted 3 years. At that time, the people heard that the weather in the neighbouring land (meaning Vietnam nowadays) was so good that the farmers had enough food for three years, even when they only cultivated crops in one year. Thus, they brought their rice seeds with them to this new area and they have stayed there ever since. This legend helps prove that dry rice pre-exists the wet rice in the Yao community, and proves that their local rice derives from China.

By searching for food in the forest at the risk of food poisoning, the people found out which wild vegetation was edible and which inedible. Unfortunately, today, no one remembers the complete category of these plants.

Apart from rice, the Yao people also domesticate other wild plants. These include the plum, some different kinds of orchids and the "*cây chân chim*." The wild damsons (*hìa pìu heng*) were previously so abundant that local people did not grow them in their home garden. Some people have grown these trees in their garden for the past four years because of their interest and the increasing rarity of these trees. However, they have not fruited yet. Orchids are domesticated due to their extreme beauty. Additionally, many nice wild orchids are being gradually rare so that it is very hard for the local people to find them in the forest. Therefore, it is obvious for the local inhabitants to withdraw wild orchids from the forest and then grow them in their home garden in order to store these wonderful flowers. The "*cây chân chim*" is both an ornamental and herbal plant. Thus, they are domesticated to serve both purposes for the local people.

The currently domesticated bamboo varieties derive from wild bamboo. It is currently very hard for people to find wild bamboos. Local people domesticate the wild bamboos and then gradually develop them in their gardens or in plots of bamboo that are mainly common in Nậm Cang commune (Sa Pa district, Lao Cai province). This is the main raw material for making productive tools, and building houses and cattle-huts.

7.2.6 Some taboos relating to gathering

The Red Yao people maintain some taboos concerning gathering, although these are less various and multiple than the taboos regarding hunting. They do not destroy the beehive in the paddy storehouse or in the granary and collect the honey there. The honeybees (*muổi mung*) sometimes come to these houses and then make their nests there. According to the local people, the bee symbolizes luck and wealth. They have a folk proverb that "*muổi mung tò bèo uồn*", meaning that the bees bring the paddy soul to the people. Good fortune will visit the people who live in the house where a beehive exists. The bees normally make their nests in the paddy storehouse as soon as the local people carry harvested rice from the field to this house. In this case, they are considered the convincing evidence of having fixed the right day for the paddy storehouse's construction. Many people begin to collect the honey only when the bees leave their storehouse and no longer live in this nest. According to the local inhabitants, if they destroy the bees' nest while the bees are still in their nest, they will lose their good fortune.

In addition, people observe particular taboos concerning the gathering and collection of some plants, mostly of rare and valuable medicinal plants, in order to maintain them for further and long-term use. For example, instead of collecting all the plants in a clump, the people always reserve some healthy plants in this clump to assure their continuous growth. They should think about the amount of plants they want to collect in order to avoid wasting these kinds of plants. In this way, people contribute to maintaining and conserving the biodiversity of the forest plants.

7.3Gender roles in the forage economy

In societies where people live mainly on the forage, or hunting-gathering economy, labour is differently divided between men and women. In studies of the forage economy practised by the Hadza people in Africa, James Woodburn (1968) reported that men were responsible for hunting while women were much more involved with gathering.[1] In the case of Australia in the period of 1950-1960, the division of labour in the communities of native Australians was similar to the case of the Hadza people.[2] Unlike these two groups, the Yao people in Sa Pa district are not pure hunters or gathers, but rather

[1] James Woodburn (1968). "An Introduction to Hadza Ecology". In: Richard B. Lee and Irven DeVore (eds.) (1968), *Man the Hunter*. Chicago: Aldine.

[2] Margaret McArthur (1960). "Food Consumption and Dietary Levels of Groups of Aborigines Living on Naturally Occurring Food". In: C.P. Mountford (ed.), *Records of the Australian-American Scientific Expedition to Arnhem Land, Vol. 2: Anthropology and Nutrition*. Melbourne: Melbourne University Press: 92.

agriculturalists. However, their economy is dominantly one of subsistence. In addition to agriculture, they also depend on the forest for their subsistence. In their communities, Yao men are mainly involved with hunting and logging while women are mainly responsible for the gathering and domestication of wild plants. However, in their communities, there is an exchange of labour between men and women. Both help collect firewood and some common kinds of vegetables. In addition, Yao women in some cases also hunt some small animals with their husbands despite their sporadic contribution.[1]

Among the Yao people in Sa Pa district, rapid population growth and high population density have made non-cultivated food sources gradually rare. The Yao people in Tả Phìn commune spend much more time in timber work, hunting and gathering than do the Yao people in two other research areas, because their forest is less extensive and far more eroded. This means that the gathering practised by the women of the Tả Phìn commune is much more time-consuming than that of the Bản Khoang and Nậm Cang women. It is evident that before new rice varieties were introduced to their communities, they had a clear shortage of cultivated food, and thus most of them had to collect wild vegetables in the forest. However, at that time, it was already hard to find these vegetables because of their scarcity. The serious problem happens to the Yao people in all communes when they need timber for their house construction. Nowadays, similar problems occur to people in all communities. However, levels of these problems differ from commune to commune depending on the forest areas. The people with less forest have much more difficulty in accessing forest products than those who have more forest accessible.

7.4Roles of institutional arrangement

Many studies of natural resource management and ecology show that government policies play a crucial role in protecting ecosystems, particularly the forest and wildlife in the forest. According to J. Fairhead and M. Leach (1996), the political aspect has a strong impact on the forest and forest products, including even wild animals and vegetation.[2] This is not only important for the protection of ecosystems in Ghana and in southern Africa, where they studied, but also for many countries in the world. Vietnam is obviously not exclusive, because mountains and hills occupy one third of the country's total areas.

In Vietnam, apart from policies of land use as one of the most important policies to develop agriculture and forestry, the government has issued many policies to protect the forest and ecosystems that are gradually being degraded. Up to 2000, the government had issued 48 legal documents; ministries and their

---

[1] The exchange of labour among men and women in the hunting-gathering economy also exists among the aboriginal Australians, as commented by Marshall Sahlins (1972) which is quite different from the study by Margaret McArthur (1960) (See more: Marshall Sahlins (1972). *Stone Age Economics*. Chicago: Aldine-Atherton, Inc.; Margaret McArthur (1960). "Food Consumption and Dietary Levels of Groups of Aborigines Living on Naturally Occurring Food". In: C.P. Mountford (ed.), *Records of the Australian-American Scientific Expedition to Arnhem Land, Vol. 2: Anthropology and Nutrition*. Melbourne: Melbourne University Press: 92).

[2] J. Fairhead and M. Leach (1996). *Misreading African Landscape: Society and Ecology in a Forest-Savana Mosaic*. Cambridge: Cambridge University Press.

branches had issued 47 documents. At the same time, local governments have also issued texts giving provincial and communal cadres specific instructions for implementation of this law. Among these, it is necessary to refer to these policies which are most remarkable and have the strongest impact on forest protection and development, as follows:

- 1991 Forest Protection and Development Law;
- 1992 Decree 327/HĐBT on policies on the use of bare land, denuded hills, forests, alluvial flats and water bodies;
- 1994 Decree 02/CP on allocation of forest land to organizations, households and individuals for long-term use for forestry purposes; and
- 1998 Decision 661/QĐ-TTg on objectives, tasks, policies and organization for the implementation of the five - million - hectare Afforestation Programme.

The 1991 Forest Protection and Development Law emphasizes that forest is an important part of ecosystems and a valuable natural source in the country. It can be renewable. It has a great value for the national economy, and is closely connected with the life of the people and with the vitality of the nation.[1] This law regulates forest management, protection, development and utilization. By this law, the government manages forest and forest land by allotting it to organizations and individual households, the so-called "master of forest," for their long-term protection, development and utilization.[2] In addition, exploitation and protection of wild animals are also involved in this law. The "masters of the forest" have the right to exploit and develop common wild animals, except rare and valuable wildlife listed in a "Red Book."[3] In particular, the law strictly prohibits the people from forest destruction and burning as well as their transgression of forest and forest land.[4]

However, this law has really influenced the rural and mountainous areas since 1992 when the government issued the *Decree 327 referring to some policies on the use of bare land, denuded hills, forests, alluvial flats and water bodies* (the so-called Programme 327). This programme is evaluated as the first large-scale attempt of the Vietnamese government to involve individual households and organizations in forest management and development.[5] It concentrates mainly on reforestation in places where forests have been destroyed, and on the protection of remaining natural forests. In addition, the *1994 Decree 02/CP aims at allocating forest land to organizations, households*

[1] *Forest Protection and Development Law* (adopted by The National Assembly of the Socialist Republic Vietnam on 12-8-1991) (Extract) (1991). In: Parliament Council of Ethnic Groups. Session X (2000), *The policy and law of ethnic groups of the Vietnam Communist Party and the government*. Hanoi: National Culture Publishing House: 280.

[2] *Forest Protection and Development Law* (1991). Chapter 1, Article 2.

[3] *Forest Protection and Development Law* (1991). Chapter 1, Article 3.

[4] *Forest Protection and Development Law* (1991). Chapter 3, Article 20.

[5] Epprecht M. and Heinimann A. (eds.) (2004). *Socioeconomic Atlas of Vietnam. A Depiction of the 1999 Population and Housing Census*. Swiss National Centre of Competence in Research (NCCR) North-South, University of Berne. Berne: 42.

and individuals for their use within 50 years for forestry purposes. The responsibility of forest users is also linked with their interests and benefits based on their allocated forest areas. As a result, after 1991, mass exploitation of forests has gradually decreased. Namely, logging by state-owned enterprises decreased from 967,700 m^3 (in 1992) down to 648,300 m^3 (in 1997) (making up 67% compared with the year of 1992).[1] The general quantity of the logging in the period of 1990-1999 is 2.1 million m^3, occupying about 46.7% compared with the period of 1986-1990.[2]

Based on the experience and lessons learned from the Programme 327, a new structure of afforestation programme began in 1998 under Decision 661/QĐ-TTg (the so-called Programme 661) and commenced in 1999. The Programme 661 envisaged the establishment of 5 million ha of forest between 1999 and 2008 to increase the forest cover to 43% (from the present 35%).[3] One significant change is the targeting of 1 million ha for rehabilitation by natural regeneration. With all the above policies, in combination with policies of land use and of socio-economic development, the central government generally aims to protect the environment and develop biodiversity, which are indispensable requirements for ecological security and sustainable development.

As a result of the implementation of different policies and programmes of forest protection and development, in the case of Sa Pa district (Lao Cai province), as mentioned in the second chapter of this study, the amount forest cover of this district is relatively high, with 48.5% of the total area of this district. With such the figure, it seems that Sa Pa district achieves the ecological security (compared with the figure of 33% for minimum ecological security defined by FAO).[4] In reality, the forest cover of this district is very different from commune to commune. In 2003, the largest forest cover existed in the San Sả Hồ commune with 78.9% of the total district area whereas the lowest amount of forest cover was in the Sử Pán commune with only 20.6%. Therefore, there is a big disproportion in forest cover in different communes of Sa Pa district, including communes populated by the Red Yao people (see more: Table 4.3). This signals ecological insecurity in this region, because people in the communes with less forest land probably go to the commune with more forest to

---

[1] Parliament Council of Ethnic Groups. Session X (1998). "Report on the implementation of the Forest Protection and Development Law in combination with the implementation of the five-million-hectare Afforestation Program", No. 215 TT/HĐDT dated 28/10/1998, present at the fourth Session of the tenth National Assembly). In: Parliament Council of Ethnic Groups. Session X. (2000), *The policy and law of ethnic groups of the Vietnam Communist Party and the government.* Hanoi: National Culture Publishing House: 1109.

[2] General Statistics Office (2000). *Figures on Social Development in "Doi Moi" in Vietnam.* Hanoi: Statistical Publishing House: 89.

[3] The figure obtained from data by Epprecht M. and Heinimann A. (eds.) (2004). *Socioeconomic Atlas of Vietnam. A Depiction of the 1999 Population and Housing Census.* Swiss National Centre of Competence in Research (NCCR) North-South, University of Berne. Berne: 42.

[4] This figure is cited in Ngo The Dan and Tran An Phong (1993). "Good exploitation and conservation of our hilly-mountainous region". In: Institute of Agricultural Programming and Planning (1993), *Agriculture in the hilly and mountainous regions - Current situation and prospects.* Hanoi: Agricultural Publishing House: 9.

exploit or seek timber there. This is similar to the case of land disputes that occurred when people in areas with less cultivated land go to other areas with more cultivated land to occupy the land and cultivate there.

In addition to the government's control of forest resources, the Yao's customary laws also play an important role in forest management. Their laws refer to the rights of all members of their communities to utilization and protection of forest resources, for these responsibilities. Their traditional laws protect property rights for a person who finds an amount of forestland for his swidden milpa which is contradictory to the land laws of the central government. In addition, there are other similar property rights of plant ownership applied in the Yao communities. Despite these contradictions of their traditional regulations with the government's laws, many rules of their customary laws are dominant and effective in protecting holy forest, watershed and wildlife, as has been presented in this chapter.

These findings prove that central government with its policies has a significant role in forest management. However, the growing interest in involving local communities in forest management reflects the fact that government cannot resolve forest problems without participation from these communities, especially when state institutions are in decline. In addition, it is found that redistribution and allocation of forestland and other forest sources to individual households and local communities has not ensured eradication of poverty; however, it has created more opportunities for local people to improve their situation.

7.5Summary

Forage economy still plays an essential role in the Yao community, although their agriculture has increased remarkably. Available food sources from the forest and the nature are diverse, including wild animals and plants as well as other forest products. Forest products help meet their demands for supplementary source of food and provide them with raw materials for basic household items and housing construction. In addition, in recent years, many people benefit from selling some forest products. The inhabitants' gathering of food from this source is their suitable adaptation to their surroundings and living environment. At the same time, it is also their traditional dealing with the food scarcity in history and in the present, especially in the hunger season and when people face natural disasters.

A fact is that natural resources in this region have been diminishing due to rapid population growth and environmental degradation in recent years in despite of all the efforts of the government and people. This situation still exists, although the local cadres and people have put many efforts into reforestation and limitation of burning forest for the farmers' shifting cultivation. In reality, the forest is gradually changing its function of a safety net for the poor into a trap laid for the people who live mainly on the hunting-gathering economy.

The variety of wild fauna and flora partly leads to a diversified knowledge of local people of these kingdoms, including their distribution, living conditions and rules of some particular species. This knowledge differs from region to region, from man and woman and from age to age. Male villagers have much experience in hunting and timbering. In comparison, female villagers are mainly responsible for the gathering, mainly gathering of non-timber forest products. However, in some cases, there is a labour exchange in this realm of economy.

An overlap in use and management of natural resources still exists in the local communities. To control and manage forest and other natural resources, particularly the forest sources, there are also two systems of institutional arrangements: the Yao's customary laws and governmental laws. Although there are some contradictions between these two systems, the customary laws still prove their importance in this realm, particularly in the protection of holy forest, watershed and some wild animals and vegetation. It is important that a shift in control of forest land from the central government to individual households and communities create more opportunities for them to improve their living situation and their access to food sources.

Chapter 8
POTENTIALS AND CHALLENGES TO MAINTAINING YAO'S LOCAL KNOWLEDGE AND ACHIEVING FOOD SECURITY

8.1 Potentials of maintaining Yao's local knowledge and achieving food security

8.1.1 Policy aspects and institutional arrangement

In the last forty years, many policies of the Vietnamese government have been made and implemented in the whole country. In addition, the government has made some other policies and special programmes for remote and mountainous regions (see Chapter 4, Part 4.3; and Chapter 7). These policies have greatly helped the mountain people to stabilize their residence and develop agroforestry. As a result, their living standard is much higher than before. The fact proves that the central governments with their policies play an indispensable role in resolving problems in the country and particularly in local communities. Government's efforts have effectively targeted the poorest segments of the population in rural and urban areas. The effects of the government's policies can be found in detail throughout this study.

However, increasing interest in involving local communities in natural resource management, particularly that of agricultural and forest land, proves that the communities also play an essential role. It is obvious that there are some contradictions between communities' customary laws and the laws of the central government. However, it is hard to deny their effects on the control and management of the community.

8.1.2 Cultural aspects

8.1.2.1 Red Yao's tradition of solidarity, of mutual affection and help in living and in production

The Yao people live mainly on agriculture which depends on the weather. Therefore, they face many risks in their life and as a result cannot live apart from their community, as they always help each other out in the face of risks and difficulties. In this way, they gradually create a good tradition and practice. These include their reciprocal protection and mutual exchange in agricultural practise, which is shown for example through their mutual labour exchange and support with food for the hungry, etc. For instance, the Red Yao in Nậm Cang commune (Sa Pa district, Lao Cai province) gave an amount of money and food to the Yao people and other ethnic groups in the same district in the recent years to help them overcome their problems. In 2000, they supported the people in Thanh Kim commune with 1 million VND to help them recover from a natural disaster. In the same year, they mobilized 16 households living distant from the communal centre to move to another place in order to protect them from a landslide. In 2004, they supplied 1,237 kg of rice to the Red Yao people in Tả Phìn commune to help them out of a food crisis caused by the extremely poor harvest that year.[1]

[1] Nậm Cang Communal People's Committee (2005). *Summary report of the term of 2001-2005 and direction and mission of the work in the period of 2005-2010.*

Additionally, their experiences in living and in production are gradually handed down from generation to generation, from individual to individual and from village to village. Until now, although their small-scale society has undergone new changes, the Red Yao have maintained these advantages of their tradition. This contributes to reinforcing the relative stabilization and justice in their communities.

In terms of their social arrangement, therefore, the above aspects of traditional culture reinforce social justice in the local community and make the local people see voluntary observance of their customary laws and regulations as a moral standard. This kind of community is surely better than a society where is "developed", but short of justice, instable and abundant in crime, as commented upon by Hoang Xuan Ty.[1] It is found that the solidarity and cooperation are indispensable conditions for a long-term and stable development in the ethnic communities, including in the Red Yao community.

8.1.2.2 The Yao's experience and knowledge in production and in access to non-cultivated food sources as an adaptable behaviour towards the environment.

Despite the Yao's application of some modern agricultural technology, their traditional knowledge and experience of production and access to non-cultivated food sources still play a significant role in supporting them with food. It is evident that their traditional classification of soil helps them to recognize the potentialities of each kind of soil, and they therefore cultivate appropriate crops. In addition, they know, none better than they, which tools should be used for tilling which kind of land. Therefore, their own artefacts are more qualitative and durable than those which are bought in the Sa Pa market.

Apart from these, in many cases, it is impossible to apply modern techniques to their cultivation because of their partitioned terraces, the weather and soil conditions in their communities which is only appropriate to the local varieties. In these cases, their traditional methods are continuously more optimal and effective than the new ones. For example, the Yao's traditional irrigation system in their sloping land reflects their adaptation to the environment, as it is impossible to construct and use modern irrigation system to irrigate some of their wet-rice terraced fields. Their traditional system is however low cost, as it is constructed from raw materials available in nature. Similar advantages of Yao knowledge are discussed in detail in previous chapters.

8.1.2.3 Educational significance of some agricultural ceremonies.

While the Red Yao people have some mystical rituals, other festivals and ceremonies are educational. For example, their harvest festival (*Nhận xèng hảng*) is both culturally and educationally significant. In their community, a rich harvest is convincing proof of the good cultivation and efforts of its owners. Their conception of food, thanks to this, becomes clear by describing their harvest. According to them, avoiding work will not bring a good result.

---

[1] Hoang Xuan Ty (1998). "Part 1: Definitions and Roles of Indigenous Knowledge". In: Center for Ecological and Forest Studies (1998), *Indigenous knowledge of agriculture and natural resource management among the people in the uplands*. Hanoi: Agricultural Publishing House: 29.

Therefore, when they achieve good harvests, they pride themselves on their achievements. Contrarily, when they get poor harvests resulting from insufficient work, they are ashamed of these bad results. This is similar to the importance of Trobrianders' yam harvests as described by Bronislaw Malinowski (1935). Every Trobrianders feels insulted if the others consider him "no food thine" or "thy hunger".[1]

In the Yao's household and community ceremonies, food is displayed as ceremonial offerings to their ancestral and other spirits. This creates good opportunities for the local people to maintain and preserve some of their flavourful local varieties. Particularly, offering the rice variety of *Bèo heng nó* to their ancestral spirits helps them to preserve this variety despite its low productivity.

Additionally, according to the Yao's tradition, after every January 15th, when the people begin to prepare for their new seasons, elder villagers and the head of the village normally organize the festival of ground breaking ("*xuống đồng*") in order to start working in the New Year. In this festival, many Yao people take part in working contests. Nowadays, local administrators have developed this festival thanks to its educational importance. This reflects their skill at cultivating and producing food.

8.1.3 Initial development of a market-oriented economy

Some studies about the mountainous regions of Vietnam show that it is difficult for the mountain people to have access to markets. This is considered one of the challenges of the uplanders to overcome poverty.[2] However, on the contrary, Sa Pa is an exception. Sa Pa has been one of the famous tourist resorts of Vietnam since the French colonization in the early 1900s. By 1915, Sa Pa, or *Chapa* called by the French, has developed a reputation as a promising summer holiday destination among French colonists in Hanoi. Dozens of villas in the French style were built over the three decades while a number of the Kinh, the so-called *Annamites* by the French, arrived to provide basic services and skilled labour required in this settlement.

The development of tourism in addition to its services in this region has created good opportunities for the local people, including the Red Yao people, to have an additional income. This source of income comes from selling their handicrafts to tourists, supporting restaurants in Sa Pa town with some of their

[1] Bronislaw Malinowski (1935). *Coral Gardens and Their Magic-A Study of the Methods of Tilling the Soil and of Agricultural Rites in the Trobriand Islands*. London: George Allen and Unwin Ltd. Ruskin House, England; American Book Company: 3.

[2] WB (2001). Project appraisal document on a proposed credit in the amount of SDR 87.9 million (US$110 million equivalent) to the Socialist Republic of Vietnam for a northern mountains poverty reduction project. Rural Development and Natural Resources Sector Unit, East Asia and Pacific Region, *Report* No: 21233-VN.

- Ha Que Lam (2002). *Hunger elimination and poverty reduction in the region of ethnic minorities in our country nowadays - current situation and solution.* A documentary book. Hanoi: National Politics Publishing House.

- Bui Minh Dao (ed.) (2003). *Some issues of poverty reduction among ethnic minorities in Vietnam.* A textbook. Hanoi: Social Science Publishing House.

valuable domestic animals or selling medicinal herbs in the Sa Pa market and in their own villages.

Particularly, in recent years, the main cash income from planting and selling *thảo quả* has remarkably changed the Yao household economy. The most important thing is that all these income sources are based on their long-term experience in production. However, there is a difference in this income in different communes and ethnic groups, depending on the quantity and quality of their forest land.

In addition to their income from selling some valuable agricultural products, the Yao also apply their traditional medicine to diversify their livelihoods. Herbalists have an additional income from treatment and healing. In some villages impacted by tourism (such as in Sả Séng hamlet, Tả Phìn commune), the people there have additional income from boiling medicinal herbs and then selling them to tourists as the bath with 50,000-80,000 VND/time of bath. However, in some cases, the price is not fixed, but is negotiated between the seller and buyer. Nevertheless, only a few people benefit from this source of income (3-4 households/village).

As another source of revenue from selling herbal plants, some Yao women gather different kinds of medicinal herbs used for baths in response to orders from Kinh people in Sa Pa town. Alternatively, as mentioned above, they gather these herbs and then sell them in the Sa Pa market. The Yao people probably maintain this income because their traditional medicine is well-known in the region. However, this source is unstable and differs from one tourist season to another. At the same time, with the increasing degradation of forest and natural sources, including of medicinal herbs, the people need to make changes in gathering or in domesticating some rare and valuable herbal plants for their long-term use.

In previous times, their experience with hunting and gathering helped them meet their domestic demands. Nowadays, the products resulting from their forage economy, such as firewood, medicinal herbs, some wild animals and some wild flowers (particularly wild orchids), have become valuable commodities. However, their exploitation has become excessive in some areas. The problem is now how to keep this exploitation at appropriate level. In this case, we meet once again a contradiction between food security and natural resource protection and development. Therefore, it is important to have specific instructions and support in training and technology to eradicate hunger and reduce poverty as well as to ensure food security in combination with protection of the environment and sustainable development. The fewer effective projects which combine development of the household-based economy and sustainable environment protection, as suggested by W. D. Sunderlin and his colleagues, also contributes to proving the importance of this combination.[1]

In Tả Phìn commune, some Red Yao and Hmong women are involved in a club for making brocade which is located near the Office of the Communal

[1] W. D. Sunderlin, A. Angelsen and S. Wunder (2003). "State of the World's Forests". In: FAO, *Forests and poverty alleviation*. Rome: Italy: 61-73.

People's Committee. A similar club exists in San Sả Hồ commune. These clubs gave work to 350 people with the average wage of 300,000 VND/person/month.[1] However, currently, it is hard for these clubs to develop well because of growing private sellers in the communities. These people, mostly little girls and women, normally follow tourists to sell them their handicrafts and brocades. Therefore, they can sell their products easier than the clubs can. However, in addition to their quickly and carelessly made of embroidery, these sellers also buy some of the embroidered items and then sell them to the tourists in order to earn as much money as possible. Unfortunately, they achieve bad results resulting from their low quality of their handicrafts.[2]

Over all, the development of tourism in Sa Pa district creates many opportunities for the people who have traditional professions and experience in production to develop their household economy. However, in the near future, one must be careful about this trade because it is not always beneficial to the poor because of its uncontrolled development.

8.2Challenges to maintaining the Yao's local knowledge and achieving food security

8.2.1 Physical constraints

The terrain in northern Vietnam is strongly partitioned, highly sloping and very complex. According to the FAO, agricultural areas in world's mountainous regions make up 65.9% of the total agricultural area in the world. Among them, some 25.5% of the upland area has a slope of more than 10 degrees. In Asia and the Pacific region, the upland agricultural area makes up 77.4% of the total agricultural areas of these regions. Among those, 45.6% of the upland has slopes more than 10 degrees.[3] In comparison, in Vietnam, 56.2% of the total mountainous area has slopes above 20 degrees.[4] The steep slopes are a main reason for the land erosion. The Yao people have a similar problem. Chapter 4 of this study refers to this characteristic of the terrain in Sa Pa district which has an average height of about 1,600m and is home to many ethnic groups, including the Red Yao people.

---

[1] Sa Pa People's Committee (2005), *Report on results of the implementation of 7 Lao Cai's Programmes towards the local levels in the period of 2003-2004*, No. 22/BC-UB dated 25/2/2005: 2.

[2] Yao's traditional ways of embroidering produce very nice products with the special streaks reflecting their specific characteristics. Tourists like them much. However, to do this, it takes them much time and labour. Therefore, in the recent years, many local people cannot completely observe their own ways of embroidering because they want to sell as much to the tourists as possible. As a result, many of their products are less traditional and well made.

[3] Cited in: Bui Quang Toan, Nguyen Van Thuan, Duong Van Xanh, and Nguyen Khang (1993). "Some surveys and studies recently done for agriculture of hilly and mountainous regions". In: Institute of Agricultural Programming and Planning, *Agriculture in the hilly and mountainous regions - Current situation and prospects*. Hanoi: Agricultural Publishing House: 18.

[4] Bui Quang Toan, Bui Thi Si, and Vu Cong Lan (1993). "Soils in our mountainous regions and the orientation for development planning". In: Institute of Agricultural Programming and Planning (1993), *Agriculture in the hilly and mountainous regions - Current situation and prospects)*. Hanoi: Agricultural Publishing House: 38.

8.2.2 Environmental constraints

Data collected from yearly surveys, from satellite imagery and photos show the increasing forest degradation. According to the General Statistical Office (2000), in the period of 1960-1990, Vietnam loses about 120,000-150,000 ha of forest per year.[1] The forest degradation has greatly increased: from 1.03% per year (1956-1966) to 1.48% per year (1966-1976) to 2.1% per year (1976-1986), and then in the period of 1986-1999 by 3.19% per year.[2]

Forest cover is different from country to country and from region to region. According to FAO, the forest cover occupies 41% of developed countries (particularly, 71% in Japan), 29.5% in the developing countries. The minimum for ecological security is considered to be 33%.[3] Compared with other countries, the forest cover in Vietnam has tended to decline, from 14.3 million ha (43.5% of the total area) of mostly primary rich forest in 1943 to less than 12 million ha nowadays (less than 35% of the total area). Among those, in comparison with the country's total forest area, the rich forests make up about 29%; the medium forests account for about 16%; and the poor forests comprise 41%.[4]

In Vietnam, the forest cover is different from region to region. According to the Forest Inventory and Planning Institute, the provinces in the Central Highland have the greatest forest cover, with about 55% of the total area. By comparison, the corresponding figures for the Northern Uplands, the North Central Coast, the South Central Coast, the Southeast and the Mekong River Delta are 36.3%; 43%; 38.5%; 20.8% and 8.5% respectively.[5] However, the forest cover in each region differs. In some areas, such as in the Northwest, the forest cover makes up less than 10%.[6] Up to 1990, the cover of the rich forest in Lao Cai province made up only 5.3%; in Lai Chau province 7.8% and in Son La province 12%.[7] In addition, many different kinds of valuable timber trees are destroyed; the wildlife is severely exploited.[8] As a result, many regions of Vietnam are in an alarming situation when it comes to ecological security. In the

---

[1] General Statistics Office (2000). *Figures on Social Development in the period of "Doi Moi" in Vietnam*. Hanoi: Statistical Publishing House: 6.

[2] Bui Quang Toan, Bui Thi Si, and Vu Cong Lan (1993). *ibid*: 40.

[3] Cited in: Ngo The Dan and Tran An Phong (1993). "Good exploitation and conservation of our hilly-mountainous region". In: Institute of Agricultural Programming and Planning, *Agriculture in the hilly and mountainous regions - Current situation and prospects*. Hanoi: Agricultural Publishing House: 8-9.

[4] Epprecht M. and Heinimann A. (eds.) (2004). *Socioeconomic Atlas of Vietnam. A Depiction of the 1999 Population and Housing Census*. Swiss National Centre of Competence in Research (NCCR) North-South, University of Berne. Berne: 42.

[5] Cited in: Epprecht M., Heinimann A. (eds.) (2004). *ibid*: 42.

[6] Bui Quang Toan, Nguyen Van Thuan, Duong Van Xanh, and Nguyen Khang (1993). "Some surveys and studies recently done for agriculture of hilly and mountainous regions". In: Institute of Agricultural Programming and Planning, *Agriculture in the hilly and mountainous regions - Current situation and prospects*. Hanoi: Agricultural Publishing House: 26.

[7] Vuong Xuan Tinh (2003). *Looking for food: The difficult journey of the Hmong in Vietnam (Anthropological Perspectives on Food Security)*. Unpublished paper.

[8] Nguyen Van Lung (2002). "Development of forestry in the upland for 10 years". In: Center for Natural Resources and Environment Studies, *Sustainable development in the upland of Vietnam: Look Back on the last ten years and problems*. Hanoi: Agricultural Publishing House: 406.

case of Sa Pa district, as discussed in previous chapters, unlike other districts in the country, forest cover here is relatively high, with 48.5% of the total area of this district. However, this cover is different from commune to commune (see more: Chapter 4). A tendency is that the people who have less forest and forest land normally have less chance to develop their agroforestry, particularly to plant *thảo quả*, their main cash crop.

There are many reasons for the forest degradation. Among them, its main causes include the political mechanism, the forest fire and the transfer of forest to other using purposes, and the shortage and the shortcoming of forest wardens.[1] In the period of 1970-1980, uplanders in the Northwest of Vietnam cleared 150,000 ha of forest every 2-3 years and used this area for 60,000 ha of dry-rice, 45,000 ha of cassava and 35,000 ha of maize.[2] In addition, many forest areas have declined partly because of the population growth which causes forest to be used for other purposes. The population growth creates increasing pressure for food, fuel and timber for domestic uses. Another reason for the forest decrease, according to Binh and Thuong (1989), is the shifting cultivation that causes forest fires. In the period of 1977-1986, 36,000 ha of forest of Hoang Lien Son province (including three current provinces of Lao Cai, Yen Bai and Nghia Lo) were destroyed because the local people burned their cultivated plots. Logging is another reason for the rapid loss of forest area. According to General Statistics Office (2000), in the period of 1986-1990, the output of timber which is cut down in the forest in the whole country reached 4.5 million m^3.[3] Since local institutions have implemented the government's policy of protecting natural forest, mass logging has remarkably declined. In the period of 1990-1999, the timber output reached 2.1 million m^3.[4]

However, in Sa Pa district, the exploitation of timber and non-timber products in the six recent years is different from the general situation of the country. According to data obtained from Sa Pa People's Committee, in the period of 2000-2003, the timber output gradually increased, from 2,042 m^3 (in 2000) to 3,720 m^3 (in 2003). In comparison, the output of timber tended to decrease in the following years, from 3,500 m^3 (in 2004) to 3,460 m^3 (in 2005) (Figure 8.1 and Figure 8.2). In addition to the reasons given above, another is that although forest rangers have tried to complete their tasks, they are short of number and lack of equipment and means for forest protection. Additionally,

---

[1] Parliament Council of Ethnic Groups. Session X (1998). "Report on the implementation of the Forest Protection and Development Law in combination with the implementation of the Five-million-hectare Afforestation Program", No. 215 TT/HĐDT dated 28/10/1998, present at the fourth Session of the tenth National Assembly. In: Parliament Council of Ethnic Groups. Session X. (2000), *The policy and law of ethnic groups of the Vietnam Communist Party and the government*. Hanoi: National Culture Publishing House: 1110-1111.
- Hoang Huu Binh and Nguyen Xuan Thuong (1989). "Potentials of Natural Resources of the Hmong's Living Area in Hoang Lien Son and Strategies for Exploitation". Hanoi: *Anthropology Review*. No. 2-3: 117-133.

[2] Hoang Huu Binh and Nguyen Xuan Thuong (1989). *ibid.*

[3] General Statistics Office (2000). *Figures on Social Development in the period of "Doi Moi" in Vietnam*. Hanoi: Statistical Publishing House: 89.

[4] General Statistics Office (2000). *ibid*: 89.

their institutional arrangement is inconsistent. Some of them are retrograde and degenerate; and they hands with forest offenders.[1] As a result, the illegal logging gradually increases despite the implementation of 1991 Forest Protection and Development Law in the mountainous regions. Illegal timber has increased from 562,600 m^3 (in 1992) to 952,100 m^3 (in 1997).[2] However, the real output is probably higher than these numbers.

Figure 8.1. Logging in Sa Pa district.

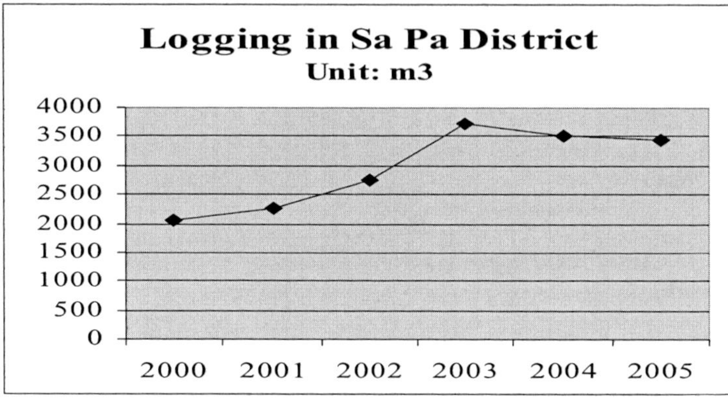

Source: Sa Pa People's Committee. 2004.

Figure 8.2. Exploitation of firewood in Sa Pa district

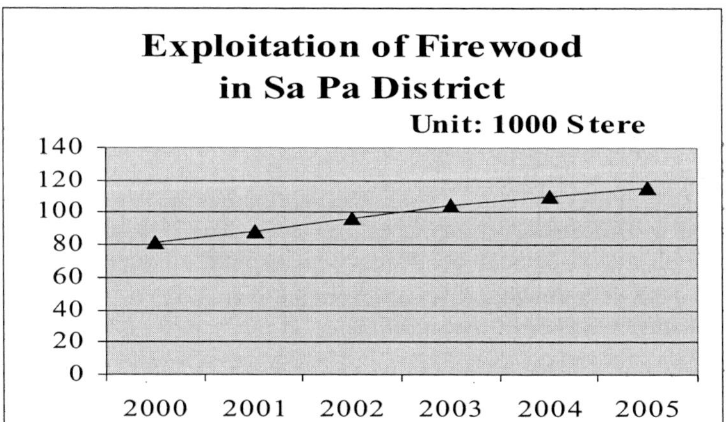

Source: Sa Pa People's Committee. 2004. ibid.

---

[1] Parliament Council of Ethnic Groups. Session X (1998). "Report on the implementation of the Forest Protection and Development Law in combination with the implementation of the Five-million-hectare Afforestation Program", No. 215 TT/HĐDT dated 28/10/1998, present at the fourth Session of the tenth National Assembly. In: Parliament Council of Ethnic Groups. Session X. (2000), *The policy and law of ethnic groups of the Vietnam Communist Party and the government*. Hanoi: National Culture Publishing House: 1111.

[2] Parliament Council of Ethnic Groups. Session X (1998). *ibid*: 1109.

It is evident that forest degradation continues to occur in many regions of the whole country in spite of the growing afforested areas. According to statistical data obtained from local administrators, although areas of reforestation have increased, this is only in the forest areas checked after planting trees there. However, in reality, the living trees in these areas make up only 70% of the total reforested area. In some regions, the reforested area does not even cover the forest that has burned. Additionally, the secondary forest areas also increase, but they are mostly young forest, and even include bare hills and mountains. This reflects the low accuracy of the data obtained from the local administrators.[1] The following figure shows the rate of income from forestry in Sa Pa district over 15 years (1990-2005). Based on this, we can recognize a difference of income from reforestation and forest exploitation in this district (Figure 8.3).

Figure 8.3. Income from forestry in Sa Pa district (1990-2005)[2]

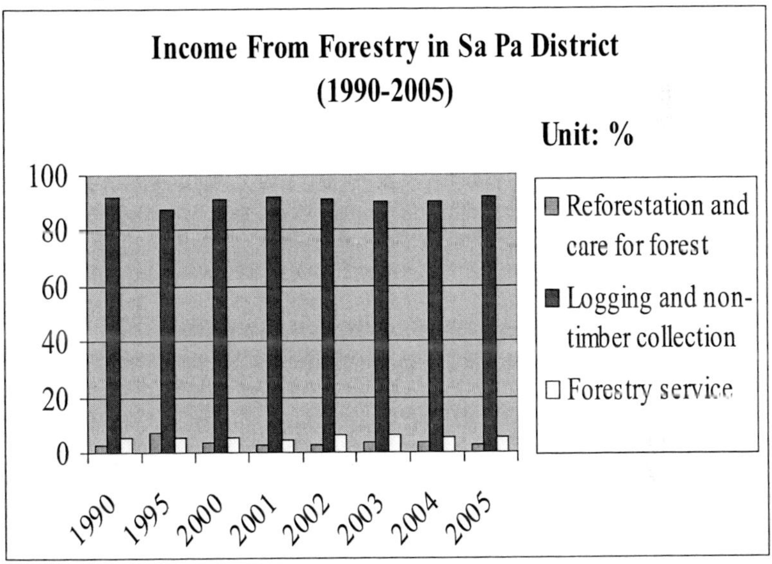

Source: Sa Pa People's Committee. 2004.

The degradation of forest and environment lead to many serious consequences, particularly for the people who live near the forest or who depend mainly on forest products. This leads to erosion and degradation of cultivated land, increased flooding and landslides, lack of water and a decrease in biodiversity. According to Vo Quy (2002), 60% of the land, mostly in the upland areas, is eroded and degraded leading to the decrease of wildlife. Many

[1] Parliament Council of Ethnic Groups. Session X (1998). *ibid*: 1109.

[2] Percentages of incomes from forestry in this figure are based on the cash income of the people in Sa Pa district (Table 3.25).

areas have a serious shortage of fresh water.[1] Therefore, crop productivity also gradually decreases. As an example, according to Ngo The Dan and Tran An Phong (1993), unterraced fields are highly subject to erosion with estimates of annual soil losses ranging from 250 to 350 tons/ha.[2] In the Red Yao communities, although I have not obtained data relating to the decrease of the soil fertility of their plots, a fact is that the productivity of their crops decreases despite their increase use of fertilizers and dung on their fields. Therefore, their demand of fertilizers gradually increases together with the erosion of their cultivated land. However, many households cannot afford to buy fertilizers for their cultivated crops, mostly for their staple food crops. The erosion results additionally from the shortening of the fallow period caused by the farmers' increasing demand for food and land. Their traditional knowledge of maintaining soil fertility is, therefore, less appropriate with the rapid land erosion and degradation of recent years. In this case, there is a close interaction of poverty, environmental degradation and biodiversity decrease. Food scarcity and poverty make farmers shorten their fallow period in order to meet their immediate demand of food. The cultivated soil is thus eroded. The land and environmental degradation accelerates the poverty. This is really a vicious circle of poverty. Therefore, in a study by Le Trong Cuc (2003), this is a process of "delitescence."[3]

In addition, environmental destruction and degradation erode the Yao's knowledge and their rich cultural diversity. Their knowledge of the environment and objects in this environment (such as the wildlife) declines along with the loss of these objects. Many valuable medicinal herbs and wild animals no longer exist in the Red Yao region. The knowledge relating to them is kept only in the memory of few elder villagers. In the near future, this knowledge will probably be lost forever.

8.2.3 Some administrative and institutional constraints

There are inconsistencies in institutional arrangements, and between the policy making and implementation. The government's policies aim at orienting and helping the uplanders to stabilize their lives and develop their household economy. However, some institutional arrangements are consistent and create roadblocks in implementation and management of these policies. For example, in the process of implementing the work of sedentarization and fixed cultivation, which has happened from 1968 until now, the government has altered the "Ministry in charge" many times. The highest responsible organ of this work was altered within a closed circle: State Committee for Ethnic Minorities ->

---

[1] Vo Quy (2002). "Review of environment issues in the mountainous regions of Vietnam in the last ten years: Real situation and problems". In: Center for Natural Resources and Environment Studies (2002), *Sustainable development in the upland of Vietnam: Look Back on the last ten years and problems*. Hanoi: Agricultural Publishing House: 103-105.

[2] Ngo The Dan and Tran An Phong (1993). "Good exploitation and conservation of our hilly-mountainous region". In: Institute of Agricultural Programming and Planning, *Agriculture in the hilly and mountainous regions - Current situation and prospects*. Hanoi: Agricultural Publishing House: 9.

[3] Le Trong Cuc (2003). "Biodiversity and human life". In: Le Trong Cuc, Nguyen Tat Canh and Tran Van On (eds.), *Proceedings on biodiversity and hunger eradication and poverty reduction in the mountainous regions of Vietnam*. Sa Pa, 26-28/5/2003: 16.

Ministry of Agriculture -> Ministry of Forestry -> State Committee for Ethnic Minorities and Mountainous Areas -> currently, Ministry of Agriculture and Rural Development. In addition, each province organizes and implements this work in inconsistent ways.[1] This leads to overlap and inconsistence in organizing and implementing the policies of the government in the localities.

As an example, Le Hong Tam (1985) points out that in the past years, there were some mistakes and limitations of specific and creative application of governmental policies. Thus, the traditional economy of ethnic minorities has not fully and extensively developed its potentials and strengths. They are not really integrated into the socio-economic structure of the large-scale socialist production which was started in the northern mountainous regions. These regions have not received proper support from the state to construct local infrastructure and apply modern technology to agriculture, particularly to intensive farming and animal husbandry, to the development of professions which are the perspectives of these regions.[2] This is more or less similar to assertions by W. D. Sunderlin and his colleagues (2003) when they refer to reasons for the tardy poverty reduction in some developing countries by timbering.[3]

In the case of Sa Pa district, irresponsibility on the part of some local administrators and their shortcomings in initiative in the instruction of production negatively influenced the farmers' food production. As a result, this led to a very poor harvest in 2004 in Tả Phìn commune and in some hamlets of Lao Chải commune. Some related departments have not had a deep understanding of the communal and village situations as well as of the farmers and their desires. In addition, their loose management of some forest wardens exacerbated continued forest destruction and the removal of forest products (including the valuable timber of *Pơ Mu*), that exists in some communes.

There are some limitations in implementation of forest protection and development laws. Although various instructions and notes for implementing these laws exist at different levels (national, regional and local), the government and local administrations have increased the spirit of responsibility and have many solutions to manage the forest and forest land throughout the country. However, the promulgation of these instructions is tardy and inappropriate with the desired achievements of these laws. Thirty-six instructions and notes are inappropriate to the forest protection and development law. Among those, it is necessary to modify five documents of the government, one document of Ministry of Agriculture and Rural Development, 26 documents of the Provincial

[1] Parliament Council of Ethnic Groups. Session X (1999). "Report on striving for narrowing a gap between the regions and between ethnic groups which is a significant objective to implement the policies of ethnic groups in the period of national industrialization and modernization", No. 392 TT/HĐDT dated 29/10/1999. In: Parliament Council of Ethnic Groups. Session X (2000), *The policy and law of ethnic groups of the Vietnam Communist Party and the government*. Hanoi: National Culture Publishing House: 1121.

[2] Le Hong Tam (1985). "Some ideas about the socio-economic development among the ethnic minorities in the northern mountainous areas". Hanoi: *Ethnology Review*, No. 1: 22.

[3] W. D. Sunderlin, A. Angelsen and S. Wunder (2003). "State of the World's Forests". In: FAO, *Forests and poverty alleviation*. Rome: Italy: 61-73.

People's Committees, 31 documents of the District People's Committees, and 5 documents of the Communal People's Committees. In addition, many documents and notes of the local administrations reveal wrong decisions on the transfer of land-use rights, and on the destruction of natural forest and reforested areas for growing coffee and tea. Apart from those, some other wrong decisions have resulted from the bureaucracy, their irresponsibility of some local administrators, or from purposeful acts against the law.[1] It is found that there are currently many positive changes in institutional arrangements and in government implementation in recent years. However, some of the situations still exist in the rural and mountainous areas.

In addition, there are contradictions between some agricultural policies and the environmental policies. In other words, there are challenges between policy makers and the people who implement and benefit from these policies; between those focused mostly an ensuring food security and those most concerned with biodiversity conservation.[2] This situation exists not only in Vietnam, but in many other countries as well. In a study by Wells and Brandon (1992) and by Gilmour (1994), since 1970, International Conservation and Development Programmes (ICDPs) have aimed at protecting the environment and forest biodiversity, along with efforts for improved livelihoods. However, most of these programmes and projects did not record great achievements, particularly in case of their conservation goals.[3] They are challenges to sustainable development which combines food security and environmental security. Therefore, although the uplanders have achieved remarkable economic development, their development is unstable and vulnerable. This results in vulnerability of food security for the mountain people.

8.2.4 Population problems - Rapid population growth and unequal population density in different communes of Sa Pa district

According to the general statistic data, the population growth of Vietnam decreased from 2.1% (in 1989) to 1.7% (in 1999).[4] However, this situation differs from region to region and from one ethnic group to another. In the case of Sa Pa district (Lao Cai province), the population has gradually increased (see: Figure 4.2, Figure 4.3 and Figure 4.4 of Chapter 4). This leads to a situation of "more people, less cultivated land". Therefore, in all cases of land disputes,

---

[1] Parliament Council of Ethnic Groups. Session X (1998). "Report on the implementation of the Forest Protection and Development Law in combination with the implementation of the Five-million-hectare Afforestation Program", No. 215 TT/HĐDT dated 28/10/1998, present at the fourth Session of the tenth National Assembly, in: Parliament Council of Ethnic Groups. Session X (2000), The *policy and law of ethnic groups of the Vietnam Communist Party and the government*. Hanoi: National Culture Publishing House: 1106.

[2] Nguyen Xuan Hong (2004). "Food security for inhabitants living in buffer zone of Bach Ma National Park: Challenges in development strategy". Hanoi: *Ethnology Review*, No. 2: 42-46.

[3] W. D. Sunderlin, A. Angelsen and S. Wunder (2003). "State of the World's Forests". In: FAO, *Forests and poverty alleviation*. Rome: Italy: 61-73.

[4] Khong Dien (2002). "Population Issues Relating to the Development in the Ethnic and Mountainous Areas in Vietnam". In: Center for Natural Resources and Environment Studies (2002), *Sustainable development in the upland of Vietnam: Look Back on the last ten years and problems*. Hanoi: Agricultural Publishing House.

defendants normally belong to the communities with numerous people, but limited cultivated land.

The rapid population growth means increased demands for food. In many upland areas, food shortages are still widespread. Therefore, to remedy temporary lack of food, in the period of 1980-1990, the government sent thousands of tons of food to the uplanders. This food support increased from 120,000 tons of food (in 1980) to 250,000 tons of food (in 1985) and 450,000 tons of food (in 1990).[1] According to General Statistical Office (2003), all levels of government and popular aids 13,600 tons of food and 36.7 billions VND to the hungry and poor. Poor households in 2002 include 30,000 households.[2] These solutions are necessary. However, this is not a solution to problems of food security for the poor.

8.2.5 Lack of means of production and lack of capital

Shortage of means of production and capital is very common in the rural and mountainous areas. Because the average population growth increases above 2.2% per year and the labour increases 3.5% per year, the area of cultivated land per household is reduced, about 0.1-0.3 ha/household. Particularly, in the South of Vietnam, about 5-7% of the total households has no cultivated land.[3] In Sa Pa district, land shortages contribute to the number of land disputes in recent years caused by pressures of population growth and the increasing erosion of cultivated land. According to data obtained from Sa Pa People's Committee (2005), there were 68 cases of land disputes as a result of 2004. Among those, there are 17 cases of Sa Pa town (occupying 25% of the total land disputes) and 51 cases of communes (making up 75%). Up to 2005, the local administrators settled 53 cases, comprising 77.9%. The rest are outstanding questions. Most communes of this district (15/18 communes, occupying 83.3%) are involved in these land disputes. In addition, there are some land disputes between communes of Sa Pa district with some communes of Bat Xat district. All these land disputes are related to cultivated land (Appendix 4).

In addition to the land, there is gradually insufficient water for farmers to irrigate all of their wet-rice fields, particularly since they are cultivating the new rice varieties. Therefore, like the case of land, there are also some conflicts relating to the availability and use of water for cultivation.

Many Yao households need more capital for investment in food production. In the case of priority loans, the amount do to lenders gradually increases. In 2003, 689 households of Sa Pa district asked banks for loans of 3,022 million VND. In 2004, the borrowers included 1,298 households with total

[1] Bui Quang Toan, Bui Thi Si, and Vu Cong Lan (1993). "Soils in our mountainous regions and the orientation for development planning". In: Institute of Agricultural Programming and Planning (1993), *Agriculture in the hilly and mountainous regions - Current situation and prospects*. Hanoi: Agricultural Publishing House: 41.

[2] Cited in: Nguyen Manh Hung (ed.) (2003). *Vietnam socio-economic of 2002, plan of 2003 - Integrate & Growth*. Hanoi: Statistical Publishing House: 23.

[3] Nguyen Quang Du (1993). "Current period and the issue of the rural development". Hanoi: *Philosophy Review*, No. 3: 36.

loans of 7,687 million VND. The average loan is 5.4 million VND/ household.[1] During the period of the Programme 135, 6,612 households in the entire district asked for banks for the priority loans of 24,965 million VND.[2] These loans are deducted from the capital source for priority which is valid from 3 to 5 years. Most of the borrowers use their loans to enhance production, such as by buying buffaloes, by claiming virgin soil and growing the *thảo quả*. However, some borrowers (mainly the Hmong people) use their loans for "wrong" purposes, such as buying rice alcohol or motorbikes. As a result, they are quickly insolvent. In addition, the banks and local administrators do not manage the loan effectively and do not speed up repayment of the loans. Thus, the source of capital is often used ineffectively. Another problem is that many Yao people do not dare to obtain a bank loan because they are afraid that they cannot repay this debt and the required interest. Therefore, they cannot develop their production as they would like.

8.2.6 Under-developed local infrastructure

In recent years, the socio-economic situation of the mountain regions has been much improved because the government, at different levels, has a combination of various development programmes funded by both the state and different non-governmental organizations in these areas. As a result of their efforts, many roads are built and upgraded. The surfacing of district-to-commune and commune-to-village roads was with naturally-occurring "as dug" gravel, where material of suitable quality is locally available, or with a mix of crushed stone and natural material. However, most village-to-commune paths remain simple footpath. Many of these have been more or less destroyed by natural disasters and the partitioning and sloping terrain in these mountain regions.

The transport and marketing networks in many communes of Sa Pa district are under-developed. Movement of the Yao people and goods into and out of their communes is very difficult, time-consuming and costly. In particular, it is normally impossible or very difficult for the people to reach communes during the rainy season because of very bad, slippery and unsafe roads. This situation exists not only in the community of the Red Yao people, but also in many communes of the whole country, particularly in the mountainous and remote areas.[3]

In the case of the national electrical system, up to 1999, 76.8% of the total communes and 65.3% of the total households of the whole country had access to

---

[1] Sa Pa People's Committee (2005). *Report on results of the implementation of 7 Lao Cai's Programmes towards the local levels in the period of 2003-2004*, No. 22/BC-UB dated 25/2/2005: 3.

[2] Sa Pa People's Committee (2005). *ibid*: 5.

[3] WB (2001). Project appraisal document on a proposed credit in the amount of SDR 87.9 million (US$110 million equivalent) to the Socialist Republic of Vietnam for a northern mountains poverty reduction project, Rural Development and Natural Resources Sector Unit, East Asia and Pacific Region, Report No: 21233-VN: 42.

- Ha Que Lam (2002). *Hunger elimination and poverty reduction in the region of ethnic minorities in our country nowadays - current situation and solution*. A documentary book. Hanoi: National Politics Publishing House.

- Bui Minh Dao (ed.) (2003). *Some issues of poverty reduction among ethnic minorities in Vietnam*. A textbook. Hanoi: Social Science Publishing House

electricity. However, the system reaches only 40% of the communes in the northern mountain. Access to this system is also different from province to province. Fifty-seven percent of the total communes in Hoa Binh province, for example, where the largest hydroelectric plant exists, access this system, but this rate falls to 31% in Cao Bang province, 22% in Lao Cai, 13% in Bac Kan, and 12% in Lai Chau.[1] In Sa Pa district, the rate of communes and households with access to this system is a little lower than the average rate for the whole country, making up about 10% of the total households of this district.[2] The objectives of the resolution of the Third National Assembly and with the Decision 22/1999-QĐ-TTg dated 13/2/1999 by the Prime Minister refer to a goal of about 60% to 80% of the total communes and about 60% of the total households of the whole country having access to and using the national electricity for living and production. However, it is very difficult to meet these objectives in the mountainous and ethnic minority areas. There, small-scale hydroelectric systems developed by the local people supplement national efforts. Most of the Red Yao people used these systems. For example, up to 2004, 190 households of Nậm Cang commune use their small-scale hydroelectric system.[3] Thanks to this, they can use the electricity for their televisions, radios, lamps and for other uses. However, their own electricity is unstable because of its small scale, and because power is normally limited in the dry season because of lack of water. Therefore, the national electric system is still very important for them.

8.2.7 Educational problems - Low and unequal educational levels

Education in Sa Pa district in recent years has obtained remarkable results. The material facilities of the education system have been greatly improved. This manifests itself by the increase of schools and classrooms. In addition, the number of teachers and pupils has gradually increased in the period of 2000-2006 (See more: Table 4.4 of Chapter 4). However, only 50% of all communes have achieved the goal of compulsory education of primary school for all children who are old enough; and few communes and the town provide compulsory education at the junior secondary school.[4]

In addition, the educational inequality between communes contributes to the decayed progress in hunger eradication and poverty reduction. Therefore, the gap between the poor and the rich tends to increase. In the communities of the Yao and of the Tay, the number of poor has increased, and those living in poverty include almost 10% of total households. In comparison, in the Hmong

[1] Parliament Council of Ethnic Groups. Session X (1999). "Report on striving for narrowing a gap between the regions and between ethnic groups which is a significant objective to implement the policies of ethnic groups in the period of national industrialization and modernization", No. 392 TT/HĐDT dated 29/10/1999. In: Parliament Council of Ethnic Groups. Session X (2000), *The policy and law of ethnic groups of the Vietnam Communist Party and the government*. Hanoi: National Culture Publishing House: 1122.

[2] Sa Pa People's Committee (2005). *Report on results of effectuation of the Programme 135 in the period of 1999-2005 in Sa Pa district*: 3.

[3] Nậm Cang People's Committee (2005). *Socio-economic situations*, Nậm Cang: 26/5/2005.

[4] Sa Pa People's Committee (2004). *Report on socio-economic situation in Sa Pa district in the period of 2000-2005*, Sa Pa: 12/2004: 13.

communities, the poor households are more numerous than in the other ethnic groups are. For example, the poverty in Hầu Thào commune reaches over 25%. Therefore, the various development projects by the government in recent years have achieved many remarkable results which have changed the face of the rural and mountainous areas in Vietnam. However, to achieve the desired results, the communes still face many difficulties.

8.2.8 Limitations of accessibility to information and to modern technology

This limitation derives from the ethnic minority people's educational constraints, the limitation of the Vietnamese language and the sense of shame in communicating with outsiders. In Red Yao communities, people mainly have access to information in the village meetings and then, from family members. In addition, the village and communal cadres and collaborators get different kinds of information through some short training courses in agricultural extension and through their meetings in the communal and provincial centres.

In recent years, many people can get information by watching television and by listening to radio. The Table 8.1 shows the accessibility of the people to the some different kinds of information by watching television.

Table 8.1. Rate of watching television of the people in Sa Pa district (Unit: %)[1]

No.	Communes and town	2001	2002	2003	2004	2005
	Whole district	23.7	27.9	36.6	44.3	50.0
1	Sa Pa Town	71.0	78.0	90.5	97.0	100.0
2	**Nậm Cang**	**54.2**	**55.3**	**64.1**	**66.1**	**97.5**
3	Suối Thầu	12.1	14.1	47.8	67.4	75.8
4	Thanh Kim	18.9	22.1	37.2	48.8	60.2
5	**Tả Phìn**	**7.0**	**11.8**	**24.9**	**37.6**	**46.4**
6	Bản Hồ	20.7	25.7	37.7	38.2	43.3
7	Thanh Phú	17.2	21.8	28.6	32.0	35.9
8	Sa Pả	3.4	5.7	17.1	31.1	41.7
9	Tả Giàng Phình	8.6	12.7	13.9	26.7	39.8
10	Bản Phùng	12.2	17.9	26.9	30.1	37.1
11	**Bản Khoang**	**12.2**	**20.6**	**26.3**	**29.5**	**34.6**
12	Trung Chải	9.3	13.8	15.7	26.9	33.2
13	San Sả Hồ	5.2	7.1	14.1	24.2	29.9
14	Sử Pán	4.7	8.0	16.4	23.2	28.6
15	Tả Van	12.6	15.9	17.8	20.0	28.4
16	Nậm Sài	17.4	17.4	19.5	21.9	26.3
17	Lao Chải	5.3	7.3	12.2	20.1	24.8
18	Hầu Thào	3.4	5.7	7.9	12,9	18.4

Source: Sa Pa People's Committee. 2004.

However, the favourite programme of most farmers is the movie channel, although some also watch the news and agricultural channels. But, they do not understand them completely because of their lack of fluency in

[1] My research areas are displayed in the boldface type.

Vietnamese. In some cases, the young people can understand something from these programmes. However, they are not sure that this information is appropriate to them. They are normally afraid of new thing and new alternatives. It takes a lot time for them to become familiar to new things. For example, when the agricultural cadres wanted to introduce something to them, they had to first do an experiment. Only when they succeed, then the other people would follow their advice.

8.2.9 Negative impacts of some cultural aspects

8.2.9.1 Traditional shifting cultivation

Shifting cultivation was a remarkable adaptation by the local people to conditions in the high mountain regions. However, nowadays, in the face of increasing environmental degradation, land erosion and shortages as well as rapid population growth, their traditional shifting cultivation with long-term fallow periods is no longer appropriate. Therefore, to maintain and increase the productivity of cultivated crops on the sloping land, it is necessary to change some methods in their cultivation, so their increasing demand of food can be met. However, to do this, the local administrations should help the local people to improve their production and their life with technical, capital and intellectual support. Nowadays, some new varieties have introduced to them. However, they have less experience in growing these well and cannot keep the new varieties for seed, but have to wait for the support of the local agricultural cadres.

8.2.9.2 Some ritual ceremonies

In addition to some nice aspects of their culture, the Red Yao maintain many ritual ceremonies which have negative influences on their production. For example, it is remarkable to refer to the worship of pests. If the people search and kill the pests in time, they can protect their crops from damage. However, in some cases, some households only organize the ritual to give the support of the spirits for the protection of their crops and they do not use another method to kill the pests. In some other cases, some households organize the worship for killing the pest; then they wait for the effect of that ritual. They only spray the pesticide for their fields damaged by the pests when they recognize that the spirits could not help them. In both cases, their cultivated crops are damaged and destroyed by the pests. Their action came too late for them to have a good harvest.

8.2.9.3 Some inappropriate traditional regulations in the current society

Nowadays, some regulations of the Yao's customary law come in conflict with the laws of the government. These include the right of land use and ownership belonging to the person who claims the virgin land first. The maintenance of these rules influences the process of the allocation of land, forest and forest land to households and organizations by the government. This also creates some land disputes by the contradiction between customary laws and the government's laws. Furthermore, this leads to a situation in which much land is concentrated in the households with few persons, and on the contrary, the household with many members own little land. The Red Yao people are patrilineal. Therefore, the son has a right to inherit land from his parents. In comparison, after the daughter gets married, she moves to the house of her parents-in-law and then lives with the family of her husband in the same house. In principle, she normally cultivates with her husband the plots which are shared by her in-laws. In this case, the number of people in her husband's family has increased, while the number in her parent's family has decreased. Meanwhile, their land area remains unchanged. In some special cases, her parent may share an amount of land with her and her husband to help them have enough land to cultivate. However, this is a rare example. It is found that when there is no change in land use and allocation from time to time in their communities, land disputes between them to obtain enough land to cultivate will arise.

8.3Summary

The ethnic minority people, including the Red Yao, have received a lot of support from different levels of government, in terms of policy, investment and special development programmes. As a result, their household economy has much improved. However, this economic development is still unstable and vulnerable because of the new changing environment. Nowadays, to achieve food security and develop their household economy, they meet with remarkable difficulties which involve all causes of poverty and challenges to local knowledge. It is obvious that the local people have to cope with the increasing shortage of the means of production (mostly, of land and water) and the diminishing of available food and natural resources together with rapid population growth. In addition, they also have to overcome many other physical, administrative, social and cultural constraints. These challenges are so great and complicated that the people cannot solve them without support from all levels of government as well as from non-governmental organizations. All of their efforts and their action programmes should aim at answering a question of how to achieve the economic development needed in combination with maintaining social and ecological security.

Chapter 9
CONCLUSIONS AND RECOMMENDATIONS

9.1Conclusions

This study shows that environmental and social conditions influence the economic structure of the Red Yao people in different communes, and vice versa. This structure is different from commune to commune. Income from tourism is much higher for the Red Yao people in Tả Phìn commune than in the two communes of Bản Khoang and Nậm Cang because the former community has been more strongly influenced by the development of tourism. However, their living standard is still worse than that of the people in the two other research areas because this income is unstable and they have a shortage of cultivated land. In comparison, the Red Yao people in Bản Khoang and Nậm Cang have a more stable income from their development of a farming system and through forestry. Their living standard is much higher than that of the Red Yao in Tả Phìn commune.

Despite this difference in income sources, this study found that all Red Yao communities live mainly on agro-forestry. Among these practices, cultivation plays a dominant role in food production for households. Up to today, local farmers maintain their traditional cultivation systems: swidden agriculture, wet-rice cultivation in the terraced fields and gardening in combination with forestry. Their farming systems mainly provide them with staple food, particularly rice and maize. *Thảo quả* (Amomum tsao ko Crev et Lem.), a cash crop which is maintained in semi-cultivated condition in the forest, contributes to remarkably improve the living standard of the Red Yao in all research areas. This is the main cash income of the local people.

Red Yao farmers have their own ways of classifying the natural resources (particularly land, water and biodiversity) that are different from those of scientists and the administrators. Their systems of land classification and their selection of cultivated crops appropriate for and compatible with the land and the weather help them to recognize the land's potential. Therefore, they work out a plan for evaluating the soil for their production.

The Red Yao's knowledge and their experience of food production and access to food manifest themselves in their relatively clear labour division. This division is based on a combination of traditional norms and comparative advantages. In agriculture, men are responsible for heavy work that requires their good health and their physical well-being. They undertake land tilling, constructions of houses for domestic animals and for keeping harvests, spraying of pesticides, making of tools for production, harvesting, and requirements of catching some animals for breeding. In comparison, women take responsibility for land clearing, sowing of seeds, transplantation of rice seedlings into the fields, putting of maize seeds into fixed holes dug by men, weeding, clearing of pests, harvesting, and feeding of domestic animals. Particularly, the Yao women have expertise in selecting and maintaining varieties of seeds. In addition, both men and women share the same work in the initial planting season and in harvesting. In the forage economy, male farmers have responsibility for hunting and timbering. Female farmers are knowledgeable about gathering, especially about the collection of non-timber products, and about the domestication of wild plants. In the case of generating cash income, excluding the sale of agricultural products, women farmers have a dominant role. They earn additional money from selling their self-made traditional handicrafts and from selling medicinal herbs that they collect. In the case of worship, male shamans play an important role in performing different ritual ceremonies. In general, women farmers have a significant role in producing and processing food for their households. They additionally spend much more time on their domestic work, which is normally considered unproductive and unprofitable.

To control the Red Yao's small-scale societies, there are parallel institutional arrangements: their customary laws and the laws of the central government. Among these, the government's laws have gradually played a dominant role in controlling the local societies. These laws help the local people to stabilize their residences, to develop their production and to create opportunities to access to food and to protect the environment. However, despite some contradictions with government land regulations, the Yao's customary laws still play a key role in their communities. This role manifests itself in community solidarity and in the protection of the environment, particularly of holy forests and watersheds.

Despite the efforts of the government and of the Red Yao, many communities are still driven into poverty. However, this situation is different from commune to commune and from ethnic group to ethnic group, and even from one sub-ethnic group to another. Except for the majority of the Kinh people in Sa Pa district, the living standard of the Red Yao people is higher than that of the other ethnic minorities in the same district. On the contrary, poverty remains in Hmong communities. However, like the Red Yao people, the poverty of the Hmong people is also different from commune to commune depending on social and environmental factors.

This study has found that the development of agro-forestry practised by the Red Yao people in Nậm Cang commune is appropriate to the environmental and socio-economic situations in this area, leading to a better life for the local people. This proves that diversified livelihoods are important. However, for the mountain people, productive sources are indispensable to obtain food and to achieve food security for their households.

9.2 Recommendations

Each mode of production has its own direct and long-term influence on the possibility of production and of the protection of natural resources and the environment. Therefore, an investment in rehabilitating the forest, managing the land and developing agro-forestry in mountainous areas is socially, economically and environmentally significant. Sustainable agriculture and food security are indispensable to achieve sustainable development. However, it is not easy to do this.

Based on this study, I suggest some solutions to questions of food security, hunger eradication and poverty reduction at the local level.

- All development projects and strategies should be appropriate to the environmental and socio-economic situations of each region. It is necessary to engage issues of ethnicity (ethnic groups, their characteristics and their culture) in these strategies to achieve desired results.

- It is important to learn about knowledge systems of local farmers in order to understand their behaviour and their interactions with the environment. It is crucial to distinguish the knowledge of men from that of women because local knowledge is gendered. With this insight, we can recognize how the Red Yao people socially and economically structure their ecosystems.

- It is necessary to combine the advantages of local knowledge with modern technology to achieve good results in these local communities. Some of the farmer's local knowledge is no longer appropriate to the changing environment, which is influenced by rapid population growth, high and uneven population density, environmental degradation and increasing shortages of productive sources.

- A fact proves that diverse livelihoods are quite important. Therefore, it is indispensable to create more opportunities for the uplanders to access to different resources which help them produce more food, access to the market and information as well as improve their daily lives in a sustainable way.

- Based on the past risks and shocks happened in the research areas, it is crucial to raise the community-based risk reduction funds at the local level in addition to reinforcement of important roles of the communities and the government in supporting the vulnerable people to overcome such the risks. These funds can help the vulnerable people timely cope with difficulties caused by the risks before they receive the outside supports from the government, different organisations and individuals which are sometimes time-consuming.

- Finally, it is necessary to have additional, similar studies because environmental, socio-economic situations are different from region to region, from commune to commune, from ethnic group to ethnic group and even from sub-ethnic group to sub-ethnic group.

BIBLIOGRAPHY

A. Terry Rambo and P.E. Sajise (eds.) (1985). *An Introduction to Human Ecology Research on Agricultural Systems in Southeast Asia.* Los Banos: University of the Philippines.

A. Vayda (ed.) (1969). *Environment and Cultural Behaviour.* Garden City. New York: Natural History Press.

Anan Poltanee (1992). *Framer as Scientist: Bringing Farmer Knowledge for Researchers.* In J. Mc. Kinninged, Marginalization in Thailand.

Arun Agrawal (1995). "Dismantling the Divide Between Indigenous and Scientific Knowledge". *Development and Change.* Volume 26, No. 3.

Be Viet Dang (1985). "Some issues of the socio-economic development in the Northern mountain provinces". Hanoi: *Ethnology Review*, No. 1.

Be Viet Dang (1998). "The Yao in Vietnam - Traditions in the contemporary period". In: *The cultural and social development of Yao people: Present and Future. Proceedings of an international workshop on the Yao* held in Thai Nguyen province in December 1995. Hanoi: 17-30.

Be Viet Dang, Nguyen Khac Tung, Nong Trung, and Nguyen Nam Tien (1971). *The Yao in Vietnam.* Hanoi: Social Science Publishing House.

Bronislaw Malinowski (1935). *Coral Gardens and Their Magic-A Study of the Methods of Tilling the Soil and of Agricultural Rites in the Trobriand Islands.* London: George Allen and Unwin Ltd. Ruskin House, England; American Book Company.

Bui Minh Dao (ed.) (2003). *Some issues of poverty reduction among ethnic minorities in Vietnam.* A textbook. Hanoi: Social Science Publishing House.

C. P. Mountford (ed.) (1960). *Records of the Australian-American Scientific Expedition to Arnhem Land, Vol. 2: Anthropology and Nutrition.* Melbourne: Melbourne University Press.

Carlos M. Correa (2001). "Traditional Knowledge and Intellectual Property. Issues and options surrounding the protection of traditional knowledge". Quaker United Nations Office Geneva. [Available at http://hostings.diplomacy.edu/quaker/new/doc/tkcol3.pdf 18.07.2003].

Cecil G. Helman (1990). *Culture, Health and Illness: An Introduction for Health Professionals.* Second Edition. Wight Publisher.

Center for Ecological and Forest Studies (1998). *Indigenous knowledge of agriculture and natural resource management among the people in the uplands.* Hanoi: Agricultural Publishing House.

Center for Natural Resources and Environment Studies (2002). *Sustainable development in the upland of Vietnam: Look Back on the last ten years and problems.* Hanoi: Agricultural Publishing House.

CH. Agrawal and S. Saigal (1996). *Joint Forest Management in India: A Brief Review.* Society for Promotion of Wastelands Development, India.

Charles F. Keyes (1999). "Approach To The Study Of Indigenous Knowledge System: Some Preliminary Thoughts", *Paper prepared for Thai -*

Vietnamese training workshop on anthropological methodology held in Chiang Mai University, Thailand.

Christina H. Gladwin, Anne M. Thomson, Jennifer S. Peterson, and Andrea S. Anderson (2001). "Addressing food security in Africa via multiple livelihood strategies of women farmers". *Food Policy*, Volume 26, Number 2.

Claude Lévi-Strauss (1979). *Myth and Meaning*. New York: Schocken Books.

Clifford Geertz (1975). "Common Sense as a Cultural System". *Antioch Review*, 33: 47-53.

Clifford Geertz (1993a). *Local knowledge: Further essays in interpretive anthropology*. FontanaPress-An Imprint of HarperCollins Publisher.

Clifford Geertz (1993b). "Local Knowledge" and Its Limits: Some Obiter Dicta". *The Yale Journal of Criticism*, 5: 129-135.

Convention 169 (1989). *Indigenous and Tribal Peoples Convention*, 5/9/1989.

Craig Calhoun (2002). *Dictionary of the social science*. Oxford: Oxford University Press.

Daniel Maxwell and Keith Wiebe (1998). "Land Tenure and Food Security: A Review of Concepts, Evidence and Methods". Madison: *Land Tenure Center*, No. 129.

David Hicks and Margaret Anderson Gwynne (1996). *Cultural Anthropology*. Second edition. New York: HarperCollins College Publishers.

Deanna Donovan, A. Terry Rambo, Jefferson Fox, Le Trong Cuc and Tran Duc Vien (1997). *Development Trends in Vietnam's Northern Mountain Region*. Honolulu: East-West Center, and Hanoi: National Politics Publishing House.

Dennis Michael Warren (1995). *The cultural dimensions of development, indigenous development system*. Leiden.

Department of Agriculture and Rural Development of Sa Pa district (2000). Report on the work on direction for the agro-forestry development in 1999 - Trend, task, and plan of the year 2000, No. 02/ BC-TK/1999.

Department of Statistics and Planning of Sa Pa District (2003). *Statistical Yearbook of Sa Pa district, Lao Cai province*.

Do Dinh Sam (1994). Shifting Cultivation in Vietnam: Its Social, Economic and Environmental Values Relative to Alternative Land Use. London: International Institute for Environment and Development. *HED Forestry and Land Use* Series No. 3.

Do Tat Loi (1991). *The Vietnamese medical herbs and ingredient medicaments*. Sixth Edition. Hanoi: Scientific and Technical Publishing House.

Epprecht M. and Heinimann A. (eds.) (2004). *Socioeconomic Atlas of Vietnam. A Depiction of the 1999 Population and Housing Census*. Swiss National Centre of Competence in Research (NCCR) North-South, University of Berne. Berne.

Esta Ungar (1994). Gender, Land and Household in Vietnam. *Asian Studies Review*, Vol. 17, No. 3: 61-72.

FAO (1998). *Women Feed the World*, World Food Day, Rome, 16 October.

FAO (2005). *Agricultural trade reform offers benefits, but the poor could be left behind*, Rome: Italy. Also available at http://www.fao.org/newsroom/en/news/2005/1000173/index.html (7/12/2005).

Food Security in Asia and the Pacific (2000). Asian Productivity Organization, Tokyo.

G. P. Murdoch (1967). *Ethnographic Atlas*. Pittsburgh: University of Pittsburgh Press.

General Statistic Office (2000). *Figures on Social Development in the period of "Doi Moi" in Vietnam*. Hanoi: Statistical Publishing House.

General Statistics Office (1962). *Population in the North of Vietnam*. Hanoi.

General Statistics Office (1979). *Vietnam population* (Vietnam general population survey dated 01/10/1979). Hanoi.

General Statistics Office (1991). *Vietnam general population census 1991 - Result of exhaustive census, Volume I*. Hanoi: Statistical Publishing House.

General Statistics Office (2001). *1999 Vietnam general population and houses census*. Hanoi: Statistical Publishing House.

General Statistics Office (2003). *2002 Vietnam Statistical Yearbook*. Hanoi: Statistical Publishing House.

Gerald G. Marten (1986). *Traditional Agriculture in Southeast Asia: A Human Ecology Perspective*. Westview Press/ Boulder and London: East-West Center.

Gerald G. Marten (ed.) (1986). *Traditional Agriculture in Southeast Asia*. Boulder and London: Westview Press: 20-53.

Grant Evans (ed.) (1993). *Asia's Cultural Mosaic - An Anthropological Introduction*. Singapore: Prentice Hall.

H. C. Conklin (1957). Hanunoo agriculture: A report on an integral system of shifting cultivation in the Philippines. *Forestry Development*. Paper 12, FAO, Rome.

Ha Que Lam (2002). *Hunger elimination and poverty reduction in the region of ethnic minorities in our country nowadays - current situation and solution*. A documentary book. Hanoi: National Politics Publishing House.

Hanoi University of Medicines - Community Health Research Department, Vietnam Red Cross Society, Danish Red Cross Society (2001). *Goodwill Medicine Practice*. Hanoi: Medicine Publishing House.

Hans Lofgren (ed.) (2003). *Food, Agriculture, and Economic Policy in the Middle East and North Africa*. Research in Middle East Economics, Volume 5. Amsterdam: JAI Press/ Elsevier.

Helen Young (1992). *Food Scarcity and Famine: Assessment and Response*. Oxford: Oxfam Practical Health No. 7.

Hoang Huu Binh and Nguyen Xuan Thuong (1989). "Potentials of Natural Resources of the Hmong's Living Area in Hoang Lien Son and Development Strategies". Hanoi: *Anthropology Review*. No. 2-3: 117-133.

Ian Scoones and John Thompson (eds.) (1994). *Beyond Farmer First: Rural people's knowledge, agricultural research and extension practice*. Intermediate Technology Publications.

Institute of Agricultural Programming and Planning (1993). *Agriculture in the hilly and mountainous regions - Current situation and prospects*. Hanoi: Agricultural Publishing House.

Institute of Ethnology (1978). *Ethnic minorities in Vietnam (in the Northern provinces)*. Hanoi: Social Science Publishing House.

Institute of Strategic Forecast (1995). *Gender, environment and development in Vietnam*. Hanoi: National Politics Publishing House.

J. A. Ekpere (Project Coordinator). "The OAU's Model Law: The Protection of the Rights of Local Communities, Farmers and Breeders, and for the Regulation of Access to Biological Resources (An Explanatory Booklet)". *Organization of African Unity*. Scientific, Technical and Research Commission, P.M.B.2359 Lagos, Nigeria.

J. E. Spencer (1966). *Shifting cultivation in Southeast Asia*. University of California Publication in Geography, vol. 19. Berkeley: University of California Press.

J. Fairhead and M. Leach (1996). *Misreading African Landscape: Society and Ecology in a Forest-Savana Mosaic*. Cambridge: Cambridge University Press.

J. W. Watson and P. B. Eyzaguirre (eds.) (2002). "Home garden and in situ conservation of plant genetic resources in farming systems", *Proceedings of the Second International Home Gardens Workshop*, 17-19 July 2001, Witzhausen, Federal Republic of Germany, International Plant Genetic Resources Institute (IPGRI), Rome.

Jean Michaud and Sarah Turner (2000). The Sa Pa marketplace, Lao Cai province, Vietnam. Victoria University of Wellington: *Asia Pacific Viewpoint*, Vol. 41, No. 1.

Jess G. Pourret (2002). *The Yao - The Mien and Mun Yao in China, Vietnam, Laos and Thailand*. London: Thames & Hudson.

Joachim von Braun and Rajul Pandya-Lorch (1992). Income Source and Diversification Strategies of the Malnourished Rural Poor.

John Dixon, Aidan Gulliver, and David Gibbon (2001). *Farming Systems and Poverty: Improving Farmers' Livelihoods in a Changing World*. Principal Editor: Malcolm Hall, FAO, Rome, Italy. Also available at: www.fao.org/DOCREP/003/Y1860E/y1860e00.htm

John Mugabe (1998). "Intellectual Property Protection and Traditional Knowledge: An Exploitation in International Policy Discourse". *Paper prepared for the World Intellectual Property Organization (WIPO)*, Geneva, Switzerland. [Available at http://www.acts.or.ke/paper%20-%20intellectual%20property.htm 18.07.2003].

Jonathan Rouse (1999). "Global Dissemination of Indigenous Knowledge - Contradiction, or the Way Forward?". Available at: http://www.worldbank.org/afr/ik/global_1k99061.htm.

Kathleen D. Morrison and Laura L. Junker (2002). *Forager-Traders in South and Southeast Asia: Long-Term Histories*. Cambridge: Cambridge University Express.

Kevin Cleaver (2002). "Issues confronting the 2002 rural development strategy of the World Bank". Unpublished paper.

Khong Dien (1995). *Population and ethnic population in Vietnam.* Hanoi: Social Science Publishing House.

Land Law (2003). Hanoi: The Eleventh National Assembly of the Socialist Republic Vietnam, Session 4, 21/10/2003-21/11/2003; Law number 13/2003/QH11.

Lao Cai People's Committee (2002). *Report on the result of work of the hunger elimination and poverty reduction in 2002 - Tendency and solution of hunger elimination and poverty reduction from 2002 to 2003.* Report No. 21/BC-UB dated on 26th March 2002.

Lao Cai People's Committee (2003). *The comprehensive poverty reduction and growth strategy in the period of 2004 – 2010.* Lao Cai: October 2003.

Lao Cai Statistics Office (2001). *Basic statistical data of Lao Cai province during the 10-year-old reestablishment from 1991 to 2001.* Hanoi: Statistical Publishing House.

Le Ba Thao (2002). *Vietnam - territory and geographic regions.* Second Edition. Hanoi: The Gioi (The World) Publishing House.

Le Hong Tam (1985). "Some ideas about the socio-economic development among the ethnic minorities in the northern mountainous areas". Hanoi: *Ethnology Review*, No. 1.

Le Trong Cuc, Dao Trong Hung and Tran Duc Vien (eds.) (1996). *Workshop on appropriate use for sustainable mountain management in Vietnam.* Hanoi: CRES and HUAF, Agricultural Publishing House.

Le Trong Cuc, Nguyen Tat Canh and Tran Van On (eds.) (2003). *Proceedings on biodiversity and hunger eradication and poverty reduction in the mountainous regions of Vietnam.* Sa Pa, 26-28/5/2003.

Lisa Ostergaard (ed.) (1992). *Gender and Development: A Practical Guide.* London and New York.

M. M. Ahmed (1994). *Indigenous Knowledge for Sustainable Development in the Sudan.* Khartoum: Khartoum University Press.

M. O. Cosven (1974). *Outline of history of the primitive culture.* Hanoi: Literature-History-Geography Publishing House.

Maria Mies (1986). "Indian women in subsistence and agricultural labour". *Women, Work and Development 12.* Geneva: International Labour Office.

Marshall Sahlins (1972). *Stone Age Economics.* Chicago: Aldine-Atherton, Inc.

Martin Linde-Rahr (2002). *Household economics of agriculture and forestry in rural Vietnam.* Göteborg University, Sweden.

Maxx Dilley and Tanya E. Boudreau (2001). "Coming to terms with vulnerability: a critique of the food security definition". *Food Policy*, Volume 26: 229-247.

Michael C. Howard (1996). *Contemporary Cultural Anthropology.* Fifth Edition. New York: HarperCollins College Publishers.

Michael R. Dove (1983). *Theories of swidden agriculture, and the political economy of ignorance.* The Hague, The Netherlands: 84-95.

Michael R. Dove (1984). Government versus peasant beliefs concerning imperata and cupatorium: A structural analysis of knowledge, myth, and agricultural ecology in Indonesia. Honolulu: East-West Center, *Working Paper* No. 54.

N. Myers (1993). Tropical forest: The main deforestation fronts. *Environmental Conservation* 20: 9-16.

Nậm Cang Communal People's Committee (2005). *Summary report of the term of 2001-2005 and direction and mission of the work in the period of 2005-2010.*

Nậm Cang People's Committee (2005). *Socio-economic situations*. Nậm Cang: 26/5/2005.

Neil L. Jamieson, Le Trong Cuc, and Terry Rambo (1998). "The Development Crisis in Vietnam's Mountains". Honolulu: East-West Center. *Special Reports*, No. 6.

Ngo Duc Thinh (1995). "Folk knowledge and development". Hanoi: *Lecture for training workshop in CRES.*

Nguyen Khac Tung (1997). "Return to the classification of Yao sub-ethnic groups in Vietnam". *Ethnology Review*, No. 3: 30-37.

Nguyen Kim Lai (1993). "Private ownership in agriculture and its potentials in our country nowadays". Hanoi: *Philosophy Review*, No. 3.

Nguyen Manh Hung (ed.). 2003. *Vietnam socio-economic of 2002, plan of 2003 - Integrate & Growth*. Hanoi: Statistical Publishing House.

Nguyen Quang Du (1993). "Current period and the issue of rural development". Hanoi: *Philosophy Review*, No. 3.

Nguyen Van Minh (2000). Agricultural adaptation of the H'mong in Vietnam (A case study of two mountain communes). Hanoi: *Vietnam Social Sciences*, No. 6 (80): 75-95.

Nguyen Van Truong (1994). "An approach to concept of mountain development of natural resources in Vietnam at commune and village levels". *Hanoi workshop presentation*. October 14-16, 1994.

Nguyen Xuan Hong (2004). "Food security for inhabitants living in buffer zone of Bach Ma National Park: Challenges in development strategy". Hanoi: *Ethnology Review*, No. 2: 42-46.

Parliament Council of Ethnic Groups. Session X. (2000). *The policy and law of ethnic groups of the Vietnam Communist Party and the government.* Hanoi: National Culture Publishing House.

Paul Richards (1985). *Indigenous Agricultural Revolution: ecology and food production in West Africa*. London: Hutchinson, Great Britain.

Paul Richards (1986). *Coping with hunger: Hazard and Experiment in an African Rice-farming System*. London: Allen and Unwin.

Paul Richards, L. Jan Slikkerveer, and Adedotun O. Philips (1989). *Indigenous Knowledge Systems for Agriculture and Rural Development: The CIKARD Inaugural Lectures*. Studies in Technology and Social Change, No. 13; Iowa State University Research Foundation.

Paul W. Lewis (1984). *People of the Golden Triangle: Six Tribes of Thailand*. London: Thames and Hudson.

Peter Hinton (1967). *Tribesmen and Peasants in North Thailand: Proceedings of the First Symposium of the Tribal Research Centre.* Chiang Mai, Thailand.

Pham Quang Hoan (1999). "Local knowledge on natural resource management of ethnic minorities in Vietnam". Hanoi: *Vietnam Social Sciences*, No. 3.

Pham Quang Hoan and Hung Dinh Quy (eds.) (1999). *Traditional culture of the Yao in Ha Giang province*. Hanoi: Social Science Publishing House.

Pinkaew Laungaramsri (2001). *Karen Ecological Knowledge and the Challenge to the Modern Conservation Paradigm*. Chennai: Earthworm Books.

Quy-Toan Do and Lakshmi Iyer (2003). "Land Rights and Economic Development: Evidence from Vietnam". *World Bank working paper* 3/2003).

R. F. Watters (1960). "The nature of shifting cultivation". *Pacific Viewpoint* 1: 59-99.

R. Neil Byron and J. E. Michael Arnold (1999). "What futures for the people of the tropical forests?". *World Development 27* (5).

R. T. Sobey (ed.) (1997). *Biodiversity Value of Hoang Lien Mountains and Strategies for Conservation, Proceedings of Seminar and Workshop*, 7-9th December 1997, Sa Pa district, Lao Cai province, Vietnam; SEE Forest Research Programme, London (ISBN 1873070 13 6).

Rerkasem B. (ed.) (1996). *Montane Mainland Southeast Asia in Transition*. Chiang Mai (Thailand): Chiang Mai University Consortium.

Richard B. Lee and Irven DeVore (eds.) (1968). *Man the Hunter*. Chicago: Aldine.

Richard B. Lee and R. Daly (eds.) (1999). *The Cambridge Encyclopedia of Hunters and Gatherers*. Cambridge: Cambridge University Press.

Robert Chambers and Melissa Leach (1989). "Trees as Savings and Security for The Rural Poor". *World Development* 17 (3): 329-342.

Robert Chambers, Arnold Pacey, and Lori Ann Thrupp (eds.) (1989). *Farmer First: Farmer Innovation and Agricultural Research*. Intermediate Technology Publications.

Robert Cooper (1984). *Resource Scarcity and the Hmong Response: Patterns of Settlement and Economy in Transition*. Singapore: Singapore University Press.

Roderick P. Neumann and Eric Hirsch (2000). *Commercialisation of Non-Timber Forest Products: Review and Analysis of Research*. Bogor, Indonesia: Center for International Forestry Research, Rome: FAO.

Sa Pa District People's Committee (2004). *Report on socio-economic situation in Sa Pa district in the period of 2000-2005*, Sa Pa: 12/2004.

Sa Pa District People's Committee (2005). *Report on results of effectuation of the Programme 135 in the period of 1999-2005 in Sa Pa district*.

Sa Pa District People's Committee (2005). *Report on the assessment of effects of irrigation systems funded by the Programme 135*, No. 75/BC-UB. Sa Pa: 7/6/2005.

Sa Pa People's Committee (2003). *Report on survey of basic household situation of agro-forestry in 2003 in Sa Pa district,* number 121/TK-ĐTH. Sa Pa 7/10/2003.

Sa Pa People's Committee (2005). *Report on results of the implementation of 7 Lao Cai's Programmes towards the local levels in the period of 2003-2004)*, No. 22/BC-UB dated 25/2/2005.

Stephen B. Brush (1996). *Valuing local knowledge: indigenous people and intellectual property rights.* Washington D.C.: Island Press.

T. P. Bayliss-Smith (1982). *The Ecology of Agricultural Systems.* Cambridge: Cambridge University Express.

Thayer Scudder (1971). "Gathering among African woodland savannah cultivators - A case study: The Gwembe Tonga". *Zambian Papers*, No. 5, Zambia: University of Zambia.

Thomas J. Barfield (ed.) (1997). *Blackwell Dictionary of Anthropology.* Oxford: Basil Blackwell.

Thomas Sikor and Dao Minh Truong (2001). "Agricultural policy and land use changes in Black Thai villages of Northern Vietnam (1952-1997)". Hanoi: *Anthropology Review*, No. 6.

Tim Ingold, David Riches, and Jame Woodburn (eds.) (1988). *Hunters and Gatherers 2: Property, power and ideology*. Oxford: Berg.

Tran Binh (2001). *Customs of economic activities of some ethnic groups in the Northwest of Vietnam*. Hanoi: National Culture Publishing House.

Tran Duc Vien and Pham Chi Thanh (eds.) (1996). *Agriculture on sloping lands: challenges and potential.* Hanoi: Agricultural Publishing House.

Tran Hong Hanh (2000). The prevention and cure of disease among the Dao Quan Chet (in some hamlets in Da Bac district, Hoa Binh province, Vietnam). Hanoi: *Vietnam Social Sciences*. No. 6: 52-74.

Tran Huu Son (1996). *The Hmong's Culture.* Hanoi: National Culture Publishing House.

Tran Huu Son (1999). *Proverb and riddle of the Yao.* Hanoi: National Culture Publishing House.

Tran Quoc Vuong (ed.) (2000). *Vietnamese cultural basis.* Second Edition. Hanoi: Educational Publishing House.

Tran Van On (2005). The medical plant resource and poverty reduction among ethnic communities in the northern mountainous area. Hanoi: *Anthropology Review*, No. 2: 36-37.

Uwe Kracht and Manfred Schulz (eds.) (1999). *Food Security and Nutrition: The Global Challenge*. Münster: LIT VERLAG.

Vandana Shiva (1998). *Globalisation, Gandhi and Swadeshi: What is Economic Freedom? Whose Economic Freedom?.* New Dehli: RFSTE.

Vandana Shiva and Gitanjali Bedi (eds.) (2002). *Sustainable Agriculture and Food Security: The Impact of Globalisation.* New Delhi: Sage Publications.

Veronika Bennholdt - Thomsen, Nicholas G. Faraclas, and Claudia von Werlhof (eds.) (2001). *There is an alternative: subsistence and worldwide resistance to corporate globalization.* North Melbourne. Victoria: Spinifex Press.

Vietnam - The Netherlands collaborative research programme (2003). *Proceedings of International Workshop on Environment and Sustainable Development*. Hanoi: Agricultural Publishing House.

VNECONOMY updated on 5 January 2005, also available at http://www.vneconomy.com.vn/eng/index.php?param=article&catid=D2&id=050105140117

Vuong Xuan Tinh (2001). "Food security of the R'mam". Hanoi: *Ethnology Review*, No. 5.

Vuong Xuan Tinh (2003). "Food system of the Hmong in food security perspective". Hanoi: *Ethnology Review*, No. 1.

Vuong Xuan Tinh (2003). *Looking for food: The difficult journey of the Hmong in Vietnam (Anthropological Perspectives on Food Security)*. Unpublished paper.

Vuong Xuan Tinh (2004). "The role of community in the use of forest land among the Northern minority people (tradition, changes and implementation of the 2003 Land Law)". Hanoi: *Anthropology Review*, No. 4: 23-34.

W. D. Sunderlin, A. Angelsen, and S. Wunder (2003). "State of the World's Forests". In: FAO (2003). *Forests and poverty alleviation*. Rome: Italy. Page: 61-73.

W. R. Gaddes (1976). *Migrants of the mountains: The Cultural Ecology of the Blue Miao (Hmong Njua) of Thailand*. Oxford: Clarendon Press.

WB (2001). *Project appraisal document on a proposed credit in the amount of SDR 87.9 million (US$110 million equivalent) to the Socialist Republic of Vietnam for a northern mountains poverty reduction project*. Rural Development and Natural Resources Sector Unit, East Asia and Pacific Region, Report No: 21233-VN.

WB (2003). *Understanding and Responding to Poverty - World Bank Poverty Net*. Available at http://www.worldbank.org/poverty/mission/up1.htm .

WIPO (2000). "Draft Report on Fact-finding Missions on Intellectual Property and Traditional Knowledge (1998-1999)". *Draft for Comment*, 3rd July 2000.

APPENDIX

Appendix 1. Household poverty in Sa Pa district

No	Communes and town[1]	2000			2003			2004			Early 2005[2]		
		Total	Poor	%	Total	Poor	%	Total	Poor	%	Total	Poor	%
1	Sa Pa town	1241	169	13.62	1315	20	1.52	1585	8	0.50	1.595	50	3.13
2	**Nậm Cang**	**161**	**23**	**14.29**	**178**	**9**	**5.06**	**190**	**7**	**3.68**	**193**	**45**	**23.32**
3	Thanh Phú	293	47	16.04	310	32	10.32	320	25	7.81	336	97	28.87
4	Bản Hồ	272	103	37.87	303	45	14.85	323	33	10.22	335	104	31.04
5	San Sả Hồ	390	93	23.85	438	35	7.99	464	29	6.25	479	157	32.78
6	Nậm Sài	226	104	46.02	238	64	26.89	258	49	18.99	267	105	39.33
7	Suối Thầu	216	128	59.26	242	42	17.36	248	25	10.08	253	117	46.25
8	Sa Pả	494	301	60.93	578	135	23.36	615	81	13.17	616	293	47.56
9	**Bản Khoang**	**266**	**57**	**21.43**	**312**	**26**	**8.33**	**343**	**20**	**5.83**	**348**	**175**	**50.29**
10	Tả Giàng Phình	361	188	52.08	394	84	21.32	409	59	14.43	437	222	50.80
11	Tả Van	394	152	38.58	449	76	16.93	454	65	14.32	473	274	57.93
12	Thanh Kim	173	92	53.18	185	40	21.62	190	16	8.42	198	120	60.61
13	Bản Phùng	196	51	26.02	207	41	19.81	213	33	15.49	217	132	60.83
14	**Tả Phìn**	**282**	**76**	**26.95**	**347**	**44**	**12.68**	**369**	**28**	**7.59**	**379**	**237**	**62.53**
15	Lao Chải	366	170	46.45	397	121	30.48	432	93	21.53	426	299	70.19
16	Trung Chải	392	158	40.31	429	98	22.84	462	83	17.97	472	352	74.58
17	Sử Pán	289	160	55.36	297	64	21.55	316	45	14.24	343	287	83.67
18	Hầu Thào	298	199	66.78	328	137	41.77	354	130	36.72	363	326	89.81
	Whole district	6310	2271	35.98	6947	1113	16.02	7545	829	10.99	7.730	3.392	43.88
	Urban area	1241	169	13.62	1315	20	1.52	1585	8	0.50	1.595	50	3.13
	Rural areas	5069	2102	22.36	5632	1093	14.50	5960	821	10.49	6.135	3.342	54.47

[1] Communes and town are listed in the ascending order of the poverty and boldface types imply the research areas.

[2] *Source*: Sample 3.2, No. 01. In: Sa Pa District People's Committee (2005). Report on the assessment of poor households in Sa Pa district in accordance with the new criteria dated in 2005, Report No. 38/BC-NV, Sa Pa: 10/6/2005.

Appendix 2. Diversity of the local rice varieties (*Lồ bèo nghim*) of the Red Yao ethnic group

Variety	Groups of variety	Local name	Meaning of local name	Naming basis	Seasonal calendar	Biological characteristics	Usage
Ordinary rice (*bèo chi*)	Upland ordinary dry-rice (*đẩy bèo chi*)	*Bèo sìn sậy*	Paddy grown in the upper soil plots	Sowing and growing location	Middle of March - End of August	Paddy is large and red, with downs at the back of its grain. Its ears are about 16-17 cm long. It is more delicious than *Tả lèng*. It bears the cold very well; therefore, it normally grows in the high, sloping land. Its average productivity is 40 kg of rice, from sowing 1 kg of rice seeds. In the past ten years, few households have grown this variety.	Cooked ordinary rice
		Bèo giàng ton	Small and yellow paddy	Size and colour of rice	Middle of March - Middle of Sept.	Paddy is yellow, long, tapering, soft and relatively balsamic. Its ears are about 17-18 cm long without down. It can bear the cold weather. However, it will be more productive when it grows in warm areas. Currently, few farmers plant this crop due to its long period of growth. Its average productivity is 40 kg of rice by sowing 1 kg of rice seeds.	Cooked ordinary rice and rice cake
		Bèo củ ton	Small and red paddy	Size and colour of rice	Middle of March - Middle of Sept.	The biological characteristics of this crop are relatively similar to that of *Bèo giàng ton*, but its husk is red. Its productivity is also similar to that of *Bèo giàng ton*.	Cooked ordinary rice and rice cake
		Bèo chìm pẹ	Dry and white rice	Sowing and growing location; and colour of rice	Middle of April - Middle of Sept.	Paddy is white. Its ears are 14-15 cm long with dense grains. Rice is dry, hard and small. It grows in bare hill areas because it cannot grow well in bushy areas. Its productivity is 35 kg of rice, from sowing 1 kg of rice seeds.	Food for domestic animals and for distillation of rice alcohol.

Variety	Groups of variety	Local name	Meaning of local name	Naming basis	Seasonal calendar	Biological characteristics	Usage
Ordinary rice (*bèo chí*)	Upland ordinary dry-rice (*đẩy bèo chí*)	*Bèo chím sí*	Dry and red rice	Sowing and growing location; and colour of rice	Middle of April - Middle of Sept.	Its biological characteristics and productivity are similar to these of *Bèo chím pẹ*, but its husk is red.	Food for domestic animals and for distillation of rice alcohol
		Tâm bèo pẹ	White rice grain	Colour of rice	Middle of March - Middle of Sept.	Paddy is white and long. Its ears are about 22 cm long with sparse grains. Rice is drier than the *Bèo giàng ton*, but it is softer than the *Tam ưu* (one of the new rice varieties grown currently in the Red Yao communities). It can stand droughts, and normally grows in the plots of the secondary forest or in the grassy hills. Its average productivity is 40 kg of rice, from sowing 1 kg of rice seeds.	Cooked ordinary rice and rice alcohol
		Tâm bèo sí	Red rice grain	Colour of rice	Middle of March - Middle of Sept.	Its biological characteristics and productivity are similar to those of *Tẩm bèo pẹ*, but its husk is red.	Cooked ordinary rice and rice alcohol
		Bèo chìm kìm	Wild ordinary rice	Wild origin of rice	End of March - Middle of Sept.	Rice is purlish-red. It is drier than the *Tâm bèo pẹ* and the *Tẩm bèo sí*. Its ears are about 18 cm long. It can endure the cold so that it is planted in the high sloping kaingins. Its average productivity is 37 kg of rice from sowing 1 kg of rice seeds.	Cooked ordinary rice
		Bèo xèng lắm	Brimful rice	Productivity of rice	End of March - Middle of Sept.	Rice is purlish-red. Its ears are about 17-18 cm long. Its taste is relatively similar to that of the *Tâm bèo pẹ* and of the *Tâm bèo sí*. It bears the cold well. It normally grows halfway down the mountain. Its average productivity is 40 kg of rice from sowing 1 kg of rice seeds.	Cooked ordinary rice and rice alcohol

Variety	Groups of variety	Local name	Meaning of local name	Naming basis	Seasonal calendar	Biological characteristics	Usage
Ordinary rice (*bèo chí*)	Ordinary wet-rice (*lình bèo chí*)	*Lở khoẻ*	Local paddy	Origin of rice	End of March - End of August.	Paddy is tall and strong. Its ears are about 18-20 cm long. Rice is white and soft. It has a low productivity: by sowing 1 kg of rice seeds, a farmer can gain 30 kg of rice. Currently, many households still grow this variety of rice and the *Tả lèng* because they are more delicious than the new ones.	Cooked ordinary rice and rice alcohol
		Tả lèng	Hard rice or "easy rice" which can grow in all soil plots	Biological characteristics of rice	End of March - Beginning of Sept.	Paddy is white with a thin, red husk. Its ears are about 20 cm long with sparse grains. Rice is hard and dry. It easily grows on nearly all sorts of land, so farmers have named it "easy rice". Its productivity is relatively low; by sowing 1 kg of rice seeds, a farmer can obtain 35 kg of rice.	Food for domestic animals, and for distillation of rice alcohol
		Tẩm lở khoảy	Big and soft rice	Size and composition of rice	End of March - Beginning of Sept.	This crop stands the cold very well so that it grows in the higher and colder area. Rice is white, big and softer than the rice of *Lở khoẻ*. Its ears are about 22-24 cm long. Nowadays, those who have a lot of cultivable land plant this variety. Its average productivity is 35 kg of rice, from sowing 1 kg of rice seeds.	Cooked ordinary rice and rice cake
		Giàng đẩy bèo	Upland dry-rice	Sowing and growing location	End of March - Beginning of Sept.	Rice is small and white with the downs at the back of its grains. Its ears are about 15 cm long with denseer grains than those of the other local paddies, but grains of its ears are still sparser than those of the new rice. It flourishes with a lot of sunshine and air. It will be less productive when it grows in bushy areas. Rice is soft and has a strong flavour. Its productivity is low; by sowing 1 kg of rice seeds, a farmer can obtain 30 kg of rice.	Cooked ordinary rice, rice cake, and rice alcohol

Variety	Groups of variety	Local name	Meaning of local name	Naming basis	Seasonal calendar	Biological characteristics	Usage
Ordinary rice (*bèo chí*)	Ordinary wet-rice (*lình bèo chí*)	*Lở khoẩy ton*	Small paddy	Size of rice	Beginning of March - Middle of Sept.	Its biological characteristics and productivity are similar to those of the *Tẩm lở khoẩy*, but its grains are smaller. Its ears are about 18 cm long with white grains. Rice is relatively soft.	Cooked ordinary rice and rice cake
		Lân suối	Paddy, which can stand the cold water	Biological characteristics of rice	End of March - Beginning of Sept.	This paddy stands the cold very well; therefore, it grows in cold areas. Its ears are as long as those of the *Tả lèng*. Paddy is white with downs like the *Bèo sìn sẩy*.	Cooked ordinary rice and rice alcohol
Glutinous rice (*bèo bụt*)	Upland glutinous dry-rice (*đẩy bèo bụt*)	*Bèo ừ củ*	Rice for old women or red glutinous rice	Users and colour of rice	Middle of March - Beginning of Sept.	Rice is dark red, round and very glutinous. Its ears are about 13-14 cm long with dense grains. Plants about 1.5 cm tall. This variety grows well in dry areas. It bears the drought and the cold. It grows both in the kaingins and in swampy fields. However, it is more productive when it grows in the kaingins. By sowing 1 kg of rice seeds, a farmer can gain 30 kg of rice (in the swampy fields) or 40 kg of rice (in the kaingins).	Steamed or cooked sticky rice, medicine (for treating stomachache and as a strong anesthetic), and distilling rice alcohol.
		Lô đau bèo	Old upland glutinous rice	Former ages	End of March - End of Sept.	Paddy can endure the cold. Its ears are 25 cm long. This is yellowish, big and relatively pointed rice with downs at the back of its grains. This crop is planted in the kaingins and in swampy fields. By sowing 1 kg of rice seeds, a farmer can obtain 30 kg of rice.	Steamed or cooked sticky rice and rice alcohol

Variety	Groups of variety	Local name	Meaning of local name	Naming basis	Seasonal calendar	Biological characteristics	Usage
Glutinous rice (*bèo bụt*)	Upland glutinous dry-rice (*đẩy bèo bụt*)	*Bèo chẳng bang*	Glutinous rice which makes its cooker collapse	Folk legend	End of March - End of Sept.	Paddy's ears are about 25 cm long with dense grains. Rice is yellow, round and glutinous. It requires a relatively large amount of air. Its name is derived from a folk legend. Before the local farmers named it *Bèo chẳng bang*, it had no name. Farmers normally cooked or steamed it. The story goes that one day, while they were cooking it, the cooker collapsed and shattered. This is where its name comes from. By sowing 1 kg of rice seeds, a farmer obtains about 30-35 kg of rice.	Steamed or cooked sticky rice, glutinous rice cake, and sweet rice alcohol
		Bèo bụt giẳng	Yellow glutinous paddy	Colour of rice	End of March - Middle of Sept.	Paddy is yellow. Its ears are about 15-16 cm long with dense grains. This crop fares well in the cold areas; thus, it normally grows in the fields near the head of the water sources. Rice is harder than the other kinds of glutinous rice. Its average productivity is 30 kg of rice from sowing 1 kg of rice seeds.	Glutinous rice cake (mostly) and steamed or cooked sticky rice (rarely, owing to its hardness)
		Bèo ông	Rice for old men	Users	Middle of March - End of Sept.	This rice requires very good land. Its ears are about 25 cm long. Its grain is light red, long and glutinous. Its average productivity is about 35 kg of rice from sowing 1 kg of rice seeds.	Steamed or cooked sticky rice and rice alcohol
	Glutinous wet-rice (*lình bèo bụt*)	*Bèo bụt sí*	Red glutinous rice	Colour of rice	End of March - End of Sept.	This crop is normally planted in the best fields, because it is extremely sensitive. If it is not planted on the right sort of land, the stalks of the plants are not strong and they often fall over. Its ears are about 17-18 cm long with dense grains. Paddy is red. By sowing 1 kg of rice seeds, a farmer can obtain about 40 kg of rice.	Steamed or cooked sticky rice, glutinous rice cake, and rice alcohol

Variety	Groups of variety	Local name	Meaning of local name	Naming basis	Seasonal calendar	Biological characteristics	Usage
Glutinous rice (*bèo bụt*)	Glutinous wet-rice (*lình bèo bụt*)	*Bèo bụt giăng*	Yellow glutinous paddy	Colour of rice	End of March - Middle of Sept.	Paddy is yellow. Its ears are about 15-16 cm long with dense grains. This crop is fond of the cold areas; thus, it normally grows in the fields near the head of the water sources. Rice is harder than the other kinds of glutinous rice. Its average productivity is 30 kg of rice, from sowing 1 kg of rice seeds.	Glutinous rice cake (mostly) and steamed or cooked sticky rice (rarely, owing to its hardness).
		Bèo bụt ngau	Curved glutinous rice	Shape of the rice grain	End of March - Beginning of Sept.	Rice grain is longer and smaller than that of *Bèo bụt giăng*. It is curved and relatively hard. Its ears are about 15-16 cm long. It stands the cold well; thus, it grows in the fields near the water source. Its productivity is similar to that of the *Bèo bụt giăng*.	Glutinous rice cake (mostly) and steamed or cooked sticky rice (rarely, owing to its hardness).
		Bèo bụt ay	Short glutinous paddy	Height of the paddy	End of March - Beginning of August.	Paddy is about 50-60 cm tall. Its ears are 15 cm long. Rice is white and rather flat with downs at the back of its grain. Its average productivity obtains 36-37 kg of rice by sowing 1 kg of rice seeds.	Glutinous rice cake (mostly) and steamed or cooked sticky rice (rarely, owing to its lack of glutinosity).
		Bèo heng nó	Everywhere glutinous rice	Popularity of rice	End of March - Beginning of August.	Paddy is about 1.5m tall. Its ears are 22 cm long. Rice is white, very glutinous and has a strong flavour. Its ripening grains make the paddy lean on the ground due to its weight. This crop does well in warm plots with a lot of air. Thus, it is normally planted in the well-exposed and spacious fields. It rarely grows well in the fields near the head of the water sources. Its average productivity is 35 kg of rice from sowing 1 kg of rice seeds.	Rice offering to the Yao's ancestor spirits because it is harvested earliest.

Variety	Groups of variety	Local name	Meaning of local name	Naming basis	Seasonal calendar	Biological characteristics	Usage
Glutinous rice (*bèo bụt*)	Glutinous wet-rice (*lình bèo bụt*)	*Bèo khọ boong*		According to Tay language, no Yao translation existing.	End of March - Beginning of October.	This is the Yao's rice, with the longest growing period. It is flourishes in warmth and sunshine. Its ears are 18 cm long with dense grains. Its grains are large and short. Its husks are relatively thick. Thus, 10 kg of paddy yields about 6.5 kg of husked rice. Rice is very white compared with the other varieties. Rice is very glutinous, has a strong flavour, and is delicious. Its productivity is low; by sowing 1 kg of rice seeds, a farmer obtains 28-30 kg of rice. Many households do not continue to plant this variety due to its long growing period. When they want to eat this kind of rice, they buy them from villagers, or from the Tay farmers for 8,000VND/kg.	Steamed or cooked sticky rice.
		Bèo bụt bưa	Ashen glutinous rice	Colour of rice	Beginning of March - Beginning of August.	This crop bears the cold well. Thus, it is planted in the cold fields near the head of water source. Its ears are 22 cm long with sparse grains. It is large, grey, and has downs around it. It is extremely glutinous, but does not have a strong flavour. Its average productivity is 30-35 kg of rice, from sowing 1 kg of rice seeds.	Steamed or cooked sticky rice, glutinous rice cake, and rice alcohol.

Variety	Groups of variety	Local name	Meaning of local name	Naming basis	Seasonal calendar	Biological characteristics	Usage
Glutinous rice (*bèo bụt*)	Glutinous wet-rice (*lình bèo bụt*)	*Bèo ừ cǔ*	Rice for old women or red glutinous rice	Users and colour of rice	Middle of March - Beginning of Sept.	Rice is dark red, round and very glutinous. Its ears are about 13-14 cm long with dense grains. It is about 1.5 cm tall. This variety grows well on dry land. It can bear drought and cold. It grows both in the kaingins and in swampy fields. However, it will be more productive when it grows in the kaingins. By sowing 1 kg of rice seeds, a farmer can obtain 30 kg of rice (in the swampy fields) or 40 kg of rice (in the kaingins).	Steamed or cooked sticky rice, medicine (for treating stomachaches and as a strong anesthetic), and distilling rice alcohol.
		Bèo chẳng bang	Glutinous rice which makes its cooker collapse	Folk legend	End of March - End of Sept.	Paddy's ears are about 25 cm long with dense grains. Rice is yellow, round and glutinous. It grows well when exposed to a lot of air. Its name is derived from a folk legend. Before the local farmers named it *Bèo chẳng bang*, it had no name. Farmers normally cooked or steamed it. One day, while they were cooking it, the cook collapsed and shattered. This is where its name comes from. By sowing 1 kg of rice seeds, a farmer can obtain about 30-35 kg of rice.	Steamed or cooked sticky rice, glutinous rice cake, and sweet rice alcohol.

Appendix 3. Some local maize varieties of the Red Yao in Nậm Cang commune

Variety	Groups of variety	Meaning of local name	Naming basis	Seasonal calendar	Biological characteristics	Growing place	Usage
Ordinary maize (*mẹ chỉ*)	*Mẹ giẳng cẳng*	Yellow ordinary maize and maize which is as hard as cast iron	Colour and composition of maize	End of Jan. - End of August	This crop is not selective about land. It normally grows in the high sloping kaingins. Its ear is big and long. Maize is yellow, very hard and has a strong flavour.	In high sloping kaingins and in secondary forestland	Food for domestic animals
	Cẵm mẹ pẹ	White ordinary maize	Colour of maize	Beginning of Feb.- Beginning of Sept.	This maize is about 3m tall. Its ears are big and long. Maize is white.	In high sloping kaingins	Food for domestic animals
	Cẵm mẹ giẳng	Yellow ordinary maize	Colour of maize	Beginning of Feb.- Middle of July	This crop is normally planted in the high sloping kaingins because it is not selective about land. It is about 2.5m tall. Its stalk is smaller than that of the *Cẵm mẹ pẹ*, but it is very hard and it bears the wind. Maize is yellow and so hard that it is difficult for farmers to eat it.	In high sloping kaingins and in secondary forestland	Food for domestic animals
	Cẵm mẹ bưa	Ashen ordinary maize	Colour of maize	Beginning of Feb.- Beginning of Sept.	This plant is about 3m tall. It requires a lot of ashes. Its ears are big, with a very thick sheath. This maize is ashen. Nowadays, few households still plant this kind of maize.	In high sloping kaingins and in secondary forestland	Food for domestic animals

Variety	Groups of variety	Meaning of local name	Naming basis	Seasonal calendar	Biological characteristics	Growing place	Usage
Ordinary maize (*mẹ chỉ*)	*Cằm mẹ mắc*	Sunken maize	Shape of maize	Beginning of Feb.- Beginning of Sept.	This crop is fond of the cold areas. Its ears are 25-35 cm long. Maize is slightly white and sunken on its surface. It is highly productive. However, it has a long growing period; thus, few households continue to plant it.	In high sloping kaingins and in secondary forestland	Food for domestic animals
Glutinous maize (*mẹ bụt*)	*Mẹ bụt pẹ*	White glutinous maize	Colour of maize	Beginning of Feb.- Middle of July	This maize is about 2m tall. Its ears are big. Maize is white, glutinous and has a lot of flavour. This is the most highly-flavoured and delicious local glutinous maize of the Yao people.	In low sloping kaingins	Food for people and domestic animals
	Mẹ bụt giẳng	Yellow glutinous maize	Colour of maize	Beginning of Feb.- Middle of August	The biological characteristics of this maize are similar to that of the *Mẹ bụt pẹ*, but it is yellow.	In low sloping kaingins	Food for people and domestic animals
	Mẹ bụt pên	Colourful glutinous maize	Colour of maize	Beginning of Feb.- Middle of August	The ears of this maize are bigger than those of the *Mẹ bụt pẹ*. Maize is glutinous and highly flavoured. It normally has three different colours: red, violet and white.	In low sloping kaingins	Food for people and domestic animals

Appendix 4. Situation of land disputes in Sa Pa district.[1]

Plaintiff	Defendant	Reason	Content of matter	Solution of local administrators
Sả Xéng hamlet (Sa Pả commune)	Hầu Chư Ngài hamlet (Hầu Thào commune)	Occupying 15 ha of forest	The people of Sả Xéng have cultivated the land belonging to Hầu Chư Ngài hamlet. In opposition, the farmers of Hầu Chư Ngài hamlet cultivate the forestland of the Sả Xéng people, because the land they own is insufficient.	Allow the people of Hầu Chư Ngài hamlet to use 5 ha of forestland from the Sả Xéng hamlet. However, the people of Hầu Chư Ngài hamlet have asked administrators to give them back all of the land that the Sả Xéng people have tilled from them. The administrators have deigned that they will give 15 ha of the forestland that they are tilling to the Sả Xéng hamlet. However, there is still dispute.
Hầu Thào commune	Giàng Tả Chải hamlet (Tả Van commune)	Cultivated land dispute	Based on the administrative boundary (Borderline 364), Giàng Tả Chải hamlet is located in the area of Hầu Thào commune. However, Tả Van commune manages the people of this hamlet. Therefore, there is a deep and significant reason for the contradiction in human and land management.	Local administrators have not yet offered a solution.

[1] To facilitate the readers, I drew this table based on information of the report by Sa Pa People's Committee (2005). In this table, in the case of communes belonging to Sa Pa district, I did not write the name of this district down. On the contrary, I specified names of other districts by adding their names together with names of the communes to which they belong.

Plaintiff	Defendant	Reason	Content of matter	Solution of local administrators
Phìn Hồ hamlet (Bản Khoang commune)	Tả Phìn commune	Dispute of wet-land and kaingins	The people in Tả Phìn commune do not have enough land to cultivate. Therefore, they till the terraced and unterraced land of Phìn Hồ hamlet (Bản Khoang commune). Borderline 364 disappears.	The dispute has already been settled, but the people haven't observed the administrator's decisions.
Bản Khoang commune	People in the area of Cửa Cải (Tả Giàng Phình commune)	Dispute of wet-land	The people of Cửa Cải do not allow the people of Bản Khoang commune to cultivate the land which they claim from the virgin land.	Ask the people to accept the current situation as regards distribution of land, and not to continue to claim land because this area is controlled by a project.
Kim Ngài-Xả Chải hamlet (Bản Khoang commune)	Phìn Ngan commune (Bát Xát district, Lào Cai province)	Dispute of wet-land and kaingins	The people of Phìn Ngan commune till the wet- and dry-land of Kim Ngài-Xả Chải hamlet.	Local administrators have not yet offered a solution.
Ky Công Hồ hamlet (Tòng Sành commune, Bát Xát district, Lào Cai province)	Vù Lùng Sung hamlet (Trung Chả commune)	Dispute of kaingins	Based on borderline 364, the current land of Ky Công Hồ hamlet belongs originally to Trung Chải commune. However, the local administrators of Sa Pa and Bát Xát districts have allowed them to cultivate that land for many years. At present, the land has been fallow for about 2-3 years.	Local administrators have not yet offered a solution.

Spektrum

Berliner Reihe zu Gesellschaft, Wirtschaft und Politik in Entwicklungsländern

hrsg. von PD Dr. Dr. Ulrich van der Heyden, Prof. Dr. Volker Lühr, Dr. Ulrike Schultz und Prof. Dr. Manfred Schulz (Freie Universität Berlin)

Manfred Schulz

Entwicklungsträger in der DR Kongo

Entwicklungen in Politik, Wirtschaft, Religion, Zivilgesellschaft und Kultur

Der erste Teil des Buches verschafft einen Zugang zum Kongo, seiner Geschichte und seinem Rohstoffreichtum. Teil zwei diskutiert neue Entwicklungen in Politik (z.B. Wahlen), Ökonomie (Ressourcengewinnung), Religion (Bildung und Gesundheitswesen der Kirchen), Zivilgesellschaft (NGOs) und Kultur (Kongo-Musik). Der dritte Teil des Bandes ist der Entwicklungspolitik gewidmet; er gibt einen Überblick über Förderansätze und Programme der einheimischen Institutionen sowie der wichtigsten multi- und bilateralen Geber. Besonders interessieren hier die Auswirkungen der beschränkten Absorptionskapazität des Kongo für Hilfe angesichts der Ausweitung der Förderung seitens der internationalen entwicklungspolitischen Community. Schließlich diskutieren in Teil vier des Bandes drei Abgeordnete des Deutschen Bundestages mit Kongo-Erfahrung die deutsch-kongolesische Kooperation.

Bd. 100, 2008, 760 S., 49,90 €, br., ISBN 978-3-8258-0425-1

LIT Verlag Berlin – Münster – Wien – Zürich – Hamburg – London

Auslieferung Deutschland / Österreich / Schweiz: siehe Impressumsseite